DEATH
A SURVIVAL GUIDE

Dr SARAH BREWER

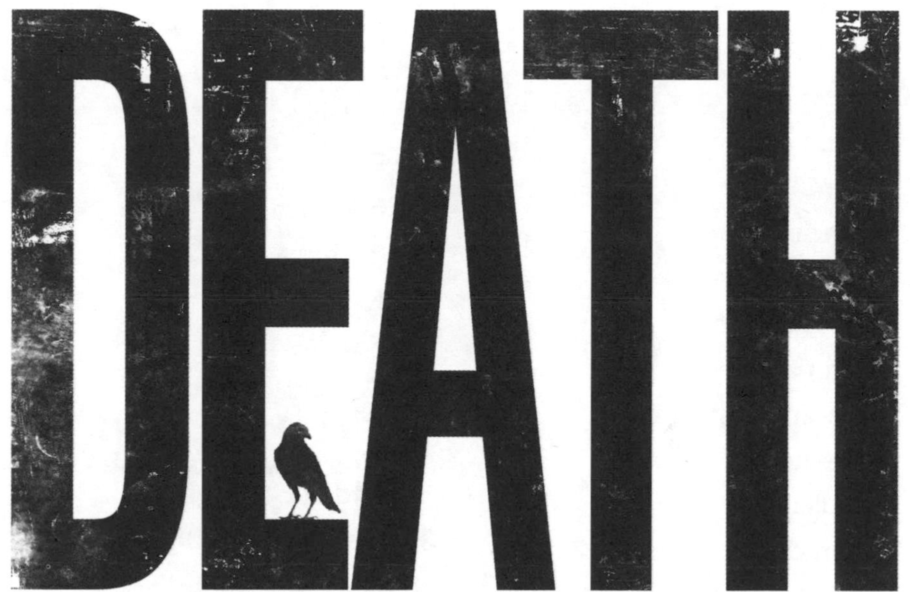

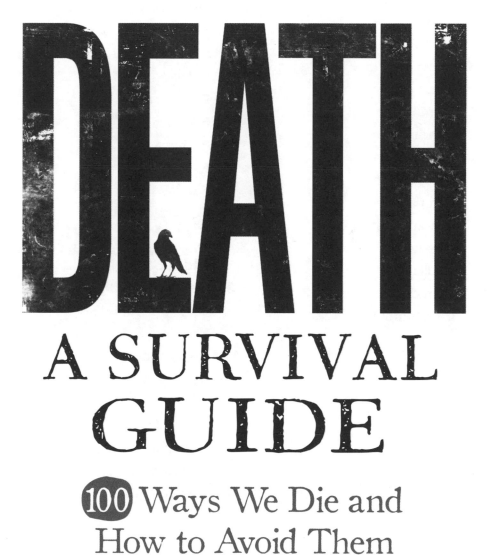

DEATH A SURVIVAL GUIDE

100 Ways We Die and How to Avoid Them

Contents

Introduction

People who die are always loved individuals rather than statistics. But sometimes there is no alternative to dicing with death and playing a numbers game. Sadly, despite increased medical advances and an ageing population, the global death rate remains constant at 100%. There is no cure. Despite millions of pounds, dollars and euros spent on research, death remains the number one killer world-wide. Good health is just the slowest possible route to getting there.

Death may be the only certainty in life, but how it gets you is anything but predictable. There are lots of ways to die. At least 100 are described in this book. You could fall off a ladder or be hit by a falling coconut, bitten by a snake, struck by lightning or shot by gangsters. You could even succumb in a plane crash – and you don't have to be on the plane to die.

However, according to the World Health Organization, the list of most frequent last gasps across the globe is topped by coronary heart disease, stroke and infections.

Disease	*Millions*	*Disease*	*Millions*
Heart attack	7,200,000	**HIV/AIDS**	1,800,000
Stroke	5,500,000	**Tuberculosis**	1,720,000
Pneumonias	4,000,000	**Lung cancer**	1,400,000
Respiratory failure (bronchitis, emphysema)	3,020,000	**Road traffic accidents**	1,300,000
Diarrhoeal diseases	2,200,000	**Prematurity and low birth weight**	1,180,000

The top ten killers vary depending on a country's level of sanitation and clean water, exposure to pathogens, nutritional quality and access to medical treatments. Depending on whether you live in a rich, poor or middling economic climate, your risk of death is shown in the table below.

'In this world nothing is certain except death and taxes.'

Benjamin Franklin

	High-income countries	*Middle-income countries*	*Low-income countries*
1	Heart attack	Stroke	Pneumonias
2	Stroke	Heart attack	Heart attack
3	Lung cancer	Respiratory failure	Diarrhoeal diseases
4	Pneumonias	Pneumonias	HIV/AIDS
5	Respiratory failure	Lung cancer	Stroke
6	Alzheimer's and other dementias	Road traffic accidents	Respiratory failure
7	Bowel cancers	Hypertensive heart disease	TB
8	Diabetes	Stomach cancer	Neonatal infections
9	Breast cancer	TB	Malaria
10	Stomach cancer	Diabetes	Prematurity/low birth weight

The same risk factors underpin all these causes of death, however – the usual suspects are smoking, uncorrected high blood pressure, uncontrolled high blood glucose, lack of exercise and being overweight or obese. Infection also plays an increasingly important role as income decreases.

Life expectancy

For many people, a population's life expectancy is considered the best measure of overall health. According to a comprehensive study of adult mortality published in The Lancet, the countries with the highest life expectancy are as shown in the table below. The highest risk of mortality is for men in Swaziland, and women in Zambia.

	Males	*Females*
1	Iceland	Cyprus
2	Sweden	South Korea
3	Malta	Japan
4	The Netherlands	Greece
5	Switzerland	Italy
6	Australia	Spain
7	Norway	Switzerland
8	Italy	Australia
9	Qatar	Sweden
10	Israel	Iceland

DID YOU KNOW?

Every year, 59 million people die – almost 1% of the population. That adds up to more than 161,600 people every day, 6735 per hour, 112 per minute or 1.87 deaths every second, on average.

Quality of life

While longevity is important, other factors affect whether or not you enjoy your prolonged years. In 2008, Forbes magazine compiled a list of the world's healthiest countries using a variety of data from the World Health Organization, World Bank and United Nations. As well as longevity, they looked at factors such as levels of air pollution, access to clean water, good sanitation, low levels of certain diseases (most notably tuberculosis), infant mortality rates and undernourishment. They also looked at standards of health care, which were assessed on the number of doctors per 1000 head of population. Out of 138 nations, their top 15 healthiest countries were:

	Healthiest country		
1	Iceland	9	Austria
2	Sweden	10	The Netherlands
3	Finland	11	USA
4	Germany	12	Israel
5	Switzerland	13	Czech Republic
6	Australia	14	Spain
7	Denmark	15	France
8	Canada		

Assessing health based on happiness

Some would argue that it's no good having a long life, flushable toilets and money in the bank if these don't make you happy. The World Database of Happiness therefore drew up an International League Table based on scientific research into 'the subjective appreciation of life'. Out of 95 countries assessed in 2009 by the Erasmus University in Rotterdam, the following were rated as happiest overall:

	Happiest country	*How much nationals enjoy their life as a whole, on a scale of 0–10*
1	Costa Rica	8.5
2	Denmark	8.3
3	Iceland	8.2
4 equal	Switzerland, Canada	8.0
6 equal	Finland, Mexico, Norway	7.9
9 equal	Sweden, Panama	7.8
11 equal	Australia, Austria, Colombia, Luxembourg	7.7
15 equal	Dominican Republic, The Netherlands, Ireland	7.6

Overall, it would seem that if you want to live the longest, healthiest, happiest life you should undoubtedly move to Iceland, Sweden, Finland or Norway. Perhaps it has to do with all those long, cold nights spent snuggling up in bed with your partner.

Raising your stakes in the survival game

We all want to live longer and enjoy a happier, healthier lifespan. Most of us know the nutritional and lifestyle steps required to achieve this. It's putting them into action that is troublesome. Follow these non-guaranteed top tips:

- Maintain a healthy weight – lose any excess weight slowly so it is more likely to stay off.
- Exercise regularly, for at least 30 to 60 minutes every day.
- Don't smoke, ever.
- Drink alcohol in moderation.
- Eat more fruit and vegetables – five to ten portions per day.
- Cut back on overall fat intake and concentrate on obtaining healthy fats (omega-3s, monounsaturates) in place of saturated fats.
- Cut back on carbohydrate intake and concentrate on following a diet that has minimal impact on blood glucose levels (low glycaemic load).
- Drink sufficient fluids to maintain pale-coloured urine.
- Heed the prevention boxes in each of the following 100 modes of death.

AIDS 1

Since it was first clinically identified in 1981, acquired immune deficiency syndrome or AIDS has infected more than 60 million people, killed over 25 million and orphaned 14 million children. No effective vaccine or cure is currently in sight.

How common is it?

An estimated 1.8 million AIDS-related deaths occur each year, including over a quarter of a million children.

Who dies?

Those with an overwhelming suppression of immunity as a result of HIV infection.

Where?

Occurs all over the world, but particularly in sub-Saharan Africa.

When?

Without antiviral treatment, HIV progresses to AIDS within 1–15 years (typically 10 years), and someone with AIDS will die within 1 year. Treatment greatly increases life expectancy by reducing viral replication.

Why?

Exposure to the human immunodeficiency virus from infected body fluids.

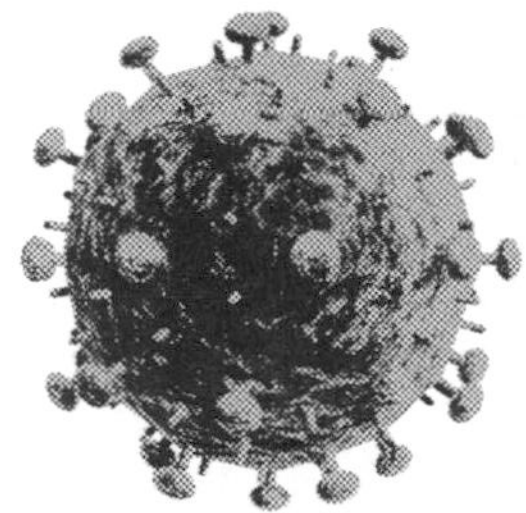

The HIV virus

Despite what ill-informed deniers have claimed, AIDS is caused by the human immunodeficiency virus (HIV). However, HIV may not progress to AIDS in every case. Although the annual number of new HIV infections and AIDS-related deaths have both steadily declined since 1999 (owing to improved education and treatment), the number of people living with HIV has increased. In 2009, an estimated 33,300,000 people were living with HIV, of whom 22,500,000 were in sub-Saharan Africa.

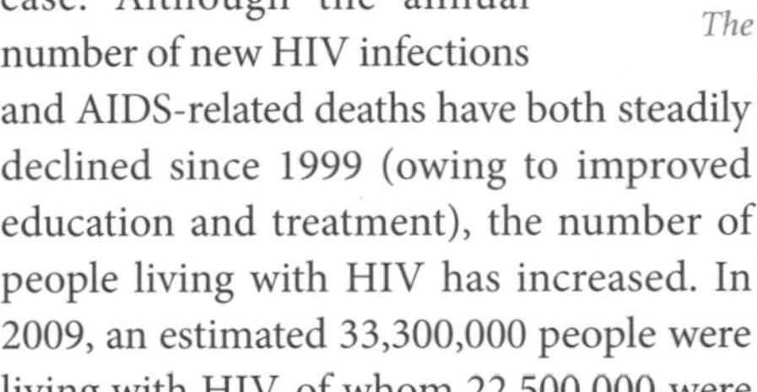

Why does it kill?

HIV decimates the host's natural immunity, so opportunistic infections can flourish. It selectively invades immune cells known as CD4 T-lymphocytes. Using an enzyme called a reverse transcriptase, it copies its genome and inveigles itself into the host cells' DNA. One of two things then happens. It either lies dormant or replicates large numbers of viral particles that invade other CD4 cells.

CD4 cells regulate immune defences, including the production of antibodies. As HIV infection becomes increasingly active, larger numbers of CD4 cells are destroyed. When their numbers are reduced to fewer than 200 per microlitre of blood, the ability to fight common infections is significantly reduced. This stage of the illness is known as acquired immunodeficiency syndrome (AIDS). Minor infections that do not trouble healthy individuals, such as the yeast-like fungi *Pneumocystis* and *Cryptococcus*, cause serious illnesses. Tuberculosis (see page 250), atypical pneumonias and cancer are common causes of AIDS-related death. Sepsis from injecting with dirty needles can also kill.

Will it happen to me?

Potentially, yes. Each year, an estimated 2.6 million people are newly infected with HIV. Most remain unaware of their infection and pass it on to others. If you have ever had unprotected sex, screening for HIV and other sexually transmissible infections is a good idea – even if you feel fighting fit.

What to look for

Many people who are HIV-positive are carriers but have no symptoms. Others develop slight swelling of the lymph glands, weight loss, night sweats or unexplained diarrhoea. Symptoms that suggest progression to AIDS include recurrent infections (oral thrush, persistent herpes, atypical pneumonia), white, furry plaques growing inside the mouth (hairy leucoplakia) or an otherwise rare form of cancer (Kaposi's sarcoma) that forms purplish-red patches on the skin or mucous membranes.

What are the chances of survival?

Progression varies from person to person. With the right treatment, people with AIDS can remain relatively well for many years. Antiviral drugs help to reduce viral replication. Antibiotic or antifungal drugs help to control secondary infections.

Although rare, a small number of people with HIV maintain high levels of CD4 cells and low levels of the virus without any treatment. These 'long-term non-progressors' may remain HIV-positive for

Estimated number living with HIV, and AIDS-related deaths during 2009

Region	Number living with HIV	AIDS-related deaths, 2009
Sub-Saharan Africa	22,500,000	1,300,000
South and South-East Asia	4,100,000	260,000
North America	1,500,000	26,000
Central and South America	1,400,000	58,000
Eastern Europe and Central Asia	1,400,000	76,000
Western and Central Europe	820,000	8500
East Asia	770,000	36,000
Middle East and North Africa	460,000	24,000
Caribbean	240,000	12,000
Oceania	57,000	1400

30 years or more without developing AIDS. An even rarer group remain HIV-negative despite high rates of exposure to the virus. Research suggests this group have had transient HIV infections that they have successfully eradicated.

HIV testing

Usually, the production of antibodies helps to eradicate an underlying infection, but because HIV hides inside T-cells, it remains safe from antibody attack. The presence of anti-HIV antibodies is a useful marker that someone has been exposed to the HIV virus and forms the basis of the HIV test. Knowing you are HIV-positive helps you avoid passing on the infection to others. It also allows you to receive early antiviral treatment that can keep you well for many years.

HOW TO AVOID IT

HIV is transmitted through contact with infected body fluids such as blood, urine, semen, breast milk and saliva. Drug-users should never share needles. In the West, at least one in seven people with HIV has caught the infection through normal heterosexual intercourse – always practise safer sex and insist on a condom. Unprotected anal sex, with a man or woman, is particularly risky as it is more likely to be associated with minor tears, abrasions and bleeding. Oral sex is also thought to increase the risk of HIV transmission (use condoms or dental dams) and, although the risk is thought to be low, you may want to avoid wet kissing with exchange of saliva.

Alcohol 2

Like many things in life, alcohol is great in moderation but lethal in excess. In the short term it acts as a sedative, initially suppressing social inhibitions to produce a mild, giggly euphoria.

How common is it?

Globally, 140 million people have an alcohol dependence, and alcohol is linked with 1 in 25 deaths.

Who dies?

Women develop health problems associated with alcohol at intakes 50% lower than for men; they are more vulnerable to alcoholic liver disease.

Where?

Everywhere, but according to one study published in 2009, more than half of all deaths in Russia in those aged 15–54 were due to alcohol.

When?

After many years of excessive intake, or after binge drinking (more than twice the recommended daily maximum), which is associated with sudden death.

Why?

Acute or long-term overindulgence in ethanol, the form of alcohol found in alcoholic drinks. On its own, ethanol is both tasteless and colourless.

As blood alcohol levels increase, this depresses parts of the brain that control movement, reaction times and coordination, before acting as a general anaesthetic, leading to respiratory failure and death.

Why does it kill?

Many things can be preserved in alcohol. Life is not one of them. Alcohol is toxic. Excess poisons the liver, brain, intestines and heart. It is responsible for more than 60 types of disease and injury, including accidents, suicide, homicide, inhalation of vomit, asphyxiation, heart arrhythmias, heart attack, pancreatitis, liver failure, stroke, epilepsy and brain degeneration (Wernicke-Korsakoff syndrome), to name but a few. Alcohol-related cancers include those of the mouth, throat, liver, colon, rectum and breast.

Cirrhosis

Alcoholic cirrhosis results from progressive liver cell death, formation of scar tissue (fibrosis), impaired blood supply and the desperate attempt by some liver cells to regenerate new tissue. Islands of regenerating liver cells, separated by bands of scar tissue, give the liver a shrunken, knobbly appearance. Fibrosis interferes with blood supply, leading to back-pressure and the formation of varicose veins within the oesophagus. These can bleed torrentially. For liver-hardened drinkers, cirrhosis eventually leads to death from haemorrhage, liver failure or liver cancer, which develops in 10% of cases as a result of abnormal cell regeneration.

Will it happen to me?

If you drink more than the safe recommended level, then it's a good bet. Alcohol kills slowly, allowing you more time to spend in the bar. While it takes up to 10 years of heavy drinking for a susceptible male to become dependent, it takes much less time (3–4 years) for a susceptible woman to develop dependency. You are at particular risk if you experience cravings (a need to drink), loss of control (being unable to quit after starting to drink), withdrawal symptoms and 'tolerance' (having to drink increasing amounts of alcohol to feel its effects). The amount of alcohol that damages health varies and not everyone who drinks heavily will suffer the same physical effects. Only 20% of heavy drinkers develop cirrhosis of the liver, for example; in others the brain or heart muscle are affected more than the liver. This effect seems to be genetically determined.

What to look for

If you answer 'Yes' to any of the following questions, you may have a problem with alcohol. Seek advice from your doctor, who can arrange a liver test and counselling.

- Do you drink every day of the week?
- Do you ever feel you should cut down on your drinking?
- Do you ever need a drink first thing in the morning?
- Do you feel annoyed if people mention your drinking?
- Do you experience mood swings or difficulty sleeping after drinking?
- Do you feel hungover or shaky the morning after drinking?
- Do you ever miss work because of the effects of drinking?
- Do you drink and drive?

Stages of alcohol poisoning according to blood alcohol level

Blood alcohol level (mg/dl)	*Clinical effect*
20–99	Impaired coordination; euphoria
100–199	Shaky movements; unsteady gait; poor coordination; mood swings
200–299	Markedly unsteady gait; slurred speech; poor judgement; increased mood swings; nausea; vomiting
300–399	Stage 1 anaesthesia, blackouts; memory lapses; mood swings
400 +	Respiratory failure; coma; death

What are the chances of survival?

If you stop drinking altogether, the chances of survival are high. If you continue to drink you may as well order a coffin with a built-in bar. A lucky few may qualify for a liver transplant and get a second chance. Don't compromise the donated liver as well.

In the UK, a unit of alcohol is defined as 10 ml or 8 grams of pure alcohol. Half a pint (300 ml) of beer, lager or cider whose strength is 3.5% alcohol by volume (ABV) therefore contains 1 unit. But many lagers now contain 5% ABV and some versions supply as much as 9%. One small (100 ml) glass of wine that is 10% ABV contains 1 unit. But most wines are now much stronger (12% to 15%) and many pubs sell wine in 250 ml glasses. Depending on its strength, a bottle of wine typically contains between 8 and 11 units of alcohol. A 25 ml pub measure of 40% spirit contains 1 unit. But many pubs now serve 35 ml measures as standard, and will often serve a double unless you specifically say you want a single.

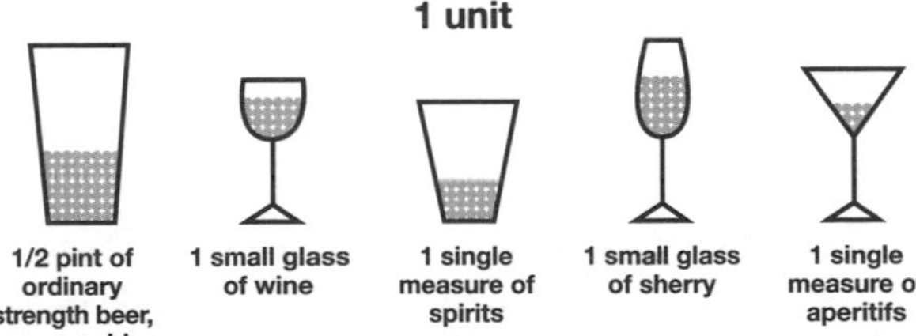

HOW TO AVOID IT

Stick to the recommended 'safe' maximum intake. Ideally, alcohol intake should not exceed 2–3 units per day (14 units per week) for women or 3–4 units per day (21 units per week) for men.

Anaemia 3

'Anaemia' literally means 'without blood' and relates to having low levels of the red blood pigment, haemoglobin.

How common is it?

Iron-deficiency anaemia is an underlying factor in 840,000 maternal and perinatal deaths per year; it is a direct cause of 134,000 deaths in young children. Sickle-cell anaemia and other haemoglobin disorders such as thalassaemia contribute to 3.4% of deaths in children aged under 5 years worldwide, and 6.4% in Africa.

Who dies?

Mostly elderly people, pregnant women and children.

Where?

Anaemia is prevalent across the globe, but anaemia-related deaths are most likely in poor countries.

When?

Anaemia becomes severe enough that vital organs no longer receive adequate blood supply; greatest mortality is during the first 2 years of life; life expectancy for adults with sickle-cell anaemia who survive childhood is between 48 and 58 years.

Why?

Poor nutrition, poor diagnosis and poor treatment.

Haemoglobin circulates within the body in doughnut-shaped bags called red blood cells (erythrocytes), each of which contains an estimated 250 million molecules of the pigment. As you have around 28,000 billion red blood cells, and produce 2 million more every second, it seems unlikely that anyone would ever run out. Yet, across the globe, almost 2 billion people – over 30% of the world's population – have anaemia.

In general, anaemia develops if you:

- Make too little haemoglobin or too few red blood cells (e.g. because of lack of iron, folic acid or B12; or because of leukaemia, bone marrow disease, kidney disease, cancer, TB, malaria, HIV).
- Lose too much blood (e.g. from general oozing of blood from cut surfaces that refuse to clot – in someone with an undiagnosed blood-clotting disorder – or from a major haemorrhage or small persistent losses such as menstruation, hookworm infestation or erosion of the stomach lining caused by aspirin).
- Recycle red blood cells more quickly than their allotted 120 days, either because they are abnormal (e.g. thalassaemia, sickle-cell disease) or because your immune system attacks them (auto-immune haemolytic anaemia).

Spinach

Half of all cases of anaemia are due to iron deficiency.

Why does it kill?

Massive haemorrhage kills through lack of blood perfusion and multi-organ failure. Chronic anaemia is seldom a direct cause of death, but poor oxygen delivery to tissues can precipitate a heart attack or stroke. It also lowers immunity, which increases the risk of succumbing to infection. Anaemia is associated with premature birth and increases maternal and infant mortality rates. Sickle-cell crises can kill as a result of organ failure, infection and stroke.

Will it happen to me?

Anyone can develop anaemia if their diet or ability to absorb essential nutrients (iron, vitamin B12, folic acid) is poor. Women and children are at greatest risk of iron-deficiency anaemia as rapid growth, pregnancy and menstruation increase their needs. A significant number of people die from anaemia as a side effect of nonsteroidal anti-inflammatory drugs (NSAIDs).

Region	*% population affected*
Africa	41%
Americas	58%
South-East Asia	15%
Europe	23%
Eastern Mediterranean	84%
Western Pacific	14%

What to look for

Anaemia can cause symptoms of tiredness, dizziness, fainting, headache, lack of energy, recurrent infections (especially *Candida*), sore tongue and mouth, ringing in the ears, shortness of breath, palpitations and even chest pain. Signs include paleness of the skin, conjunctivae and lips. Iron-deficiency anaemia can also cause spoon-shaped fingernails (koilonychia).

What are the chances of survival?

If the anaemia is due to poor nutrition and is diagnosed and treated, the chances of survival are excellent. If anaemia results from an underlying condition such as sickle-cell disease, kidney failure or cancer, the prognosis will depend on these.

Population group	*Number affected*
47% of preschool children	293 million
25% of school children	305 million
42% of pregnant women	56 million
30% of non-pregnant women	468 million
13% of men	260 million
24% of elderly	164 million
The data is incomplete, but it is estimated that, worldwide, at least 1,620,000 people are affected.	

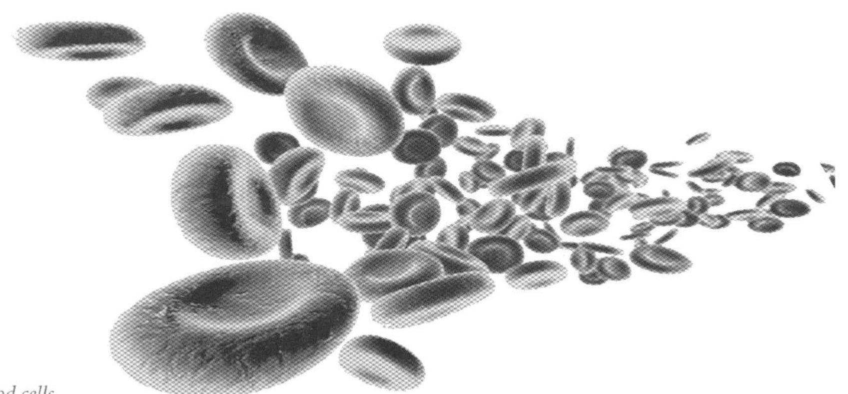

Red blood cells

HOW TO AVOID IT

The form of iron found in red meat (haem iron) is up to 10 times more easily absorbed than the non-haem iron in vegetables. Meat-eaters are therefore less prone to iron-deficiency anaemia than non-meat-eaters. The form of iron found in nuts, whole grains and green leafy vegetables is absorbed more easily if eaten together with a source of vitamin C, such as fresh orange juice.

Anaphylactic shock

4

Anaphylaxis is a severe, life-threatening allergic reaction. It occurs when an overvigilant immune system mounts an excessive reaction against a particular foreign protein.

How common is it?

More than 1% of the population is affected and it is becoming more common. In the USA alone, 11 million people have suffered a life-threatening reaction; 1 in 5000 exposures to penicillin or cephalosporin antibiotics causes anaphylaxis; worldwide, 1 person dies per 2.8 million people each year, which is equivalent to around 2500 people.

Who dies?

Perhaps surprisingly, adults are more likely to die than children; women are twice as likely as males to be admitted to hospital with anaphylaxis.

Where?

Usually a long way from hospital, without access to antihistamines, adrenaline or corticosteroids.

When?

Typically within 5 minutes if drug-induced, 15 minutes if venom-induced, and 30 minutes if food-induced.

Why?

Half of all anaphylactic deaths are iatrogenic (doctor induced), 25% are due to food allergies, and 25% are caused by insect or animal venom.

Rapid swelling of the tongue and airways compromises breathing. Histamine and other powerful immune chemicals cause widespread dilation of the blood vessels, so blood pressure plummets. Heart rhythm abnormalities and cardiac arrest can develop. Risk of death is greatest in those with pre-existing asthma, especially if it is poorly controlled. The majority of deaths (90%) occur because no adrenaline (epinephrine) was available for use at the time of the reaction.

When an allergen is encountered, mast cells found in the skin and lining of the respiratory and intestinal tracts suddenly release histamine and other powerful chemicals. Potentially catastrophic symptoms reach a peak within 15 minutes, although potentially fatal reactions may be delayed by half an hour or more. Without emergency medical treatment it is rapidly lethal.

Why does it kill?

Half of all victims die from asphyxia, and half from shock (circulatory collapse).

Will it happen to me?

Often a combination of factors that each increase gut 'leakiness' is needed, so that incompletely digested allergens cross the gut wall into the circulation: for example, walking up a steep hill, after eating prawns and drinking alcohol, during a heat wave. Researchers suggest the risk of experiencing anaphylaxis at some point during your life lies somewhere between 1 in 33 and 1 in 100. However, with proper treatment, 98% of people experiencing anaphylaxis will survive. You are probably more likely to die from base-jumping or being hit by lightning than from suffering anaphylactic shock.

DID YOU KNOW?

Reported triggers for anaphylaxis include: foods (nuts, especially peanuts, seafood, fin fish, milk, egg, soya, wheat, chickpeas, bananas and snails), Hymenoptera insect venoms (bees, wasps, yellowjackets, hornets, fire ants), snake bites, antibiotics (especially penicillins and cephalosporins), anaesthetic drugs (especially suxamethonium), ibuprofen, aspirin, iodine, latex, hair dye. In many cases, however, no cause is identified.

What to look for

Victims often report an initial 'sense of doom' and a metallic taste in the mouth. Anaphylaxis is associated with severe tissue swelling (angio-oedema), usually around the face and tongue. Spasm of airways causes wheeziness and shortness of breath similar to asthma. In the skin, histamine release causes flushing and an itchy, raised rash (urticaria or hives). If the intestinal lining is affected, this leads to vomiting, abdominal pain and diarrhoea. If not treated quickly, a severe reaction will result in low blood pressure and a rapid pulse; collapse may follow. The more rapid the onset, the more serious the reaction.

What are the chances of survival?

Speed is vital. Rapid medical treatment with antihistamines, adrenaline and corticosteroids are life-saving in 98% of cases. Those with known severe allergies should carry their own supply of antihistamines and adrenaline wherever they go (see below). Avoid known allergens. Carry a medical alert identifier (jewellery engraved with details of your allergy).

HOW TO AVOID IT

If you have ever had a severe allergic reaction, carry an adrenaline pen (an injector) with you. The chance of experiencing another severe reaction is as high as 1 in 12.

5

Animal attack

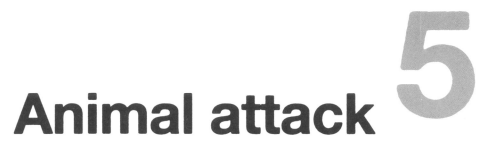

As human beings are usually at the top of the food chain, it comes as a shock to be attacked by species other than our own. The vast majority of animal-related deaths are due to lowly creatures such as the scorpion and snake.

How common is it?
More frequent than most people realize, except for shark attacks, which are rarer than commonly assumed; if animal-borne diseases such as rabies (see page 201) and malaria (see page 157) are excluded, then, worldwide, around 110,000 people die from an encounter with wildlife.

Who dies?
Males are three times more likely to die an animal-related death than females; the very young and very old are most at risk of venom-related deaths; children are most at risk of a dog-related fatality.

Where?
Mostly Africa, Asia and Latin America.

When?
More deaths occur during summer.

Why?
Animal attacks can kill as a result of physical injury or poisoning with the animal's venom.

According to the WHO (World Health Organization), as many as 5 million people are bitten by snakes every year. Half of these involve a venomous species and at least 100,000 people die as a result. Although the stuff of legend, attacks by giant squid are at the bottom of the list in frequency. While being attacked by an animal may imply a glamorous safari lifestyle, it is still possible to be killed by a domesticated animal, such as a dog, in your own back garden.

Why does it kill?

Different animals have different methods. Some claw, gore or trample you to death, some rip out your throat or puncture your

Animal	*Average world fatalities per year*
Snake	100,000
Scorpion	5000
Wildcat	1700
Alligator/crocodile	1000+
Dog	600
Elephant	500
Hippopotamus	300
Wasp/bee/hornet	100 (not counting anaphylaxis)
Rhinoceros	100
Buffalo/bison	100
Bull	100
Jellyfish	50
Shark	4
Bear	3
Spider	2
Stingray	Less than 1
Blue-ringed octopus/giant squid	Less than 1

DID YOU KNOW?

The hippo kills more people in Africa than any other large animal. When size is discounted, however, the female *Anopheles* mosquito (or more accurately the parasite that it transmits) wins hands down (as long as we exclude human beings).

skull, while others just sting or bite then run away. Some kill because they feel threatened, some because they see red (allegedly), while others simply view you as a passing snack.

Will it happen to me?

Your lifetime risk of being attacked by a shark is, apparently, 1 in 11 million. The chance of being killed by one is 1 in 264 million. This obviously depends on whether or not you are swimming in shark-infested waters. Your annual chance of being killed by a snake, however, is a mere 1 in 68,700.

What to look for

Anything with the potential to bite, sting, crush, gore, stamp, buck, peck, scratch or nibble you to death.

What are the chances of survival?

If close to intensive medical care and venom antidotes, the chance of surviving any potentially lethal animal interaction is high.

DEADLY DELICACY

Puffer fish are the world's second most deadly vertebrate, after the golden poison frog. Puffer poison is contained in the liver and sometimes the skin. One puffer fish carries enough toxin to kill 30 people, yet their flesh is considered a delicacy in Japan, where it is prepared by specially trained chefs.

HOW TO AVOID IT

If you encounter an aggressive animal, back away slowly. Don't run. Eye-to-eye contact should be avoided with some species (bears) but not others (cougars) so bone up in advance on the potential predators you are most likely to meet. Curling up and 'playing dead' often fools an aggressive bear into thinking you really are dead – but don't get up until you're positive it has gone. This tactic is unlikely to work with a charging elephant.

Anthrax 6

Anthrax holds a special interest for most microbiologists. In 1877, it was the first disease conclusively shown to be due to a bacterium, *Bacillus anthracis*. There's more.

How common is it?

Although classed as a rare disease, anthrax infection is endemic in some countries and sporadic in many others.

Who dies?

Those exposed to anthrax spores who are not immune. While an effective vaccine is available, it is usually offered only to laboratory workers and others who may be exposed during the course of their work.

Where?

See map on page 26.

When?

Symptoms usually appear within 7 days of inoculation with anthrax spores, but in the case of inhalation, anthrax can lie dormant in the lungs for as long as 100 days before germinating.

Why?

Exposure to *Bacillus anthracis* spores, either accidentally or as a result of malicious action.

Global Incidence of Anthrax

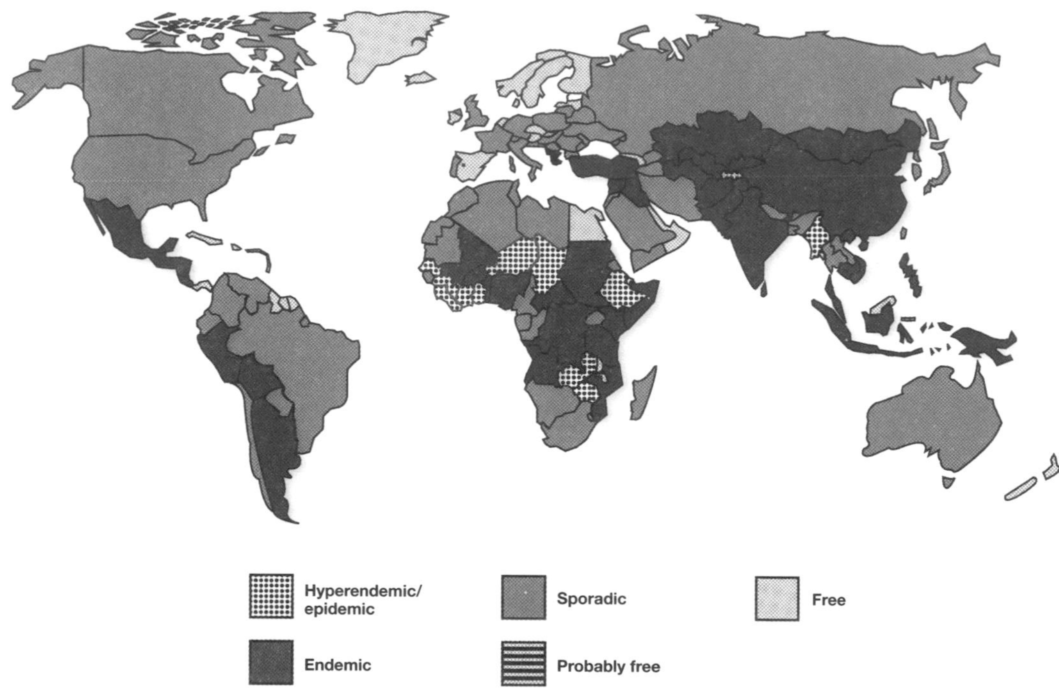

Bacillus anthracis is also the only bacterium to synthesize a protein capsule and the only one to secrete a three-part toxin, one bit of which carries the inspired name of 'lethal factor'.

The anthrax bacterium lives in soil, where it produces spores that can survive adverse conditions for years, possibly even centuries. Because of its protein capsule, it is highly resistant to just about everything nature can throw at it, including temperature, antiseptics and attack by our own immune cells. Luckily, it's no match for synthetic antibiotics.

Whether or not anthrax kills depends on how its spores enter your body. Skin penetration (cutaneous) is preferable to ingestion or inhalation. Cutaneous anthrax (the most common type) causes a localized, black, necrotic lesion known as an eschar. Although this in itself is disturbing, cutaneous anthrax is usually quickly diagnosed and successfully treated with an extended 60-day course of antibiotics. Those who ingest or inhale the spores and subsequently develop gastrointestinal or pulmonary anthrax are less fortunate, however.

Why does it kill?

One component of anthrax toxin (cell-binding protein) acts as a Trojan horse, escorting the other two proteins, oedema factor and lethal factor, into a host cell. Once inside, oedema factor upsets fluid balance while lethal factor snips the end off important cell enzymes to inactivate them. The cell then dies in a cascading mini-implosion.

Biohazard sign

Will it happen to me?

It takes just one spore to initiate an infection. When standing downwind of a heavily contaminated site and breathing calmly at a rate of 20 breaths per minute it will take 2½ minutes to inhale that one spore (assuming you don't have a biohazard mask). In contrast, an exercising horse with a respiratory rate of 77 breaths per minute will inhale that one spore in 20 seconds. Based on this sort of logic, scientists seriously suggest that human beings are relatively resistant to anthrax compared with the herbivorous animals on whom the disease usually preys.

While in theory only one spore reaching the right place can cause anthrax, in practice a higher inoculation is needed, as shown in the table below.

What to look for

In the skin, anthrax causes an itchy bump like an insect bite, surrounded by a ring of vesicles. The lesion ulcerates and dries to form the classic black eschar. Death, when it occurs, is usually due to sepsis (see page 208). In addition, with pulmonary anthrax, massive swelling of the lungs produces shortness of breath and cardiovascular shock. Gastrointestinal anthrax produces fever, vomiting, severe stomach pains and bloody diarrhoea.

Route of infection	*Dose that is lethal in 50% of cases (number of spores)*
Cutaneous inoculation	10–100
Inhalation	15,000–100,000
Ingestion	100 million+

DID YOU KNOW?

Anthrax has been hijacked as a lethal weapon by bioterrorists. In the USA in 2001, letters containing anthrax powder caused 22 cases of pulmonary anthrax. On a brighter note, anthrax has been harnessed in the search for a magic bullet that kills cancer cells but leaves normal cells intact.

What are the chances of survival?

Cutaneous anthrax offers the best hope. Even without treatment, 80% of victims live to tell the tale. Between 25% and 60% of those with gastrointestinal anthrax die, while pulmonary anthrax attracts a 50% fatality rate.

Bacillus anthracis

HOW TO AVOID IT

There are no documented cases of anthrax spreading from person to person. It develops when spores are inoculated into the skin (e.g. from faeces in soil), inhaled from infected animal products (e.g. goat-skin rugs, wool) or ingested by eating undercooked meat from infected animals. So the following may help with prevention:

- **Do not work in laboratories that handle *Bacillus anthracis.***
- **Do not open mail that you suspect has been sent by a bioterrorist, especially if it is contaminated with white powder.**
- **Ironing suspicious mail with a steam iron supposedly disinfects anthrax spores, but if you are concerned, call the police and stay as far away from the envelope as possible.**
- **Avoid contact with livestock and animal products imported from endemic countries (see map), although sporadic cases can occur just about anywhere.**
- **Ensure meat products are thoroughly cooked before eating.**
- **Drink tea, whose polyphenols inhibit both *Bacillus anthracis* and anthrax toxin (but probably only in a test-tube). Do not add milk, which neutralizes the anti-toxin effect.**

Aortic aneurysm

The aorta is the body's equivalent of Highway 401, one of the largest motorways in the world, which in parts is 18 lanes wide. As blood surges through the aorta with each heartbeat, its walls are subjected to immense pressure, making it a hotspot for hardening and furring up (atherosclerosis) of the lining.

How common is it?
A ruptured aortic aneurysm is the 15th-leading cause of death in the world and looks set to become more common as the population ages.

Who dies?
Mostly males over the age of 60 years who smoke.

Where?
Often in bed.

When?
There is a marked early-morning peak between midnight and 6 a.m.

Why?
Blood pressure falls during deep sleep, then rises significantly before waking to rupture an already weak aneurysm.

'What do I dislike about death? Probably the hours.' Woody Allen

Continued pressure in the artery then causes the damaged lining to bulge, forming a dilation called an aortic aneurysm. Abdominal aortic aneurysms are three times more common than thoracic aortic aneurysms. One in every thousand people will develop an abdominal aortic aneurysm between the ages of 60 and 65, and this number continues to rise with age, so that 13% of men and 6% of women over the age of 65 are affected. If an aortic aneurysm remains intact, you're fine. If it ruptures, you're in big trouble.

Why does it kill?

If an aortic aneurysm ruptures forward (20%), blood pumps freely into the abdominal or chest cavities. Few patients survive to reach hospital. If the aneurysm ruptures backwards (80%) into the retroperitoneal space (behind the peritoneal membrane), the resistance of surrounding tissues may slow blood loss long enough for a surgeon to intervene. An aneurysm can also split lengthways, like a pitta bread, when blood seeps into its wall (dissecting aortic aneurysm). Other complications that can kill include pulmonary embolism (see page 198), sudden blockage (acute aortic occlusion) and reduced kidney function.

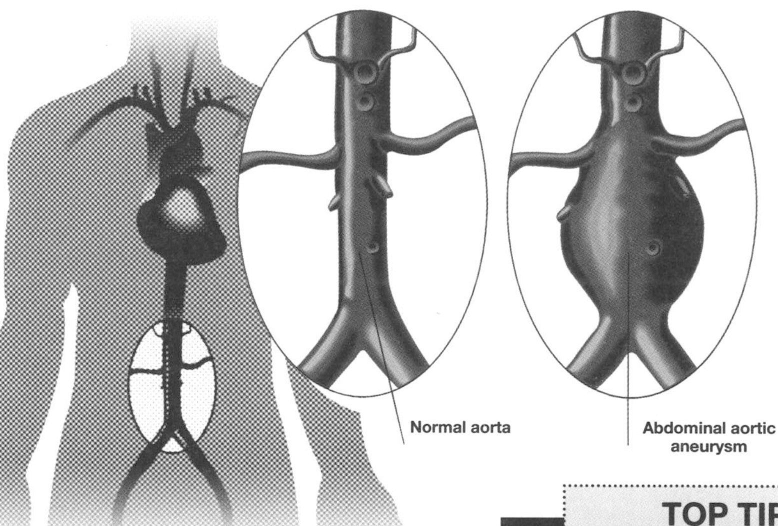

Location of Aorta

TOP TIP

Choose your surgeon carefully if having an elective operation. In one study, only 2.2% of patients operated on by a vascular surgeon died, compared with 4% for cardiac surgeons and 5.5% for general surgeons.

Will it happen to me?

Men are up to nine times more susceptible than women. Once an aneurysm expands to a diameter of 5.5 cm (2.2 in) there is a 1 in 3 chance it will rupture within the next 5 years. Early detection and elective surgical repair once the aneurysm has reached a critical size can be life-saving. Elective surgical grafting (the equivalent of a bicycle inner tube repair) is usually advised if an abdominal aortic aneurysm:

- causes symptoms
- grows at a rate of more than 1 cm (0.4 in) in diameter per year
- is larger than 5.5 cm (2.2 in) in diameter

What to look for

An aortic aneurysm often displays no symptoms. As it slowly dilates, it may cause stretch pains and pulsating sensations in the chest, abdomen, back or scrotum (unusual as that may sound). An acute rupture is diagnosed from a triad of abdominal pain, low blood pressure (shock) and the presence of a pulsating abdominal mass.

What are the chances of survival?

An acute aneurysm rupture is invariably fatal unless a heroic surgeon is able to repair it. Even then, the chance of survival is not good. Fewer than 50% of patients survive to reach hospital, and another 20% die before reaching the operating theatre. Survival following emergency surgery for acute rupture is just 10% to 20%.

Survival following planned, *elective* surgery, using the traditional open method, is 95.3%. Survival with new, less invasive techniques, in which an abdominal aortic graft is inserted, under X-ray control, via small incisions in the groin, is as high as 98.3%.

HOW TO AVOID IT

Elective surgery to insert a graft is strongly advised before an aneurysm ruptures. As most aneurysms occur over the age of 60 years, there have been calls for routine ultrasound screening, especially of males, to allow earlier diagnosis. In addition:

- **Beware of your genes – an inheritable aortic defect may be involved. This could be carried on the Y chromosome, explaining why abdominal aortic aneurysms are nine times more common in men than women.**
- **Do not smoke – inhaling just 100 cigarettes during your life increases the risk. All other healthy diet and lifestyle advice applies, too. Ensure blood pressure, cholesterol and glucose levels remain well controlled.**

8 Asphyxiation

Asphyxiation, or suffocation, results from a lack of oxygen entering the body. It can be accidental (inhaling a foreign body, vomit), homicidal (smothering, strangulation), suicidal (plastic bag over the head) or the result of disease (bronchial cancer).

How common is it?

Birth asphyxiation causes over a million deaths per year. Between the ages of 1 and 10 years, the risk of accidental asphyxiation is 1 in 50,000, falling to 1 in 500,000 between 10 and 14. Of as many as 30,000 adult deaths due to auto-erotic asphyxiation, most are sanitized as 'suspected suicide'.

Who dies?

Young children, men and elderly people are especially vulnerable.

Where?

The riskiest room in the house is the bedroom.

When?

Breathing is compromised.

Why?

Accident, homicide, suicide or respiratory arrest.

Sadly, accidental asphyxiation also occurs in children, though the risk is low. One study found that 19% of these deaths were due to inhaling a foreign body, 12% from facial occlusion (smothering when sleeping with a parent), 38% from entanglement with scarves or ropes (especially home-made swings) and 31% were due to becoming trapped (including in cots and bedding).

In recent years, increasing numbers of deaths have resulted from auto-erotic asphyxiation going wrong. Deliberately suffocating yourself for sexual kicks (hypoxyphilia) is incredibly dangerous. If you black out before activating your improvised, so-called fail-safe mechanism, death or severe brain damage results.

Why does it kill?

Lack of oxygen leads to loss of consciousness and brain death within minutes.

Will it happen to me?

Accidents, homicide and diseases that compromise breathing are generally unpredictable. The risk of auto-erotic asphyxiation is firmly in your own hands.

What to look for

Cyanosis (blueing) of lips, peripheries and other parts of the body, shortness of breath, rapid pulse, seizures, coma ...

What are the chances of survival?

Slim unless you choke near someone who knows what to do, which is:

- Remove an obstructing object if it is clearly visible; sweeping blindly with your fingers should be avoided unless you know what you are doing – you may just push the object farther down the airway, which could prove fatal, especially in children.
- Give up to five blows on the back to help dislodge the food/foreign body.
- If this fails, give up to five abdominal thrusts by placing one hand on top of the other just above the navel and thrusting upwards (do this only on adults and children over 1 year; use chest thrusts for infants).

Continue alternating five back blows with five abdominal thrusts.

But be warned. Abdominal thrusts can lead to injury if performed too vigorously. Deaths have resulted from ruptured ribs, liver, spleen, aorta or oesophagus – especially in children.

HOW TO AVOID IT

- **Never put yourself in a situation where your airway or oxygen supply could become compromised.**
- **Don't talk with your mouth full.**
- **Encourage children to sit down when eating, and not to run around with hardboiled sweets or other objects in their mouth.**

Asthma 9

Asthma is an inflammatory disease of the lungs that causes reversible airway obstruction. Worldwide, an estimated 300 million people are affected, with the prevalence ranging from 1% to 18% of the population in different countries.

How common is it?

Asthma accounts for 1 in every 250 deaths worldwide.

Who dies?

The incidence rises with age, so the over-65s are at greatest risk; asthma deaths are more common in women than men, possibly due to their smaller airways, which are more easily compromised.

Where?

Most deaths occur outside hospital, frequently after a visit to the emergency department when symptoms recur after initial recovery; sudden death can occur in the early hours of the morning when asphyxiation wakes the victim but unconsciousness intervenes before they can summon help.

When?

Symptoms are exacerbated by a trigger, such as a viral respiratory infection (half of all cases), exercise, emotion, allergens or exposure to cold air.

Why?

Inadequate control of symptoms, often from not taking medication correctly.

Despite being a totally treatable condition, asthma is tragically underdiagnosed and undertreated. As a result, as many as 255,000 preventable deaths are attributed to this disease every year. This death toll is set to rise. The prevalence of asthma has increased by 50% over the past decade, and the number affected will increase by another 100 million by the year 2025.

Why does it kill?

Asthma causes inflammation of lung airways, which become red and swollen and go into spasm. Constriction of these airways (some of which have the diameter of a human hair) initially causes cough, wheeze, chest tightness and shortness of breath. As the attack progresses, the swollen airways secrete excess mucus to trigger a second bout of tightness and wheezing, 6–8 hours later (often after leaving the hospital emergency department). Mucus blocks oxygen absorption, and waste carbon dioxide gas builds up – a life-threatening situation.

Will it happen to me?

Surveys suggest 1 in 10 people with asthma lives in constant fear that their next attack will kill them. If you're one of them, see your doctor. Do it now. Asthma deaths are totally preventable when you have the correct medication and take it EXACTLY AS PRESCRIBED. Time and again, researchers find that people with asthma fail to take their preventive medication as often as they should. Inhaled corticosteroids do not produce instant results, like bronchodilators, so many people don't think they are

DIETARY TIPS

Consume more anti-inflammatory omega-3s, which are found in:

- oily fish (two to four portions per week), such as mackerel, herring, salmon, trout, sardines, pilchards, fresh tuna (not tinned)
- wild game meat, such as venison and buffalo
- grass-fed beef
- omega-3 enriched eggs
- omega-3 fish oil supplements

Cut out excess inflammation-promoting omega-6s by consuming fewer:

- omega-6 vegetable oils, such as safflower oil, grape-seed oil, sunflower oil, corn oil, cottonseed oil or soyabean oil (replace with healthier oils such as rapeseed, olive, walnut, almond, avocado, hempseed or macadamia oils, which contain good amounts of omega-3s and/or monounsaturated fats)
- margarines based on omega-6 oils, such as sunflower or safflower oil
- convenience foods
- fast foods
- manufactured foods, such as cakes, sweets and pastries

important. They are. They are damping down the inflammation in your airways. They may stand between you and death's door.

What to look for

Signs that your asthma is poorly controlled include:

- Poor peak flow readings.
- Waking with symptoms such as cough or wheeze.
- Having to use your reliever inhaler more than once a day.
- Having to make compromises in your life because of symptoms.

What are the chances of survival?

Your chances are 100% if your symptoms are controlled by taking the right medications at the right times. Ask your doctor for a personal management plan so you know how to step your treatment up and down according to your peak-flow readings and other symptoms.

Allergic asthma is triggered by allergens, notably:

- grass and tree pollens
- house dust mite
- animal fur
- fungal spores and moulds
- certain foods, such as peanuts, eggs and milk products
- work hazards, e.g. some chemicals
- viral infections
- cigarette smoke and other air pollutants
- cold or damp air
- exercise
- strong emotions, stress
- cosmetics and perfume
- volatile chemicals in solvents, paint, polishes and glues

DID YOU KNOW?

Coffee contains caffeine and theobromine, which suppress cough and reduce airway spasm. Those with a regular coffee habit are 30% less likely to have asthma symptoms compared with non-coffee drinkers.

HOW TO AVOID IT

Asthma is linked with ill-understood interactions between our genes, immune system, 21st-century diet, lifestyle and environment. Identify your triggers, if any, and try to avoid them (see above).

Bleeding diseases 10

Bizarrely, the word 'haemophilia' comes from the Greek for 'love of blood', which seems somewhat inaccurate. It is a blood-clotting deficiency in which prolonged bleeding (for days, weeks or even months) can follow even a minor injury. Spontaneous internal haemorrhage can also occur.

How common is it?

An estimated 500,000 people worldwide have haemophilia, but 75% remain undiagnosed and untreated.

Who dies?

Mostly males.

Where?

Developing countries where diagnosis and safe treatments are less readily available.

When?

Life expectancy of severe undiagnosed haemophilia averages 11 years. With proper treatment, life expectancy is just 10 years shorter than for males without haemophilia.

Why?

Excessive bleeding and blood-borne infections acquired during transfusion treatment.

DID YOU KNOW?

People with haemophilia are a third less likely to die of a heart attack than those without.

Blood clotting involves the interaction of at least 12 different proteins or clotting factors. Most are produced in the liver, and some require vitamin K. This complexity gives plenty of scope for things to go wrong.

Prolonged bleeding can result from acquired conditions such as liver disease, vitamin K deficiency or leukaemia. It can also result from inheritable abnormalities such as haemophilia A (Factor VIII deficiency), haemophilia B (Factor IX deficiency), haemophilia C (Factor XI deficiency) and von Willebrand's disease (lack of a protein that sticks platelets together).

The genes associated with haemophilia are carried on the X-chromosome. Women, who have two X-chromosomes, doubling the chance of their owning at least one healthy version of the gene, are rarely affected. Men have only one X-chromosome and when a faulty gene crops up, symptoms develop.

Worldwide, haemophilia A affects 1 in 5000 males and haemophilia B affects 1 in 25,000 males. In a third of cases, there is no family history: the condition arises from a spontaneous gene mutation at conception. In contrast, von Willebrand's disease affects as many as 1 in 100 people, including as many as 1 in 6 women with persistent heavy periods, but only 1 in 10,000 is ever diagnosed.

Why does it kill?

Intracranial bleeding accounts for one-third of deaths due to haemorrhage. Bleeding can also compromise internal organs and obstruct the airways. Sadly, viral infections from infected blood transfusion products mean that hepatitis, cirrhosis and HIV are among the most common causes of death. Improved screening, and the development of recombinant clotting factors (using DNA biotechnology) are reducing these risks.

Will it happen to me?

If you bleed normally after a minor injury, you are unlikely to be affected. Acquired blood coagulation disorders can result from vitamin K deficiency or severe liver disease, but the risk is low.

What to look for

Excessive bleeding or bruising, including excessive nose bleeds that are difficult to stop, and (for women) heavy menstrual periods.

What are the chances of survival?

Overall, the mortality rate for haemophilia is between two and six times that of the healthy male population. The mortality rate from intracranial bleeding is 30% in patients with severe haemophilia.

HOW TO AVOID IT

Eat more cauliflower (for vitamin K), look after your liver and avoid excessive alcohol.

Boredom 11

If you've ever complained of feeling bored to death, you're probably not wrong. Researchers took 7500 civil servants, aged 35–55, who did not have any known pre-existing heart disease and asked whether they'd felt bored over the past 4 weeks. Participants could respond with 'not at all', 'a little', 'quite a lot' or 'all the time'.

How common is it?
Boredom, or ennui, affects everyone at some time.

Who dies?
Women are twice as likely to feel bored as men.

Where?
Any office, in fact, anywhere.

When?
Office hours, waking hours.

Why?
Dearth of stimulating activities, e.g. lack of interesting paper to push.

'One must choose in life between boredom and suffering.'

Madame de Staël

The same question was asked 3 years later – at the risk of boring them again – before the group were followed for a total of 25 years. Guess what? Those who reported quite a lot, or a great deal, of boredom, were more likely to die during the follow-up period than those who were not bored at all.

Why does it kill?

In this study, boredom increased the risk of death from any cause by 37%, but increased the risk of dying from heart attack or stroke by two and a half times.

Will it happen to me?

If you often feel bored, then it may well affect your mortality rate.

What to look for

Boredom may be a marker of other risk factors, such as lack of exercise, smoking, excessive alcohol, taking illicit drugs and having poor health.

What are the chances of survival?

Good, if you keep mind and body busy.

HOW TO AVOID IT

Never sit still long enough to feel bored. If you do feel bored, get up and go for a brisk walk. It could save your life.

DID YOU KNOW?

Even after adjusting for physical activity level, employment grade and self-rated poor health, those experiencing a great deal of boredom were still twice as likely to die from a heart attack or stroke during follow-up than those without boredom, though this could have been a chance finding.

Botulism 12

The term 'botulism' was derived from *botulus*, the Latin for 'sausage', after a spate of German outbreaks involving, presumably, contaminated frankfurters. The causative bacterium, *Clostridium botulinum*, was later isolated, in 1895, from a home-cured ham that poisoned three people.

How common is it?
Rare, with a yearly worldwide incidence of 1 case per 1.77 million people.

Who dies?
Infants and elderly people are particularly susceptible to botulism as they produce less stomach acid to inactivate ingested spores.

Where?
Usually in a hospital intensive care unit.

When?
Typically 12–36 hours after intoxication.

Why?
Exposure to *Clostridium botulinum* spores through ingestion, inhalation or wound contamination.

Lightly preserved foods are the most common source of contamination, especially home-canned vegetables, fermented, salted or smoked meat, fish and honey. The bacteria and spores are also present in soil and can enter the body through wounds.

Clostridium botulinum bacteria are 'obligate' anaerobes – which means they are rapidly poisoned by oxygen. Unlike other sporulating (spore-forming) bacteria, they do not produce spores to see them through when conditions are hostile – they produce spores only when happily ensconced in a low-oxygen environment. During sporulation, they also secrete powerful neurotoxins, of which seven types (A to G) with numerous subtypes have been identified.

Injections of purified botulinum toxin (type A) are used cosmetically to paralyse facial muscles and iron out wrinkles; these can also prove lethal. In the USA alone, between 1997 and 2006, 180 people developed life-threatening complications after botulinum toxin injections, with 16 deaths.

Why does it kill?

Botulinum toxins act at the neuromuscular junction (where nerve and muscle cells communicate) to cause a flaccid, muscular paralysis. Death results from paralysis of respiratory muscles, leading to suffocation, or from an inability to swallow (dysphagia) resulting in pneumonia and a buildup of fluid in the lungs.

Will it happen to me?

If you eat food contaminated with *Clostridium botulinum*, or if a wound is infected with the bacterium, then yes. Botulinum toxin is one of the most lethal substances in nature. A minute dose of just 1 nanogram (a billionth of a gram) per kilogram can kill, especially if injected into a vein. Unfortunately, contaminated food offers few clues in the form of odour or taste changes. Contaminated canned food may show black discoloration, but more often it looks perfectly fine.

What to look for

With ingestion of the toxin, vomiting and diarrhoea can occur. Fatigue, weakness and dizziness are followed by blurred vision, dry mouth and difficulty swallowing or speaking. Muscle weakness may then spread to the respiratory muscles, with paralysis making it difficult to breathe.

What are the chances of survival?

Rapid diagnosis and treatment with antitoxin immunoglobulin (antibodies), and, if needed, artificial ventilation, increase the chance of survival. Typical survival rates are shown on page 43.

DID YOU KNOW?

Purified botulinum toxin type A is used medically to treat facial tics, stroke, paralysis, squints, urinary incontinence, severe headaches and excessive sweating, as well as wrinkles.

Type of intoxication	*Survival rate*
Infant botulism	99.5%
Adults over 60 years of age	70%
Wound botulism	90%
Overall	90% (Type A neurotoxin) to 95% (Type B neurotoxin)

HOW TO AVOID IT

- **Good food preparation, preservation and hygiene are vital. Pre-formed botulinum toxin is a protein that is inactivated by heating to 85 °C (185 °F) for 5 minutes, but the spores will survive to produce toxins when conditions are right. To kill these, commercially canned goods must be cooked at 121 °C (250 °F) for 3 minutes.**
- **Only eat preserved food that has been properly tinned or cured.**
- **Avoid canned foods that are bulging or leaking.**
- **Don't give honey to infants under the age of 12 months.**
- **Choose your cosmetic surgeon carefully.**

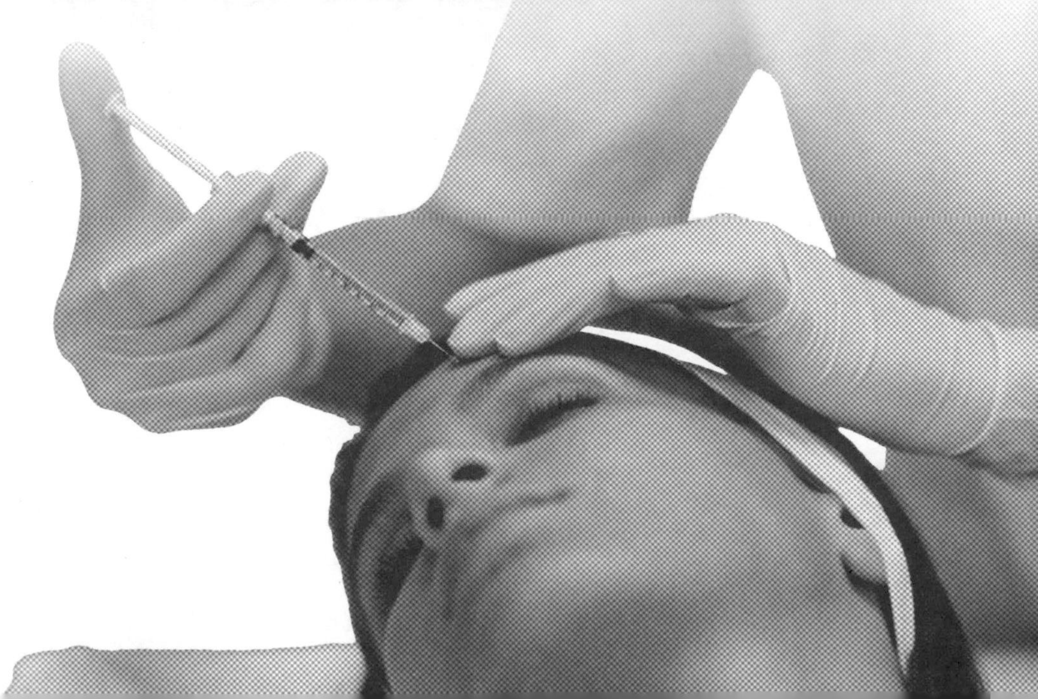

13

Brain death

Brain death is diagnosed when all higher and lower brain functions have ceased. This includes the brainstem, which regulates vital activities such as breathing, heartbeat and blood pressure. Someone who is declared 'brainstem dead' or 'whole-brain dead' is 'alive' only because of medical intervention in the form of artificial ventilation. Once a decision is made to remove life support, the body cannot breathe on its own.

How common is it?
The true incidence is unknown; various studies suggest that brainstem death accounts for around 1 in 10 deaths within intensive care units.

Who dies?
Children and adults alike.

Where?
In developed countries where advanced life support is available.

When?
Following major damage to the brain.

Why?
Lack of blood, oxygen and/or glucose supply to the brain.

The heart will also stop beating within a few minutes, owing to lack of oxygen. Even when life support is maintained, the heart often stops beating on its own within a few days, but occasionally continues to beat for weeks or even months.

In contrast, a persistent vegetative state is diagnosed when no higher brain functions are detectable, but the brainstem still functions. Someone in a persistent vegetative state has periods of wakeful consciousness, but, as far as we know, remains unaware of their surroundings and cannot feel mental distress or pain. There is a small chance that higher brain functions may recover.

Why does it kill?

Technically, the patient dies from another cause – lack of blood/oxygen/glucose to the brain can result from heart attack, stroke, serious head injury, meningitis, brain tumour, drowning, hypoglycaemia (e.g. from insulin), surgical complications or suicide, say. Medical intervention may revive the heartbeat, but not brainstem function.

Will it happen to me?

Technically, everyone who dies experiences brainstem death.

What to look for

Essentially, someone who is not conscious and does not respond to any form of stimulation, including pain, loud noise or withdrawal of artificial respiration.

Tests used to determine brainstem death include:

- Shining a torch in both eyes to see if they react to the light.
- Stroking the sensitive cornea of the eye with a tissue or piece of cotton wool.
- Applying pressure to the forehead and pinching the nose.
- Squirting ice-cold water into each ear to see if the eyes move (nystagmus).
- Inserting a thin plastic tube down the trachea (windpipe) to see if this triggers a gagging or coughing reflex.
- Withdrawing ventilation briefly (for 5 minutes) to see if spontaneous breathing movements start.

If none of these elicits a response, then a diagnosis of brainstem death can be made. An EEG, a radionuclide cerebral blood-flow scan or a brain PET scan may be helpful in showing absence of brain activity.

What are the chances of survival?

If the diagnosis of brainstem or whole-brain death is accurate, then the chance of recovery is zero. There are no verified reports of anyone who meets the criteria for brainstem death recovering brainstem function. Recovery has occasionally occurred in those who have been diagnosed with a persistent vegetative state, however.

HOW TO AVOID IT

You cannot avoid it, but you can influence the outcome with a living will. This records your wishes about how to be treated if you are ever diagnosed as being in this unfortunate state.

Brain tumour

14

As the brain is an incredibly delicate organ, it is bathed in fluid and placed in a strong 'box', the cranium, for ultimate protection. Unfortunately, this box leaves little room for expansion.

How common is it?

Half of all brain tumours are benign. Globally an estimated 186,700 benign brain tumours are diagnosed each year; mortality rates are unavailable, but likely to be in the region of 20,000 per year; brain tumours are the second-leading cause of tumour-related death in males aged 45 and younger.

Who dies?

Meningiomas and pituitary adenomas are more common in women; males are 50% more likely to develop a brain tumour than females.

Where?

Incidence of benign brain tumours is twice as high in Western Europe and North America as elsewhere.

When?

Deaths peak during late winter/early spring – low vitamin D levels may be involved.

Why?

Cells that escape normal control mechanisms overgrow within a closed space.

Although everyone rightly fears malignant brain tumours (cancers), which kill an estimated 175,000 people a year worldwide, benign (non-cancerous) brain tumours also cause problems. While they do not physically invade surrounding brain tissue, they press into it, causing damage and increasing pressure within the skull. If not successfully treated, they are also life-threatening. The term 'benign' is therefore misleading, especially as a benign tumour sometimes becomes malignant. Benign tumours are classed as Grade 1 (least malignant): this means they are generally slow-growing, are less likely to recur after removal, are unlikely to spread to other parts of the brain, and may just need surgery rather than radiotherapy or chemotherapy to treat them. There are more than 140 different types of brain tumour, many of which are rare. Some of the most common 'benign' tumours are listed in the box below:

Why does it kill?

Increased intracranial pressure can affect control of normal body functions, including breathing, heart rate and consciousness; and there can be complications associated with surgery and/or radiotherapy treatment.

Will it happen to me?

Your lifetime risk of a benign brain tumour is around 1 in 170. Factors that increase the risk include family history, neurofibromatosis (in which multiple nodules arise from nerve cells), receiving radiotherapy as a child (e.g. for leukaemia) and exposure to certain chemicals (formaldehyde, vinyl chloride). One in five people with a benign brain tumour has a family history of the condition.

Types of Grade 1 brain tumour	*How they arise*	*Frequency*
Meningioma	Arachnoid cap cells on the meningeal membranes surrounding the brain	20%
Schwannoma (acoustic neuroma)	Tumour arising from insulating cells wrapped round the auditory nerve	9%
Pituitary gland	Hormone-secreting pituitary gland cells	8%
Pilocytic astrocytoma	From star-shaped brain cells called astrocytes	2%
Haemangioblastoma	Blood vessels within the brain	2%
Craniopharyngioma	Developmental remnants from early foetal development, often forming a cyst	3%
Choroid plexus papilloma	Tissues that secrete cerebrospinal fluid	1%
Epidermoid and dermoid cysts	Pearly tumours arising from 'skin' cells trapped in the brain during foetal development	1%

What to look for

Recurrent headache, seizures, changing sense of smell, nausea, loss of vision in one or both eyes (especially if peripheral), blurred or double vision, weakness of eye movement, hearing loss, problems with balance, dizziness, speech difficulty, memory loss, gradual loss of movement or sensation in part of the body, a change in behaviour or personality.

What are the chances of survival?

For malignant brain tumours, survival depends on age. Survival in children is 70%. Five-year survival in young adults (20–44 years) is 50%, falling with age to less than 5% for the over-65s. For those with benign tumours, survival can be as high as 90% but for some 'benign' brain tumours prognosis is worse than for breast cancer. Survivors of benign brain tumours currently outnumber those with malignant brain tumours by more than four to one.

HOW TO AVOID IT

Not easy. Live as healthy a life as possible. Don't smoke. Although evidence of harm is not conclusive, it makes sense to limit your exposure to mobile-phone radiation as much as possible. This is especially important for children.

- Select a low-emission model.
- Use your mobile phone only when essential – try to use a land line instead, or text.
- Keep essential calls short.
- Avoid using your phone when the signal is weak, which increases power output – find somewhere with a strong signal.
- Avoid using your phone in a confined space such as a lift or train – using it outdoors, or near a window, helps to increase signal strength.
- Keep the phone (especially the aerial) away from your head.
- Use a hands-free device – preferably one that is wired, rather than wireless.
- Avoid touching the aerial while your phone is turned on.
- Switch off the phone when not in use, such as at night.
- Avoid playing games on your mobile.

Broken heart syndrome 15

It's quite possible to die from a broken heart. It even has a medical name: tako-tsubo cardiomyopathy, which translates from the Japanese as 'fishing pot for trapping octopus'. Apparently, acute emotional stress causes the tip of your left ventricle to dilate temporarily so that it resembles a fishing pot.

How common is it?
More common than previously thought; one study found 5% of those admitted to hospital with sudden heart pain had tako-tsubo cardiomyopathy.

Who dies?
Of those affected, 80% are postmenopausal females, aged 49 and over.

Where?
Cases were initially reported in Japan, then identified in the United States, Belgium, Italy, Germany – anywhere that doctors started to look, basically.

When?
After an intense emotional shock such as unexpected bereavement, domestic abuse, cancer diagnosis, devastating financial/gambling losses or natural disasters.

Why?
Stress hormones play havoc with your heart.

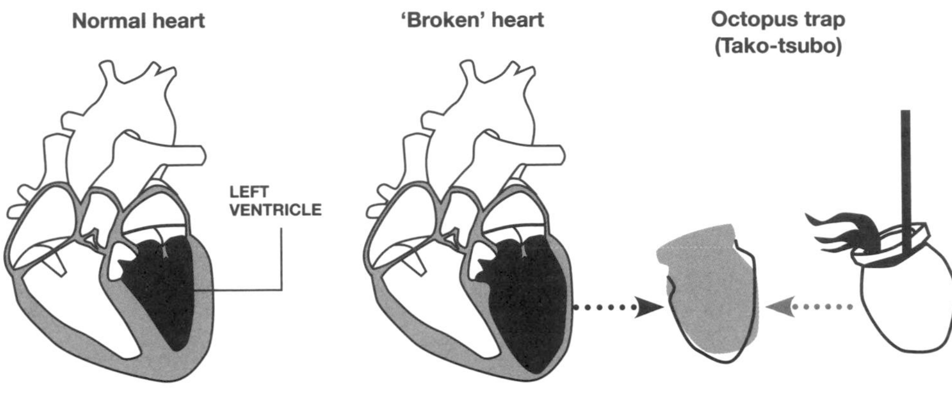

The shape of a normal left ventricle after it contracts to pump blood into the aorta.

In a person with broken heart syndrome, the left ventricle takes on a different shape.

The disorder was first identified in Japan and named after a tako-tsubo octopus trap because of its similar shape.

Although the ballooning at the heart's apex during tako-tsubo cardiomyopathy passes, it causes sudden heart pain, shortness of breath, changes in the electrical activity of the heart, and elevated levels of heart muscle enzymes. Without rapid medical care, it can prove fatal.

Why does it kill?

The mechanism of this stress-induced sudden heart failure (cardiomyopathy) is not fully understood. Sudden spasm of coronary arteries may reduce blood flow to heart muscle. Stress hormones may also 'stun' nerve fibres supplying heart muscle.

Will it happen to me?

If you are female and postmenopausal, and you tend to flap when the unexpected happens, you are the perfect candidate.

What to look for

Sudden chest pain and shortness of breath following an intense emotional shock.

What are the chances of survival?

Pretty high. With hospital care, over 92% of patients make a full recovery. In those who survive the acute episode, the condition usually resolves within 1–4 weeks. In a study following 100 patients, 31% continued to have episodes of chest pain and 10% had a recurrence of heart failure. The 5-year survival ratewas 83%; however, this was similar to that expected in women of this age.

HOW TO AVOID IT

Try to keep calm, no matter what life throws at you.

Cancer 16

Cancer is not called the 'big C' for nothing: including all forms, it is the leading cause of death worldwide. Every year, an estimated 13 million new cases are diagnosed, and around 8 million people succumb. And numbers are rising by around 1% per year.

How common is it?

Although heart attack is the number one killer in the Western world, cancer is the leading cause of death globally, accounting for 13% of all deaths worldwide.

Who dies?

Cancer can strike at any age; the risk generally increases with age.

Where?

Everywhere, but more than 70% of deaths are in low- and middle-income countries; numbers are increasing, especially in China, Russia and India.

When?

Half of people diagnosed with cancer live for more than 5 years; some cancers have 5-year survival rates of 90%.

Why?

Cancers result from ill-understood interactions between our genes, environment, diet and lifestyle.

The number of cancer deaths doubled between 1975 and 2000, will double again by 2020 and is expected to triple by 2030.

Cancers develop when a single cell starts to divide repeatedly, producing abnormal copies of itself, rather than dividing occasionally just to replace worn-out cells. If the immune system does not recognize and destroy these abnormal cells they continue to divide and invade surrounding tissues, so that a detectable lump develops.

Cancer can affect any part of the body, from the skin and lungs (common) to the belly-button and big toe (rare). Once the tumour has reached a certain size, a few abnormal cells may break away and spread through blood and lymph vessels to other parts of the body. These secondary cancers (metastases) most commonly take root and continue to grow in the lungs, bones, liver and brain.

Why does it kill?

It depends on the type of cancer and the part of the body affected. Not all cancers kill. Many are so slow-growing that you die *with* them rather than *from* them. Others affect eating or absorption of nutrients and reduce immunity, so you are prone to serious infections, such as septicaemia or bronchopneumonia. Some lead to organ failure and a buildup of waste toxins, salts or fluid imbalances. Others trigger severe weight loss (cachexia) and increase blood stickiness so you succumb from a heart attack or stroke. Alternatively, a cancer may invade blood vessels or affect blood clotting, so that haemorrhage or internal bleeding occur. Anaemia may develop if the marrow or kidneys are affected or if there are persistent blood losses. Many people with cancer just pass away quietly in their sleep, however. Opiate painkillers help to reduce discomfort, but may contribute to death by suppressing respiration and consciousness. Euthanasia and suicide are other factors.

DETECTION BOX

Check your breasts and/or testicles for lumps. Attend for regular health screening – anything and everything you are offered: mammography, cervical smears, hidden occult faecal blood tests, blood tests for Prostate Specific Antigen (PSA), dental checkups for mouth cancer, endoscopy, imaging (ultrasound, CT, MRI) scans, colonoscopy, cystoscopy. Some screening tests are only available privately but the costs must be weighed up against the benefits. We incur 60% of our healthcare costs during the last 6 months of our life. Rather than saving for the rainy day that never comes, why not invest some of your savings earlier in the umbrella of private health screening? You may live longer as a result. It's definitely something to think about.

Most common cancers	*Annual number of deaths worldwide*	*Most common cancers*	*Annual number of deaths worldwide*
Lung	1.4 million	**Prostate**	260,000
Stomach	800,000	**Leukaemia**	258,000
Liver	700,000	**Lymphoma**	222,000
Colon/rectum	640,000	**Brain**	175,000
Breast	520,000	**Bladder**	151,000
Oesophagus	410,000	**Ovary**	141,000
Uterus	280,000	**Mouth/lip**	128,000
Cervix	275,000	**Kidney**	117,000
Pancreas	270,000	**Malignant melanoma**	60,000

Will it happen to me?

If you smoke, then probably, yes. Otherwise, your lifetime risk of receiving a cancer diagnosis is 1 in 3. Your chance of dying from cancer before the age of 75 is currently 1 in 9. This risk is higher if cancer runs in your family.

What to look for

Symptoms you should never ignore include:

- a change in bowel habits
- urinary difficulties
- recurrent heartburn
- a nagging cough or shortness of breath
- pain or discomfort that keeps coming back
- weight loss for no apparent reason
- unexpected blood loss from any orifice (including postmenopausal and postcoital bleeding)
- difficulty swallowing
- feeling full despite eating very little
- hoarse voice or sore throat lasting more than 3 weeks
- any persistent health problem that worries you

What are the chances of survival?

Mortality rates vary with each cancer. Basal-cell carcinoma (affecting the skin) rarely kills, for example, while the prognosis for malignant melanoma is poor. Some cancers are so prevalent (prostate, thyroid) that many people die with them without ever knowing they are affected. Early detection increases the chance of a cure by at least one-third.

'You show me something that doesn't cause cancer, and I'll show you something that isn't on the market yet.'

George Carlin

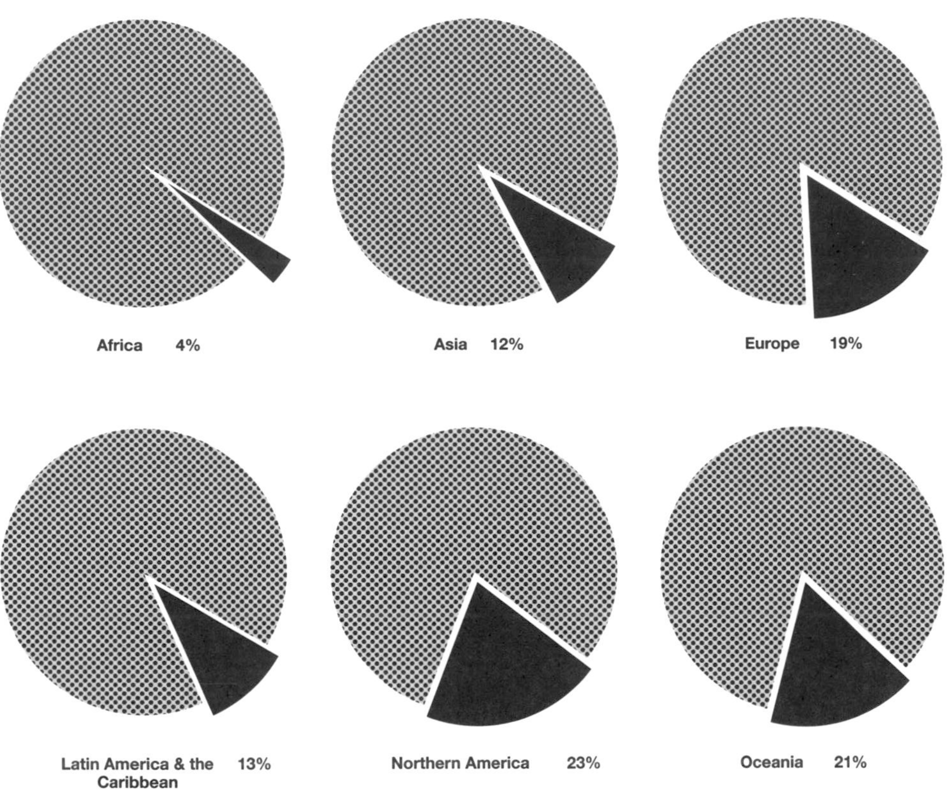

HOW TO AVOID IT

At least 40% of cancers can be prevented by lifestyle changes. It comes down to controlling: tobacco use, alcohol use, fruit and vegetable intake, obesity, exercise levels, urban air pollution, workplace carcinogens, indoor smoke from solid fuels, hepatitis viruses, and some types of human wart (papilloma) virus. Reducing exposure to sunlight lowers the risk of skin cancer but also decreases levels of vitamin D, which boosts anti-cancer immunity. Use sunscreen, but take vitamin D supplements too.

Carbon monoxide poisoning 17

Carbon monoxide is a colourless, odourless, tasteless, non-irritant gas, and therefore undetectable without instruments.

How common is it?

Exposure to carbon monoxide is the most common cause of lethal poisoning worldwide, accounting for more than 50% of fatal poisonings in industrial countries. It is estimated to cause at least 250,000 deaths per year, and contributes to 1.6 million premature smoke inhalation-related deaths worldwide, including resultant pneumonia and lung cancer.

Who dies?

Anyone – children, women and elderly people have higher rates of exposure from indoor sources.

Where?

In a confined space contaminated with fumes; often in a bedroom near a faulty central heating system or blocked flue, many in their own home.

When?

Epidemics of carbon monoxide poisoning occur in winter months; deaths are often at night, during sleep.

Why?

Fumes from a poorly maintained heater or boiler.

Carbon monoxide leaks from old motors and poorly maintained gas-powered tools, heaters and cooking equipment, can kill.

This gas binds 200 times more tightly than oxygen to the red blood pigment, haemoglobin. It therefore displaces oxygen from circulating red blood cells to form carboxyhaemoglobin, which imparts a healthy-looking cherry-red glow. As a result, the tell-tale blue (cyanosis) that usually signals lack of oxygen fails to cause alarm in those finding you, apparently sleeping peacefully, in your bed.

An estimated 2 billion people worldwide are at risk as half of the world's population burn wood, charcoal, dung and coal that releases carbon monoxide and other toxins into their home.

Why does it kill?

Lack of oxygen to the brain causes convulsions, loss of consciousness and death; lack of oxygen to the heart causes cardiac arrest.

Will it happen to me?

If you are in a confined space with a poorly maintained motor, heater or cooking equipment, then it is a possibility. Suspect the diagnosis if symptoms rapidly clear on breathing fresh air, especially if two or more people are simultaneously affected.

What to look for

Mild poisoning causes headache, dizziness, irritability and confusion. The speed at which symptoms appear and escalate depends on the concentration of carbon monoxide (expressed in parts per million) to which you are exposed.

What are the chances of survival?

If removed from the source and treated with oxygen (preferably at high pressure), you are in with a chance. However, brain damage can result from prolonged lack of oxygen.

HOW TO AVOID IT

Have chimneys and flues cleaned and checked regularly. Get gas appliances and heating systems professionally inspected every year. Never run cars, motorbikes or lawn mowers in a closed garage. Fit a carbon monoxide alarm in your home.

Chagas' disease 18

Named after the Brazilian physician who first described it in 1909, Chagas' disease is most commonly spread by infected blood-sucking insects, known by evocative names such as the assassin bug, or the kissing bug, because it feeds around victims' mouths while they sleep.

How common is it?

Ten years ago, Chagas' disease affected 20 million people throughout the Americas, and killed 50,000 per year; these figures have now dropped by half owing to improved control of insect carriers and screening of blood donations and organ transplants.

Who dies?

During the acute phase of infection, children are most vulnerable; the heart and gut manifestations almost exclusively affect adults.

Where?

Mostly in Southern, Central and North America.

When?

Usually several decades after infection with the parasite *Trypanosoma cruzi.*

Why?

Exposure to *Trypanosoma cruzi* via the assassin, or kissing, bug.

When the kissing bug bites an infected person (or animal) it becomes a carrier for the protozoon *Trypanosoma cruzi*, a less lethal relative of the organism that causes sleeping sickness (see page 213). The parasite multiplies within its gut and is deposited on future victims' skin when the bug defecates during feeding. Infection then becomes smeared into the bite wound, the mouth or the eyes. *T. cruzi* can also be transmitted by wild animals, especially the opossum (whose anal gland allows the parasite to develop), through blood transfusion, in breast milk, across the placenta, and from eating contaminated food or juice.

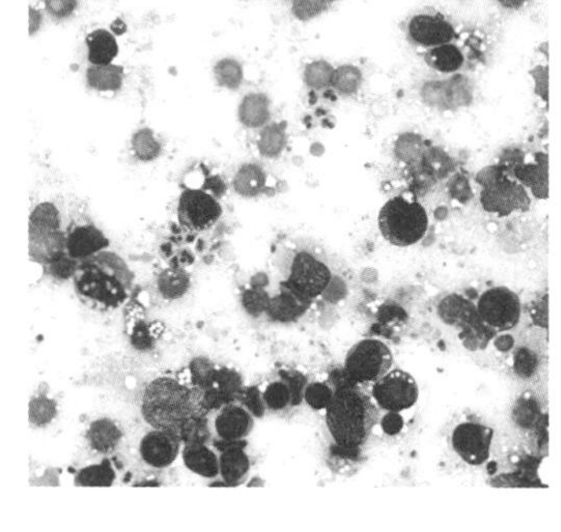

Trypanosoma cruzi *in a blood smear*

Why does it kill?

Trypanosoma cruzi enters body tissues and is particularly fond of heart muscle cells. Nests of dividing protozoa cause infected cells to rupture, causing cell death (necrosis), inflammation (myocarditis), scarring (fibrosis), blocking of the heart's electrical conduction and disruption of the cardiac cycle. During the acute stage, death may result from myocarditis or, less commonly, inflammation of the brain (meningoencephalitis). Chronic (long-term) infection kills as a result of abnormal heart rhythms, enlargement of the heart (cardiomyopathy) and heart failure. Gross swelling of the oesophagus or colon can lead to malnutrition and death due to volvulus (see page 62) if not treated surgically.

Will it happen to me?

It could do, if you sleep near an infected assassin/kissing bug. The WHO estimates that more than 25 million people are at risk of the disease. Around 41,000 new cases occur every year, and over 14,000 infants are born with congenital Chagas' disease.

What to look for

A red nodule called a chagoma develops at the site of inoculation. During the initial phase, when blood is teeming with parasites, symptoms are mild and non-specific, such as fever, a purplish swelling of one eye (if infection enters via that route), lethargy, headache, muscle aches and chest or abdominal pain. These symptoms usually resolve within 8 weeks. The disease then enters a latent phase.

DID YOU KNOW?

Charles Darwin was plagued by undiagnosed health problems after being bitten by a 'great black bug' during the voyage of the *Beagle*; his remains have yet to be tested for DNA evidence of Chagas' disease. He said, 'Constant attacks make life an intolerable bother and stop all work.'

What are the chances of survival?

During the acute stages, the chance of survival is 95%. Unless treated, there is a 30% risk of progressing to chronic Chagas', in which parasites invade the heart and digestive smooth muscle. Complications develop over the course of several decades. Antiparasitic drugs (benznidazole, nifurtimox) are most effective during the first year of infection, when the cure rate is between 60% and 85%. Treatment is less effective for chronic disease, and drug resistance is growing. Heart arrhythmias can be treated with the heart drug amiodarone, with a pacemaker or with a heart transplant (using low doses of immunosuppressant drugs to prevent activation of the parasite).

Assassin Bug

HOW TO AVOID IT

- There is currently no vaccine, and prevention involves using insecticides to eradicate carriers, and improving housing and sanitation.
- Avoid camping in the wilds in endemic areas.
- Avoid sleeping in hostels and mud, thatch or adobe houses, which are more likely to harbour assassin bugs.
- Avoid contact with opossums.
- Use an insecticide-impregnated mosquito net at night.
- Try not to rub your skin or eyes if bitten.

19 Congenital abnormalities

The development of a human foetus is extraordinarily complex. A single fertilized egg divides to form trillions of cells, each of which dances to the tune of a plethora of genetic, chemical and hormonal signals.

How common is it?
30–50% of infant deaths are due to congenital malformations; an additional 20–30% are related to genetic disorders.

Who dies?
Those with the most severe disorders.

Where?
Developing countries, where exposure to toxins is higher; prenatal screening in developed countries gives parents the choice of selective termination for serious life-threatening abnormalities.

When?
When foetal development goes wrong.

Why?
Some cases are linked with poor nutrition or maternal exposure to smoking, alcohol, drugs, pesticides and other toxins; most have no obvious underlying risk factors.

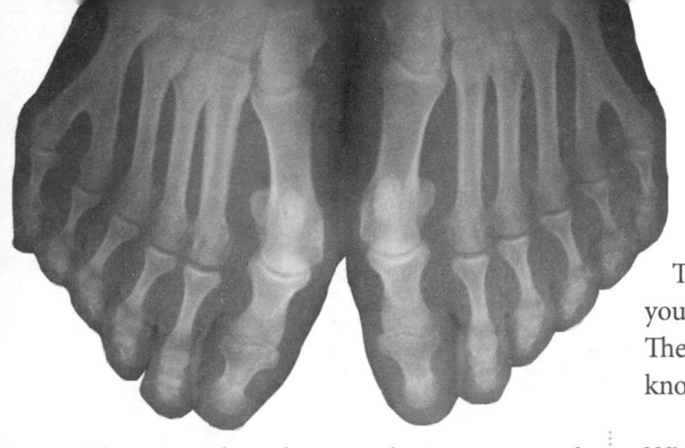

Will it happen to me?

There is a greater than 19 in 20 chance that you do not have a congenital abnormality. The risk of your having a child whom you know to be affected is around 1 in 20.

These signals orchestrate the movement of foetal cells into the right place, and their differentiation into the right type of tissue. Why things don't go wrong more often is a mystery. As it is, only 1 in 20 babies is born with a genetic disorder, and an additional 1 in 20 has a congenital malformation. The majority are mild and often go unnoticed (such as an additional nipple). Others are readily treatable (a sixth finger, a club foot). Some, however, are life-threatening, especially if they affect vital internal organs. Overall, congenital malformations, deformation and chromosomal abnormalities are the number one cause of foetal and infant deaths.

Why does it kill?

If a major organ or metabolic pathway is affected, this can interfere with normal vital functions.

What to look for

Maternal age is one factor known to increase the chance of chromosomal abnormalities. The mechanism that separates duplicated chromosomes during cell division does not work as well in older eggs, making abnormalities more probable, such as Down's syndrome (in which a fertilized egg retains three copies of chromosome number 21, rather than the usual two).

Another risk factor is alcohol intake. If a woman regularly drinks 2 or 3 units of alcohol per day throughout pregnancy, her baby has an 11% chance of developing malformations associated with foetal alcohol syndrome. The risk rises to 19% with 4 units per day, and to 30% with 5 units per day. A pregnant woman who regularly drinks more than 9 units of alcohol per day is almost certain to have an affected child.

Mother's age	*Risk of conceiving a child with Down's syndrome*	*Mother's age*	*Risk of conceiving a child with Down's syndrome*
28	1 in 1000	**40**	1 in 100
30	1 in 880	**42**	1 in 70
32	1 in 720	**44**	1 in 40
34	1 in 460	**46**	1 in 25
36	1 in 280	**48**	1 in 15
38	1 in 180	**50**	1 in 10

Constipation 20

It's easy to see why diarrhoea might prove lethal. With constipation the mechanism is less intuitively obvious, but kill it can and does.

How common is it?

Chronic constipation affects a staggering 12% of the population worldwide – over 820 million people. Volvulus (see opposite) is the third-leading cause of intestinal obstruction after cancer and diverticulitis. Volvulus occurs during 1 in 1500 pregnancies.

Who dies?

Those with constipation-associated volvulus are in their 70s or 80s; those with malrotation-associated volvulus are more likely to be infants or children; those in the high-fibre volvulus belt (see opposite) are mostly in their 60s; pregnant women are also at risk as the expanding uterus tilts a distended colon the wrong way.

Where?

People in the Americas and Asian Pacific are twice as likely to suffer from constipation as those living in Europe. Volvulus associated with constipation is most common in Africa, Asia and the Middle East, in the so-called 'volvulus belt'.

When?

More wastes build up in the colon than you can comfortably evacuate, leading to acquired 'megacolon' in which the colon becomes abnormally stretched and unresponsive to the need to evacuate the bowel.

Why?

Many underlying factors may be involved – see opposite.

A loaded, constipated colon can form an elongated, redundant loop that twists over on itself to cause an intestinal volvulus. This is especially common if your bowel did not fully rotate during foetal development, if you eat a low-fibre diet (and have constipation) or, paradoxically, if you eat a very high-fibre diet that excessively loads the colon. This is especially common in Africa, the Middle East and Brazil, which is known in surgical circles as the 'volvulus belt'. Overloading of the colon can also result from intestinal infestation with worms or Chagas' disease.

Constipation and straining can also cause outpouchings, or diverticula, to form where the lining of the colon ruptures through its overlying muscle. As well as making constipation worse (by interfering with muscle contraction), diverticula frequently fill with compacted faeces that become inflamed and toxic (diverticulitis).

Constipation can also encourage overuse of laxatives, leading to habituation, a need to take increasing doses, drug dependency and a slack, distended megacolon. In some cases, the only available treatment is total abdominal colectomy.

Constipation is a symptom rather than a disease, and a surprisingly long list of underlying factors can be involved:

- poor fibre intake
- not drinking enough fluids
- lack of exercise
- weight-loss diets
- pregnancy
- irritable bowel syndrome
- diverticular disease
- poor muscle tone in pelvic floor
- hernia
- anal pain due to fissure or piles
- depression
- old age

DID YOU KNOW?

Constipation has variably been defined as infrequent defecation, painful defecation, or both. To put things on a scientific footing, an international team of gastroenterologists drew up the Rome III criteria, which allow constipation to be diagnosed when patients who do not have irritable bowel syndrome experience at least two of the following for 3 months:

- **fewer than three bowel movements per week**
- **straining**
- **lumpy or hard stools**
- **sensation of anorectal obstruction**
- **sensation of incomplete defecation**
- **manual manoeuvring (wriggling around or using fingers) to defecate**

The world constipation record is allegedly 102 days.

- prostate problems
- drugs and medications (especially opiate painkillers and anti-cholinergic agents)
- hormone or electrolyte imbalances (e.g. underactive thyroid, low potassium levels, high calcium levels)
- abdominal mass pressing on bowel (e.g. ovarian cyst, tumour, fibroid)
- disorders of the central nervous system (e.g. MS, Parkinson's, Chagas' disease)
- bowel obstruction (e.g. stricture due to scar tissue or colon cancer)

Why does it kill?

Twisting of a loaded colon leads to strangulated bowel, gangrene, peritonitis and sepsis.

Will it happen to me?

You have a 1 in 8 chance of becoming constipated. Minor gut malrotation occurs during foetal development in 1 in 7 people, and 1 in 4 people have a gut that is mobile enough for volvulus to occur. If you visit the Andes Mountains and follow a high-fibre diet, your risk increases 50-fold owing to the low atmospheric pressure and the higher relative gas volume taken up by the gases produced during bacterial fermentation in the colon (carbon dioxide, methane, hydrogen).

What to look for

Bloating, abdominal discomfort, headache, coated tongue, straining when passing a stool, inability to pass motions. Volvulus causes cramping abdominal pain, distension and obstruction, so that you can't even pass wind. Vomiting of faecal material can occur.

What are the chances of survival?

It depends on how quickly the problem is diagnosed and whether part of the strangulated bowel has died (necrosis). Despite surgical correction, volvulus has at least a 15% mortality rate, rising to 25% for emergency procedures, 50% if obstruction is present, and 65% if a significant length of bowel is necrosed.

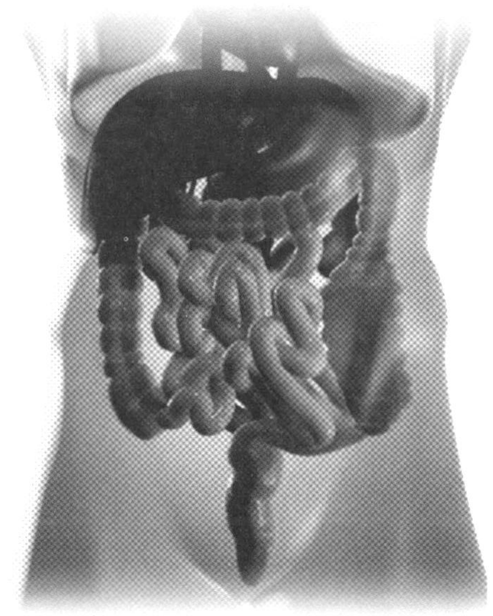

An obstruction caused by constipation

HOW TO AVOID IT

Follow a wholefood diet containing just the right amount of fibre – not too much and not too little; drink plenty of water; take fibre and probiotic supplements; exercise regularly; don't abuse laxatives.

Dangerous sports

Some sports are about advertising revenue and the joy of taking part. Others are all about the fear. Adrenaline junkies are so addicted to the frisson of danger that they constantly seek bigger and bigger risks. Those taking part in extreme sports appear to have a distinctive psychological makeup.

How common is it?
Limited information is available on death from sport and recreational activities worldwide; overall, the average rate of death is less than 1 per 100,000 participants per year.

Who dies?
Mostly young, testosterone-driven males.

Where?
Away from the safety of home.

When?
Something goes horribly wrong.

Why?
For the thrill.

'A life without adventure is likely to be unsatisfying, but a life in which adventure is allowed to take whatever form it will is sure to be short.' Bertrand Russell

People who take part in extreme sports have low harm-avoidance instincts, are less prone to anxiety and are relatively immune to post-traumatic stress.

But you don't need to participate in extreme sports to die. Everyday sports from rugby, soccer and horse-riding to golf, fishing and croquet come with their own unique mortality rate.

Males are five times more likely to experience serious injury and 15 times more likely to die from a sport- or recreation-related cause than women.

Why does it kill?

Head injury, fractured neck, crushing of internal organs, drowning, burning and being run through with a fencing epée are among the causes of death. Heart attack and abnormal heart rhythm can result from physical exertion and adrenaline rush. For example, sudden death on the squash court is a notoriously common end for middle-aged males (average age 46 years). Most of these die instantaneously during play, but a quarter collapse during the early post-exercise period. Blunt, non-penetrating blows to the chest can cause the heart to stop (commotio cordis) and are a recognized risk with some sports, especially those involving a stick, such as hockey. Goalies are at particular risk, even when wearing protection.

Will it happen to me?

Ask an actuary for a life-insurance quote, and see the premiums multiply as you start listing your dangerous pastimes.

What to look for

You may be addicted to the adrenaline rush if you:

- feel high after a dangerous or demanding activity
- deliberately pile on the pressure
- always play to win
- find it difficult to relax and do nothing

What are the chances of survival?

This depends on the activity and whether you play for fun or for kicks. If you take part in any sport, especially the following, ensure your affairs are always up-to-date.

- Base-jumping
- Powerboat racing
- Bull-riding
- Free diving
- Canyoneering
- Heli-skiing
- Parachuting
- High-altitude mountaineering
- Bungee-jumping
- White-water rafting
- Speed-skiing
- Horse-racing
- Cave diving
- Cliff diving

HOW TO AVOID IT

Avoid any sport that affects your life-insurance premiums. Exercise for heart health, not for heart-stopping moments.

Sport	*Odds of dying each time you take part*
Base-jumping	1 in 2300
Swimming	1 in 56,500
Cycling	1 in 92,300
Running	1 in 97,500
Skydiving	1 in 101,100
Football	1 in 103,200
Hang-gliding	1 in 116,000
Tennis	1 in 116,900
Running a marathon	1 in 126,600
Horse-riding	1 in 175,400
American football	1 in 182,200
Scuba diving	1 in 200,000
Table-tennis	1 in 250,600
Rock-climbing	1 in 320,000
Canoeing	1 in 750,000
Skiing	1 in 1,556,800

Death sentence 22

A judicial decree that sentences certain convicted criminals to death is still carried out in around a third of the world's countries. According to Amnesty International, as of 2010 139 countries have abolished or no longer use the death penalty. Unfortunately, 58 still retain it – including some otherwise civilized societies.

How common is it?

In 2009, 18 countries are known to have carried out executions. Outside China, over 700 people were executed; although China did not divulge its final tally, it is believed to have hit the thousands.

Who dies?

Mostly convicted murderers, but some are condemned for 'ordinary' crimes such as adultery or political dissent. Innocent people, wrongly convicted, are not infrequently involved.

Where?

In countries that should know better.

When?

After all appeals for clemency are lost.

Why?

In the name of justice.

In the United States of America, on January 1, 2010 there were 3261 inmates on 'Death Row', including 61 women. By the end of the year, 46 inmates had been executed but 112 replacements were found. Texas executes more people than any other US state – 464 since 1976. Second was Virginia (108) and third was Oklahoma (95).

Why does it kill?

Methods vary but include: beheading, electrocution, firing squad, gas chamber, hanging, stoning and lethal injection. The electric chair remains an option in some US states but its use is infrequent, as prisoners retain the right (their only one) to select a lethal injection instead. Traditionally, this consists of three drugs:

- a barbiturate to render the victim unconscious (e.g. sodium thiopental)
- a muscle relaxant to paralyse breathing (e.g. pancuronium bromide)
- potassium chloride, which interferes with the electrical activity of heart muscle and induces cardiac arrest

A newer, single-drug protocol now used by some American states involves intravenous sodium thiopental. Two intramuscular 'fail-safes' remain in case the victim's veins refuse to cooperate. These are midazolam, a benzodiazepine muscle relaxant to suppress breathing and intensify coma, and hydromorphone, a narcotic respiratory suppressant.

35 American states retain the death penalty:

Alabama	Idaho	Montana	South Carolina
Arizona	Illinois	Nebraska	South Dakota
Arkansas	Indiana	Nevada	Tennessee
California	Kansas	New Hampshire	Texas
Colorado	Kentucky	North Carolina	Utah
Connecticut	Louisiana	Ohio	Virginia
Delaware	Maryland	Oklahoma	Washington
Florida	Mississippi	Oregon	Wyoming
Georgia	Missouri	Pennsylvania	plus US federal courts and the US military

Will it happen to me?

If you commit an appropriate crime in a country, state or territory that retains the death penalty, it is a distinct possibility. You don't even have to be guilty. In the United States over 130 people have been released from Death Row since 1973 following irrefutable evidence of innocence.

What to look for

When the death penalty was still in use in the UK, a convicting judge put a square of black cloth on top of his wig before passing a death sentence – which served as a clue. The black cap is still carried into the High Court as part of a judge's official regalia.

What are the chances of survival?

Once sentenced, long-term chances of survival are slim. Short-term chances are better in some countries, where appeals can prolong the time on Death Row to over 10 years. Currently, the average time between sentencing and execution in the US is 169 months. Although New Mexico repealed the death penalty in 2009, this was not retrospective and two people remained on Death Row in Santa Fe.

VOODOO

Death curses can also work. The power of suggestion is strong enough for some targets to die from fear, accident, suicide or extreme stress. This is known as psychogenic death.

HOW TO AVOID IT

Do not break the law (or at least don't get caught) in the 58 countries, territories or states that retain the death penalty. These are:

- Afghanistan
- Antigua and Barbuda
- Bahamas
- Bahrain
- Bangladesh
- Barbados
- Belarus
- Belize
- Botswana
- Chad
- China
- Comoros
- Democratic Republic of Congo
- Cuba
- Dominica
- Egypt
- Equatorial Guinea
- Ethiopia
- Guatemala
- Guinea
- Guyana
- India
- Indonesia
- Iran
- Iraq
- Jamaica
- Japan
- Jordan
- Kuwait
- Lebanon
- Lesotho
- Libya
- Malaysia
- Mongolia
- Nigeria
- North Korea
- Oman
- Pakistan
- Palestinian Authority
- Qatar
- Saint Kitts and Nevis
- Saint Lucia
- Saint Vincent and the Grenadines
- Saudi Arabia
- Sierra Leone
- Singapore
- Somalia
- Sudan
- Syria
- Taiwan
- Thailand
- Trinidad and Tobago
- Uganda
- United Arab Emirates
- United States of America
- Vietnam
- Yemen
- Zimbabwe

23

Dementia

Dementia is one of the prices we pay for a longer lifespan. Neurons exceed their use-by date more quickly than other body cells, causing a decline in intellectual function that creeps up with age. Dementia is not considered a disease of ageing per se, however, as it is not inevitable.

How common is it?

An estimated 40 million people have dementia worldwide, with 4.6 million new cases diagnosed annually – one every 7 seconds. Thanks to an ageing population, the number is predicted to exceed 115 million by 2050.

Who dies?

Dementia almost always (98% of cases) strikes those over 65.

Where?

Mostly in developed and developing countries – few people survive to the age of 65 in very poor countries.

When?

Four to seven years after diagnosis.

Why?

Loss of brain-cell function.

Alzheimer's is the most common type (77%) of dementia and is linked with an accumulation of altered protein inside brain cells (neurofibrillary tangles) and abnormal protein outside brain cells (amyloid plaques). These are only noticeable under a microscope and, owing to the inadvisability of brain biopsy, are usually detectable only after death. Dementia with Lewy bodies (26%) is also associated with the appearance of abnormal proteins within brain cells. In contrast, vascular dementia (18%) results from reduced blood flow to the brain, so that neurons succumb from a lack of oxygen and nutrients. Hippocampal sclerosis (13%) and frontotemporal dementia (5%) involve a selective loss of brain cells from particular parts of the brain.

Some readers may have noticed that, collectively, these percentage points exceed 100%. That's because it's common to have more than one type of dementia. Other forms of dementia also exist, such as those associated with infection – e.g. syphilis (see page 235) and mad cow disease (see page 155) – brain tumours and poisoning with alcohol (see page 13) or heavy metals.

DID YOU KNOW?

Researchers have discovered that the gene that codes for apolipoprotein E (a protein that carries cholesterol around the circulation) has three forms: one protects against Alzheimer's, one does not affect risk, and the other increases it.

Why does it kill?

As more and more brain cells degenerate, there comes a time when the regulation of vital processes, such as breathing, swallowing and remembering to eat or avoid the traffic, are affected. Although dementia is a life-shortening illness, it will usually cause other conditions such as bronchopneumonia, heart attack, embolism or accident, which therefore usually appear as the main causes of death on death certificates. It is claimed that one in three people over the age of 65 will die with (though perhaps not from) some form of dementia.

Will it happen to me?

This mostly depends on your age. Only 2% of those with dementia are under 65. After this milestone, the risk of dementia rises exponentially with no sign of levelling off, as follows:

Age (years)	*Risk*
Under 65	1 in 1000
65 to 75	1 in 30
75–85	1 in 10
85–95	1 in 5
95–105	1 in 3
Over 105	0.999 in 1

As with just about everything else, smokers have a higher risk. It's also worth checking your predecessors – most forms of dementia have a hereditary component.

The vitamin folic acid may help to protect against Alzheimer's disease by lowering blood levels of an amino acid called homocysteine. Too much homocysteine in the circulation hastens hardening and furring up of the

'I don't mind dying. I just don't want to be there when it happens.' Spike Milligan

arteries. This in turn increases the risk of heart disease, stroke and several forms of dementia – including Alzheimer's. In fact, researchers have found that people with raised levels of homocysteine are at least twice as likely to develop Alzheimer's as those with low levels.

What to look for

Problems with thinking, language, memory and judgement. Those affected experience difficulties with words, understanding, familiar tasks and planning, as well as loss of memory and initiative.

What are the chances of survival?

As yet, there is no cure. Life expectancy of someone with dementia is unpredictable, but the average duration from onset to death is 4 years; however, newer drugs may slow the progression of the disease. Early diagnosis means you can take an active part in decisions that will affect your future. Psychological treatments, behaviour therapy, mental stimulation, reality orientation therapy and regular exercise can also help. With good care, survival can be as long as 10 years.

BRAIN BOX

For each additional year of education you gain an 11% decrease in the risk of developing dementia. Brain pathology remains the same, but education helps you compensate for the effects of dementia. Just reading this book has already reduced your risk.

HOW TO AVOID IT

The usual advice (healthy diet, regular exercise, don't smoke, moderate alcohol) applies. But the most important advice is to keep challenging yourself mentally. With brain cells, it's a case of 'use 'em or lose 'em'.

Depression 24

Few people are blessed with a happy mood all the time. One day you may feel cheerful and the next you are gloomy and withdrawn for no obvious reason. This is a normal part of everyday life, but if your mood swings too low, a full-blown depressive illness can result.

How common is it?

Depression affects 121 million people worldwide; it leads to 850,000 deaths by suicide (see page 229) every year; 14% of teenage deaths are linked with depression and suicide.

Who dies?

The age of onset is decreasing: 50 years ago depression appeared around the age of 29; now it is appearing at the age of 15. Females are two to three times more likely to be affected than males, owing to hormonal influences associated with menstruation, pregnancy and menopause.

Where?

All geographic locations.

When?

Hospital admissions for depression are more common in winter.

Why?

Loss of self-care; loss of interest in life, which no longer seems worth living.

Depression occurs when the level of chemical messengers in the brain becomes unbalanced. These neurotransmitters, such as serotonin, noradrenaline and dopamine, pass messages from one brain cell to another by crossing the tiny gap (synapse) between them. Once across the gap, they trigger an electrical response in the next brain cell so that the message continues on. If neurotransmitter levels fall too low, however, messages are not propagated from one brain cell to another and clinical depression develops.

The WHO predicts that by the year 2020 depression will be the second-leading cause of disability in the Western world. This is not necessarily because depression is becoming more common – it may be that the stigma attached to having a psychiatric or emotional illness is starting to disappear, so people are more likely to be diagnosed.

Why does it kill?

Although depression can lead to suicide, this accounts for less than 20% of deaths among depressed patients. Other causes include coexisting chronic physical illnesses that may have contributed to the depression, including obesity, smoking, alcohol abuse, poor self-care (for example, in maintaining diabetes control) and accidents.

Will it happen to me?

Your lifetime risk of a major depressive illness is 1 in 10 if you are male, and 1 in 4 if you are female.

What to look for

Typical symptoms include feelings of sadness and hopelessness and crying for no apparent reason. There is little interest or enjoyment in activities, low sex drive, lack of energy, aches and pains, loss of appetite and sleep difficulties, such as early-morning waking.

What are the chances of survival?

If you think you may be depressed, or if you feel suicidal, it is important to seek medical help. Antidepressant medications and psychotherapy are effective for 60–80% of cases.

HOW TO AVOID IT

- **Exercise improves symptoms of depression, but needs to be continued long term to maintain benefits for mood. Try to exercise for at least 30 minutes on most days. Select a form of exercise that you enjoy, so you are more likely to keep it up.**
- **Fish oils contain omega-3 fatty acids (DHA, EPA) that are important for brain function and serotonin metabolism. Population studies suggest that people who eat fish regularly are less likely to develop depression than those who eat very little fish.**
- **A light source that emits bright white fluorescent light (2500 lux) that is 'cool' in colour (similar to natural daylight), can improve low mood linked to seasonal affective disorder.**

Diabetes 25

Your body normally maintains a tight control on your blood glucose level, keeping it within the narrow limit of around 3.9–5.6 mmol/l, or 70–100 mg/dl (mmol/l, or millimole per litre, and mg/dl, or milligrams per decilitre, are both units in which to express the concentration of a dissolved substance).

How common is it?

A minimum of 12% of deaths are linked with diabetes, which claims more than 4 million lives every year. The WHO expects this number to double by the year 2030. In some countries it is the sixth-leading cause of death and may rise to fifth place.

Who dies?

Children aged 1–4 years (from late-diagnosed ketoacidosis) and obese, middle-aged adults (from heart disease and stroke).

Where?

Over 80% of diabetes-related deaths occur in low- and middle-income countries.

When?

Glucose levels move significantly above or below the normal range.

Why?

Poor diet, poor lifestyle, poor diagnosis and/or poor compliance with treatment.

Insulin escorts excess glucose into muscle and fat cells, where it is burned as a fuel or stored as fat. If you produce too little insulin (Type 1 diabetes, 5% of cases), or if your overstuffed fat cells ignore the insulin that is present (Type 2 diabetes, 95% of cases), glucose can't enter these cells, and it builds up in your circulation instead. Muscle and fat cells that can't access this glucose 'starve in the midst of plenty', leading to dangerous acid, fluid and salt imbalances.

Diabetes may relate to sugar, but the facts are anything but sweet. Worldwide, more than 246 million people currently live with diabetes, with another person added every 7 seconds. Type 2 diabetes is becoming so prevalent that in some communities half of all adults over 35 are affected. By the year 2025 as many as 380 million people will be diabetic. Unfortunately, for every person who knows they are diabetic, there is someone else unaware of his or her health condition.

Why does it kill?

In the short term, high circulating glucose levels (hyperglycaemia) and abnormal cell metabolism (ketoacidosis) lead to coma and death. Overzealous treatment that excessively lowers glucose levels (hypoglycaemia) is also potentially lethal. In the long term, a persistently raised glucose level hastens hardening and furring up of the arteries (atherosclerosis). As a result, people with diabetes are six times as likely to develop coronary heart disease, and more than twice as likely to die from it, as those without diabetes. They are also four times more likely to have a stroke. Persistently raised glucose levels attract complications such as infection, kidney failure, leg ulcers and gangrene, possibly requiring the amputation of a limb; all of these outcomes carry their own additional risks.

DID YOU KNOW?

For people with diabetes, optimal blood fat levels are:*

- **'Bad' LDL cholesterol: less than 2.6 mmol/l (less than 100 mg/dl).**
- **'Good' HDL cholesterol: greater than 1.1 mmol/l (greater than 45 mg/dl) for men; greater than 1.4 mmol/l (greater than 55 mg/dl) for women.**
- **Triglyceride levels: less than 2.3 mmol/l (less than 200 mg/dl).**

Suggested target blood glucose levels for people with diabetes are:

- **4–7 mmol/l (72–126 mg/dl) before meals.**
- **Less than 9 mmol/l (162 mg/dl) when checked 90–120 minutes after a meal.**

*** Levels may become even more stringent – check with your doctor. He or she will tell you how to increase or reduce your food intake and/or medication if your blood glucose levels are usually too high or too low.**

Will it happen to me?

If your father has diabetes, your risk of experiencing the disease during your lifetime is between 1 in 20 and 1 in 40. If your mother has diabetes, the risk is between 1 in 40 and 1 in 80. If both parents are diabetic, your chance is around 1 in 20. As your weight increases above the healthy range for your height, so does your risk of Type 2 diabetes – especially if you store fat around your middle (central obesity). For people of Asian origin, the risk is greatest in those with a waist circumference above 90 cm (36 in) for men and 80 cm (32 in) for women. In people of other ethnic origins, the risk is highest once waist size reaches 102 cm (40 in) for men or 88 cm (35 in) for women. Complications develop even more quickly if you also smoke, or have uncontrolled high blood pressure, or have elevated blood levels of LDL-cholesterol or triglycerides.

What to look for

A raised blood glucose level. Have yours checked regularly by your doctor, at least once a year if you are not knowingly diabetic. Monitor levels yourself, at least two to four times a day if you are diabetic.

What are the chances of survival?

If you maintain tight control of your blood glucose, blood pressure, cholesterol and weight, then in theory your life expectancy should be the same as for someone without diabetes. In practice, however, good control is the exception rather than the norm. As a result, life expectancy in people with poorly controlled diabetes is 25% shorter than it could be.

HOW TO AVOID IT

If your waist size is in the danger zone, losing 10 kg (22 lb) of excess fat can reduce your fasting blood glucose levels by 50%, your blood pressure by 10/20 mmHg, your triglycerides by 30% and your 'bad' LDL-cholesterol levels by 15%. It also increases your 'good' HDL-cholesterol by at least 8%. As a result, for someone with diabetes who is obese, losing 10 kg reduces their overall risk of a premature diabetes-related death by as much as 30%. In someone with both diabetes and hypertension, bringing blood pressure down to normal levels can reduce the risk of a diabetes-related death by 32%, stroke by 44% and heart failure by 56%.

Diarrhoeal infections 26

Your intestines process around 9 litres (19 pints) of fluid per day: 2 litres (4 pints) from your diet and 7 (15 pints) in the form of recycled digestive juices. Normally, 95% of these fluids are reabsorbed before you go to the toilet. Diarrhoea is what happens when they aren't.

How common is it?

Out of 4 billion cases of diarrhoeal disease every year, 2.2 million deaths occur; 1.5 million are children under the age of 5; diarrhoea causes 4% of all deaths.

Who dies?

80% of victims are under the age of 2 years, or are malnourished, or are living with HIV, or some combination of these.

Where?

Mostly in low-income countries, especially South-East Asia and Africa, where it accounts for 7% of infant deaths.

When?

Rotavirus tends to strike in winter, while bacterial pathogens prefer warm and wet weather.

Why?

Death is from dehydration, leading to fluid and salt imbalances.

Diarrhoea is no joke, especially if your liquid stools are mixed with blood, pus, and slime.

Worldwide, diarrhoeal disease is the second-leading cause of death in children under the age of five (after pneumonia). Most cases result from faecal contamination of food or water supplies with bacterial, viral or parasitic pathogens (disease-causing organisms). Some diarrhoeal diseases also spread from person to person where hygiene is poor.

Pathogens cause diarrhoea in a number of ways. Some cause the body to secrete more fluid into the intestines, producing a watery diarrhoea (rotavirus) that can be as high as 10–20 litres (21–42 pints) per day (in cholera); some stop lining cells from absorbing fluids but don't actually kill them (norovirus); others do kill them, either by producing nasty toxins (*Escherichia coli*) or by physically invading them and blowing them up (as in salmonellosis). These latter mechanisms are invariably violent and tend to produce bloody diarrhoea or even dysentery in which diarrhoea features the aforementioned blood, mucus and pus (shigellosis).

The good news, if you can call it that, is that as many as 1 in 4 people infected with a diarrhoeal pathogen do not develop symptoms. The bad news: they act as carriers and pass on infection to others.

Why does it kill?

Diarrhoea can lead to severe dehydration with salt/electrolyte imbalances. A buildup of potassium or sodium in the blood can cause the heart to stop beating. Diarrhoea is also a leading cause of malnutrition, which lowers immunity against other infections and infestations.

Will it happen to me?

Diarrhoea is the commonest health problem to strike travellers abroad. Up to 50% of those visiting tropical regions are

DID YOU KNOW?

The anal sphincter is the only muscle in the body that consistently knows the difference between solid, liquid and air.

Pathogen	*Disease*	*Annual Deaths*
Shigella dysenteriae	Shigellosis	1.1 million
Rotavirus A	Infant diarrhoea*	580,000
Noroviruses	Winter vomiting disease	200,000
E. coli	ETEC (enterotoxigenic E. coli)	170,000
Salmonella enterica	Salmonellosis	155,000
Vibrio cholerae	Cholera	120,000

** By the age of 3, virtually all children worldwide have become acquainted with this.*

affected. Although many cases are mild and self-limiting, 30% of sufferers become bedridden and another 40% have to curtail their activities. You don't even have to travel far. Ten per cent of those visiting Europe are also affected. However, access to medical treatment means most victims survive to tell graphically embellished tales.

What to look for

The symptoms, signs and smell of diarrhoea are unmistakable. Vomiting and stomach pains are also common. Moderate dehydration causes thirst, restlessness, irritability, decreased skin elasticity and sunken eyes. Severe dehydration causes worsening symptoms with clinical shock (rapid weak pulse, low blood pressure, cool pale skin, confusion and reduced consciousness).

What are the chances of survival?

With appropriate fluid and electrolyte replacement, and antibiotics where indicated, the chance of survival is excellent. Very young children, elderly people and those debilitated by other serious disease are most at risk.

HOW TO AVOID IT

- Access to safe drinking-water, sanitation and good personal and food hygiene are vital.
- Exclusive breastfeeding for the first 6 months of life helps to protect infants.
- Vaccination is available against some pathogens (e.g. rotavirus, cholera).
- When travelling, drink only bottled water from reputable sources (check it isn't just filled from a tap) or use water-purifying tablets.
- Probiotic supplements offer some protection against diarrhoeal infections.
- Zinc supplements can reduce stool volume by 30% and duration of illness by 25%.

Diphtheria 27

Diphtheria is a disease caused by the bacterium *Corynebacterium diphtheriae*, which is usually inhaled. On its own, it produces a mild sore throat. But if the bacterium is itself infected with a promiscuous virus (a bacteriophage), it acquires the ability to kill.

How common is it?

Once a leading cause of death among children, the global burden has now decreased to between 5000 and 10,000 deaths per year.

Who dies?

Mainly children aged 4–6.

Where?

Mostly in India, Nepal, Bangladesh and other areas where vaccine coverage is low. A massive re-emergence of diphtheria occurred in the newly independent states of the former Soviet Union during the 1990s. Over 140,000 cases and 4000 deaths were reported, mainly in adolescents and adults.

When?

Diphtheria cases used to cluster around the beginning of term in the autumn, when children returned to school. Cyclical epidemics occurred every 7–10 years.

Why?

Exposure to a toxigenic strain of *Corynebacterium diphtheriae.*

The virus impregnates the bacterial cell with a gene that codes for a powerful toxin. In non-immune people, this toxin causes the larynx and tonsils to swell alarmingly. A white exudate forms a leathery membrane across the tonsils and larynx from which the affliction gains its name: *diphthera* is the Greek for 'two leather scrolls'. If the toxigenic bacterium enters through a wound, instead of the throat, a deep skin ulcer may form.

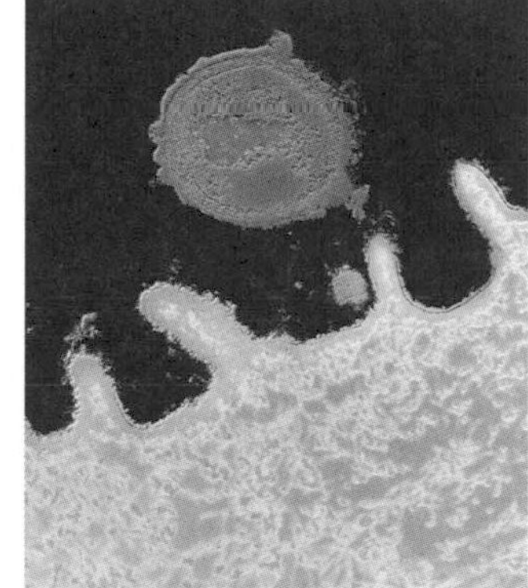

Diphtheriae *bacterium in throat*

Why does it kill?

Gross swelling of the throat (bull neck) together with the white exudate interferes with breathing. The diphtheria toxin inhibits the synthesis of cell proteins, causing local tissue destruction. It can also damage heart muscle (diphtheric myocarditis), the nervous system and the adrenal glands, resulting in heart attack, heart failure and adrenal shock (lack of response to the severe stress of illness).

Will it happen to me?

If you have received a full course of vaccinations, you might hope your risk is low. However, immunity wanes with age. Testing suggests that 38% of UK blood donors are susceptible to diphtheria, including 25% of people aged 20–29 and 53% of those aged 50–59. The number of susceptible people in the community is therefore rising, which means the infection could make a comeback, as happened in the former Soviet Union (see page 82). Have a booster before travelling to endemic areas.

What to look for

Infection is spread in the same way as other respiratory tract infections: by direct contact, coughing, spluttering and sneezing. These symptoms develop 2–5 days after exposure. Patients remain infectious for 2–3 weeks, or until 24 hours after receiving appropriate antibiotics. Occasionally the skin is also infected, causing deep ulceration.

What are the chances of survival?

Treatment with antibiotics and diphtheria antitoxin antibodies can boost survival to between 77% and 95% of cases.

HOW TO AVOID IT

An effective vaccine (an inactivated form of the bacterium) has been available since the First World War. The primary course of three injections in infancy, and a preschool booster, protects in 70% to 90% of cases. A further booster is recommended on leaving school or if visiting an endemic area.

Domestic accidents 28

Your home is where you are most likely to have an accident.

How common is it?

In the UK, 4000 people a year die as a result of domestic accidents; in the USA, the figure is in the region of 20,000. Global figures are difficult to find, but extrapolation from UK/US data suggests the figure will be in the region of 5 million or more, as few other countries have such stringent health and safety legislation.

Who dies?

A third of all accidental childhood deaths occur in the home; within Europe alone, 72 children die as the result of a domestic accident every day. That's one every 20 minutes. Elderly people are also at higher risk, and females are twice as likely as males to experience an unintentional domestic accident.

Where?

The highest levels of domestic accident-related deaths are in low- and middle-income countries; by definition, they occur within the home or its immediate grounds.

When?

More common during winter than summer months.

Why?

Momentary lapse of concentration or vigilance and just bad luck; some also cite 'safety-warning fatigue' (e.g. we are so used to seeing warnings on plastic bags that we no longer notice them, yet they pose a significant risk of suffocation for young children).

Surveys of hospital emergency department records reveal the proportion of accidents occurring inside the home (42%), on the roads (20%), during leisure and sport activities (17%), at work (15%) and in school and childcare (5%). Of domestic accidents, two-thirds occur inside the home itself, and one-third in the garden, grounds and boundaries.

Not surprisingly, the kitchen is the most dangerous place of all. It is where you wield sharp knives, boil kettles, use heat to cook and plug in electrical appliances on a daily basis. Other dangerous places are bedrooms (particularly for homicides, but that's another topic: see page 125), bathrooms, stairs, high balconies and second-storey windows.

Why does it kill?

Deaths in domestic accidents mostly result from falls (36%), fire (21%), poisoning (21%), choking and suffocation (11%). Less common causes include swallowing items such as a toothpick – or a bay leaf, whose sharp, serrated edges can puncture the oesophagus to cause a surprising amount of damage.

Will it happen to me?

One in two people will injure themselves in their home each year. Most injuries are not life-threatening. The risk of experiencing a home accident-related death is around 1 in 1500.

What to look for

Trip hazards, spillages, dodgy wiring, tired electrical appliances, open fires, hot surfaces, slippery stairs, open windows, rusty nails, wobbly ladders ... it's not rocket science.

What are the chances of survival?

The overall chance of surviving a domestic accident is 99.9%.

HOW TO AVOID IT

Most domestic accidents are avoidable. Stay out of the kitchen as much as possible, look out for trip hazards, especially near stairs; don't leave cooking pans, kettles, irons or candles unattended or within reach of children; fit childproof locks to windows; avoid glass doors; use a sturdy kick-step to reach high shelves; lock away poisons, cleaning items and drugs; fit smoke alarms and carbon monoxide detectors; don't overload electric sockets; get heaters, fires and electric circuits checked regularly; keep plastic bags out of the reach of children; fence off areas of open water; obtain local home-safety information appropriate to your circumstances.

Drought 29

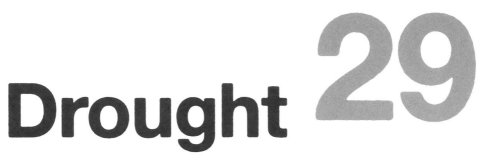

Political prisoners on hunger strike have lasted as long as 73 days without food. Deprive someone of water, however, and they succumb within 2–14 days, depending on the ambient temperature.

How common is it?

Between 1990 and 2006, the average number of people dying as a result of drought was just 185 per year worldwide, and falling. But it remains among the top three climate-related threats to life, as many drought-related deaths are classed as famine.

Who dies?

Anyone, but especially the very old, very young and debilitated.

Where?

Those living in Africa and Asia are most at risk.

When?

Lack of rain, depletion of ground water.

Why?

Changes in climate, ocean temperatures, ocean currents, jet streams, deforestation.

Two-thirds of body weight is water. Lose 10% of your body water and you can usually recover with no long-term ill effects. Lose 15% and you may not make it. During times of prolonged drought, the death toll can be enormous. According to the International Disaster Database, between 1900 and 1989 an average of 130,042 people died from drought every year. Since 1990, this figure has dropped by almost 99.9% – an extraordinary testament to international aid. If global warming is a real phenomenon, however, this figure is set to rise.

Why does it kill?

Dehydration reduces mental and physical function, leading to acid and salt imbalances, low blood pressure, muscle cramps, convulsions, heart arrhythmias, heart failure, kidney failure, confusion, coma and death. Drought can also lead to economic losses, famine, disease, civil unrest and mass migration, which bring additional threats.

Will it happen to me?

If caught in a hot climate without sufficient water, then yes.

What to look for

Extreme thirst, dry skin, sunken dry eyes, dry mouth and tongue, loss of skin tone, weakness, cramping, rapid deep breathing, fast weak pulse, passing reduced amounts of dark urine, or none at all.

What are the chances of survival?

If you can access clean water within a couple of days, the risk decreases.

HOW TO AVOID IT

You can do your bit by conserving water. Stop washing the car and watering the lawn (except with recycled dish water or rain water). Shower rather than bath. Always respect hosepipe bans.

Country	*Year of drought*	*Number killed*	*Country*	*Year of drought*	*Number killed*
Kenya	2008	4	**Ethiopia**	1983	300,000
China	2006	134	**Sudan**	1983	150,000
Burundi	2005	120	**Ethiopia**	1973	100,000
Kenya	2004	80	**India**	1965	1,500,000
Mozambique	2003	9	**Bangladesh**	1943	1,900,000
Malawi	2002	500	**India**	1942	1,500,000
Pakistan	1999	143	**China**	1928	3,000,000
Indonesia	1997	672			

30

Drowning

We may have evolved in water, but somewhere along our evolutionary journey we lost the ability to extract oxygen from anything other than air.

How common is it?

Around 388,000 people are known to drown every year – 7% of all deaths. This figure is recognized as an underestimate, however; data is limited and excludes drowning from floods and tsunamis, as well as boating and water transport accidents. The real figure exceeds half a million.

Who dies?

Children under the age of 5, and young males with access to water; males are twice as likely as females to die by drowning.

Where?

Sea, rivers, lakes, pools, streams, hot tubs, baths, garden ponds, swimming pools; 96% of drownings occur in low- and middle-income regions, especially Africa, China and India; the death rate from drowning is more than eight times higher in Africa than in Australia or the USA, for example.

When?

Entering water alone or unsupervised, especially after drinking alcohol; in unexpected flash floods or storms; when there is an injury, such as spinal injury from diving in head-first; epilepsy, hypoglycaemia, stroke, heart attack or muscle cramping play a role in some cases.

Why?

Unfamiliarity with water; lapse of supervision of young children; diving accidents; boating accidents; derring-do behaviour of young males, who are more likely to go fishing, swim alone, jump in without thinking, or drink alcohol beforehand.

As a result of our inability to survive without air, drowning is the third-leading cause of death by unintentional injury worldwide.

Why does it kill?

Drowning is a form of asphyxia in which liquid in the lungs prevents access to oxygen. Water in the airways also impairs the ability to shout and call for help. Death quickly results from lack of oxygen to the brain (cerebral hypoxia) and heart muscle. In some cases the heart stops beating from the 'shock'.

Will it happen to me?

If you enter water, it always remains a possibility – especially if you can't swim. Some people hold their breath underwater for so long that they pass out and sometimes drown.

What to look for

'We arrived on the scene and all five of them were in the water; some clinging to debris, some not. As we hovered ... two of the victims appeared to be looking up at us, treading water. I hurriedly changed into my wetsuit when I heard the pilot say, "They don't look like they are in any immediate danger. They can wait for the boat." I said, "No, Sir, they look like they are drowning!"'

This story from the journal of the US Coast Guard Search and Rescue, shows that those who are drowning do not always splash, yell or wave for help (aquatic distress). An instinctive drowning response may take over, causing them to extend their arms sideways and press down in an attempt to leverage themselves upwards. They may remain upright, looking up, and seem as if they are OK and just treading water. In reality, they are unable to kick their legs voluntarily, or reach for rescue equipment, and are about to go down for the last time.

What are the chances of survival?

If you are rescued, survival depends on how long you were submerged and the resuscitation skills of those assisting. If drowning in ice-cold water, chilling reduces the oxygen needs of the brain and may trigger a primitive mammalian diving reflex that slows heartbeat and redirects blood flow from the peripheries to the heart and brain. This diving reflex is stronger in children than adults, and increases the chance of resuscitation after prolonged submersion.

HOW TO AVOID IT

- **Learning to swim is vital.**
- **Always wear a lifejacket when boating.**
- **Ensure garden ponds and swimming pools are fenced in.**
- **Never enter water after drinking alcohol.**
- **Never swim alone.**
- **Only swim in areas patrolled by lifeguards.**
- **Never dive into unfamiliar or shallow water.**

31

Electrocution

Now that the electric chair is (mostly) retired from duty, electrocutions tend to result from accident, suicide or torture. The tiny current drawn by a 7.5-watt 120-volt lamp can kill if it passes from hand to hand across the chest. You don't even have to have a weak heart. Death has occurred simply from touching a broken light bulb in the home – you don't always need contact with overhead power lines.

How common is it?
Close to 1 million people are electrocuted worldwide every year.

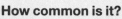

Who dies?
Infants and electrical/power-line workers are most at risk; males are more likely to be affected than females; three people die out of every 10,000 patients receiving electroconvulsive therapy (ECT) for severe depression.

Where?
In the workplace, at home, or near power lines, especially in Asia.

When?
Coming into contact with a live current; most deaths occur in the summer.

Why?
Faulty wiring, electrical overload, damaged cords, exposure to power lines, lack of warning or shielding devices.

High-voltage electroshock guns are allegedly fired almost a thousand times per day across the world. There is a potential risk of death for victims, especially when used multiple times on those taking certain drugs. Their use has been associated with at least 245 deaths worldwide, although it is unclear if they were the direct cause of demise.

Why does it kill?

Electricity kills by interfering with the electrical conduction of messages in the brain and heart, leading to respiratory arrest and cardiac arrest; by heating tissue and causing internal burns, and by falls caused by contact with electrical energy. Other causes of death following electric shock include septicaemia and renal failure.

Will it happen to me?

Most electrical injuries are preventable with simple safety measures. For those living in countries with robust health and safety laws, the lifetime chance of being electrocuted is 1 in 5000. For those living without such legislation, electrocution is the leading cause of workplace deaths.

What to look for

Old or frayed wiring combined with inexperience or lapse of attention.

What are the chances of survival?

This depends on the current, voltage, resistance, duration and frequency of the alternating current to which you are exposed (a direct current offers little hope). If a domestic current passes from hand to hand through the heart there is at least a 60% chance of death; if the current passes from hand to foot through the heart, the risk of death is 20%. If you have a pre-existing heart condition, the chance of survival is slim.

HOW TO AVOID IT

- **Be safety-conscious. Have wiring checked by a professional on a regular basis.**
- **Shut power off before working on an electric circuit – then test to ensure it is really off, and put a warning label on the circuit so that someone doesn't inadvertently switch it back on before you've finished.**
- **Don't make that mistake yourself – check a circuit-breaker isn't turned off for a reason before switching it back on.**
- **Don't use a metal ladder for electrical projects – invest in an insulated, fibreglass ladder.**
- **Don't work in wet areas. Wear rubber boots and gloves.**
- **Limit the use of extension cords.**
- **Use outlet covers to protect infants.**

32

Epilepsy

Epilepsy is a tendency to have recurrent seizures. It is caused by excessive electrical activity within the brain, which disrupts the normal transmission of messages that control body functions. Most episodes are brief, but prolonged seizure (status epilepticus) can occur. Forty per cent of those affected will die an epilepsy-related death.

How common is it?
50 million people have epilepsy worldwide.

Who dies?
Men are twice as likely to die from epilepsy as women. Most cases of sudden, unexpected death occur between the ages of 20–40.

Where?
90% of people with epilepsy are in developing regions, three-quarters of whom do not receive the treatment they need.

When?
Usually during or soon after a seizure.

Why?
Disruption of normal brain control of body functions.

IF SOMEONE HAS A FIT

- Put a cushion under their head or place your hands or forearms under their head to protect them.
- Place them in the recovery position once the seizure is over, but do not move them during the seizure unless they are in danger of harming themselves.
- Do not put anything in their mouth or between their teeth.
- Do not try to restrict their movements.
- Do not leave them until they are fully recovered.
- Call an ambulance if:
  - it is their first seizure
  - the fit lasts more than 5 minutes
  - two or more seizures occur without full recovery in between

As a result, people with epilepsy are between two and nine times more likely to die prematurely than those without epilepsy.

Will it happen to me?

The overall global risk of developing epilepsy is 1 in 137. Most cases are 'idiopathic' – having no known underlying cause. A family history of epilepsy increases the risk. Secondary epilepsy can be triggered by scarring associated with brain damage (birth trauma, head injury, meningitis), congenital abnormalities, tumours or stroke. Poor blood flow to the brain (cerebrovascular disease) is a common cause in elderly people.

In people with severe epilepsy it is estimated that about 1 in 200 dies of SUDEP (sudden unexplained death in epilepsy) each year. In people with mild idiopathic epilepsy (epilepsy of unknown cause), it is estimated that about 1 in 1000 dies of SUDEP each year.

What to look for

Epilepsy can be divided into two main types. *Generalized seizures* affect the whole brain and cause initial stiffening followed by falling over unconscious. Rhythmic, convulsive jerking of some or all muscles is then followed by drowsiness and confusion, which may last for several hours. *Partial seizures* affect just part of the brain, and symptoms can include suddenly going 'blank' and staring into space as if day-dreaming. Blinking, twitching or rhythmic movements of one part of the body may occur, along with hallucinations affecting vision, hearing or sense of smell. Sometimes there is confusion and repetitive behaviour.

What are the chances of survival?

Excellent. In 70% of newly diagnosed epilepsy, drugs successfully control seizures. These can often be withdrawn (under medical supervision) after 2–5 years without relapse.

HOW TO AVOID IT

Reduce your risk of head injury by wearing appropriate helmets when riding bikes or playing certain sports. Take anti-epileptic medication exactly as prescribed.

33

Euthanasia

The term 'euthanasia' is derived from the Greek for 'a good death' and is the deliberate ending of a life to relieve suffering. Advocates believe it should be done only for the benefit of the patient.

How common is it?

The true extent of euthanasia is far from clear; it undoubtedly occurs in every country, even where illegal. Researchers from London University estimate that 1 in 500 British deaths involves voluntary euthanasia, and 1 in 300 involves involuntary euthanasia – equivalent to 3000 deaths a year. During 2009, 2636 Dutch people died via euthanasia (1.8% of all deaths). If the passive withdrawal of treatment is included, estimates increase 20-fold.

Who dies?

Mostly those who are terminally ill from cancer or AIDS, suffering intractable pain or who are severely physically disabled by stroke or multiple sclerosis; some, however, may have a treatable depression that might skew their view.

Where?

In the Netherlands, 80% of euthanasia patients die at home.

When?

When life is no longer bearable.

Why?

To end physical suffering.

While acceptable in veterinary practice, euthanasia is illegal for humans in most countries.

Euthanasia is classed as voluntary when performed with consent; non-voluntary when the patient is not competent to consent (a child, an unconscious patient or one who is not of 'sound mind'); or involuntary if it is against the will of the patient. It can also be divided into active (involving lethal drugs or forces) or passive (withdrawal of necessary medical treatment) and, depending on your philosophy, viewed as consensual homicide, suicide, self-deliverance or murder. The European Association of Palliative Care Ethics Task Force considers the '... medicalized killing of a person without the person's consent, whether non-voluntary or involuntary, is not euthanasia: it is murder. Hence, euthanasia can be voluntary only.'

Voluntary euthanasia and/or assisted suicide is legal in a few countries, including Albania, Belgium, Germany, Luxembourg, the Netherlands and Switzerland. In addition, physician-aided death (in which the patient administers the lethal dose while a doctor holds their hand) is legal in three American states: Oregon, Washington and Montana.

In some countries, such as the UK, those who accompany patients to legal euthanasia centres abroad may escape prosecution in certain circumstances: for example, if they act out of compassion rather than for financial gain, if the patient was competent and, without being pressured, if the patient made a 'clear and settled' decision to die.

Why does it kill?

Legal euthanasia mostly involves medical drugs such as diamorphine (AKA heroin, which sedates and suppresses breathing) or those used on Death Row (sodium thiopental, pancuronium bromide, potassium chloride). Some illegal devices kill through the inhalation of inert gases, so death results from lack of oxygen (asphyxia).

Will it happen to me?

Only you can decide that.

What are the chances of survival?

A Dutch review found that complications occurred in 1 in 3 cases of legal euthanasia or physician-assisted suicide. In 12%, the time to death was longer than expected (45 minutes to 14 days), in 9% there were problems administering the drugs (difficulty accessing a vein, patient's inability to swallow all the medications), in 9% of cases nausea, vomiting and muscle spasm occurred, and in 2% patients awoke from their drug-induced coma. As a result, in 18% of cases the doctors had to provide euthanasia because of problems with assisted suicide. However, the eventual survival rate was zero.

DID YOU KNOW?

Voluntary refusal of food and fluids is viewed by some people as a legal alternative to passive euthanasia.

Falls 34

Just to be clear, the WHO defines a fall as 'an event that results in a person coming to rest inadvertently on the ground or floor or other lower level'. This covers a surprisingly wide range of situations.

How common is it?
Falls are the second-leading cause of accidental death worldwide, accounting for 424,000 fatalities; falls are the second-leading cause of work-related deaths.

Who dies?
Mostly the over-60s, young adventurous adults and children; males are more likely to die from falling than females, owing to higher levels of risk-taking behaviour and occupational hazards.

Where?
Eight out of ten lethal falls occur in low- and middle-income countries, especially in the Western Pacific and South-East Asia.

When?
Usually shortly after your feet leave contact with solid ground.

Why?
Lack of health and safety legislation and/or bad luck.

While it is possible to fall over 1000 m (3280 ft) and live, it is also possible (even common) to trip on perfectly flat ground and die. You can also be felled by coconuts, which can reach velocities of 80 km per hour (50 mph) after falling from a high palm. Despite these skull-crushing impacts, there is no truth in the rumour that more people die from falling coconuts each year than as a result of parachute failure.

Of the estimated 3,730,000 falls that are severe enough to need medical treatment each year, 1 in 11 is fatal. Falls are therefore classed as a major public health concern.

Why does it kill?

Death may be instantaneous from head or internal injury, or occur later, owing to infection (e.g. in a compound fracture), surgical complications, or as a result of immobility (bronchopneumonia, blood clot, pulmonary embolism).

Will it happen to me?

Over the coming year, on average, you have a 1 in 1850 risk of experiencing a fall that requires medical treatment, and a 1 in 20,350 risk of dying from one. If you are a steeplejack, however, assume your risk is significantly greater (1 in 888).

What to look for

Signs saying 'Stop', 'Danger Ahead', 'Falling Rocks', 'Cliff Edge' or 'Beware Falling Coconuts' – as well as uneven or slippery ground, unlit places, even if familiar, and dark stairwells.

What are the chances of survival?

If, on average, 1 in 11 serious falls is lethal, then the chance of surviving one is in the region of 91%.

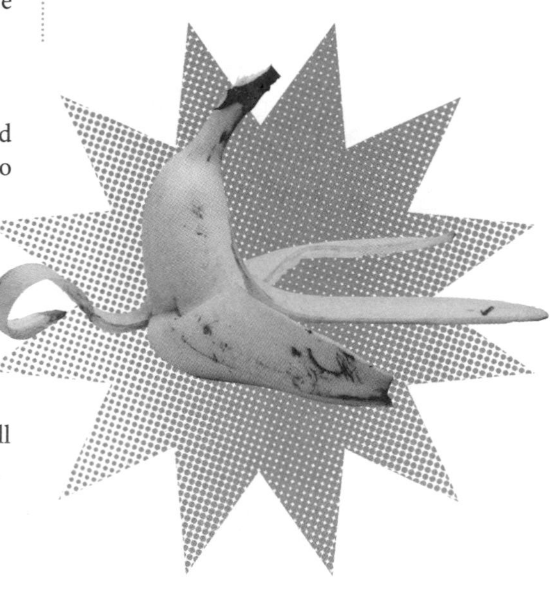

HOW TO AVOID IT

Don't work as a steeplejack, high-wire artiste or tightrope walker. If you must work at heights, use a personal fall-arrest system. Avoid hobbies that involve climbing ladders, cliff-walking, rock-climbing, horse-riding, base-jumping, parachuting or hang-gliding. Stay at home when there's ice or snow on the ground.

Famine 35

It is iniquitous that people still die of hunger when so-called developed countries are struggling with an obesity epidemic.

How common is it?

Over a billion people suffer from hunger and malnutrition. Every year, hunger plays a direct or indirect role in 36 million deaths (58% of all deaths) – that's 100,000 deaths each day through lack of adequate nutrition.

Who dies?

Mostly women and children; every year, 6 million children die as a direct or indirect result of hunger: that's 16,000 child deaths per day, one child every 5 seconds.

Where?

About 98% of the world's hungry people live in developing countries; two-thirds live in just seven countries: Bangladesh, China, Democratic Republic of Congo, Ethiopia, India, Indonesia and Pakistan.

When?

If poverty and harmful economic systems collide; death is especially likely if malnutrition is combined with exposure to infection.

Why?

90% of the world's hungry people live with chronic hunger that does not go away; the other 10% experience acute famine as a result of crises such as flood, drought, climate change, epidemics or conflict/war.

According to the WHO, hunger is the single gravest threat to public health. As a result of the global economic recession, rising food prices and agricultural neglect, around a billion people are currently undernourished or starving.

An energy intake of 2100 kcal per day is the minimum standard set by humanitarian agencies providing food aid. In the United States average energy intake is 3800 kcal per day, almost double that of Eritrea's 1520 kcal per day. For the starving, even this amount of energy would be a luxury.

But it is not just a question of energy intake. Hidden hunger affects an additional 2 billion people who consume adequate calories and protein, but lack one or more micronutrients. Every year:

- vitamin A deficiency causes 800,000 deaths among women and children
- iron deficiency leads to 814,000 deaths in women and infants
- zinc deficiency results in 665,000 child deaths, with millions more experiencing stunted growth, failure to thrive and reduced immunity

Females are especially vulnerable as, in many cultures, they traditionally 'eat last, and eat least'. After malnourishment during childhood and adolescence they marry young, have underweight babies and are unable to breastfeed for long, and so the cycle perpetuates.

In addition to famine and poverty, starvation can result from wasting diseases (this is called cachexia and can be due to malabsorption of nutrients, cancer, AIDS, renal failure, coma), neglect, lack of self-care (owing, for example, to depression or old age) and prolonged fasting by choice (anorexia nervosa, hunger strike).

Why does it kill?

Famine frequently kills as a result of weakened immunity, which occurs with micronutrient deficiency, kwashiorkor (severe protein malnutrition) and marasmus (severe protein and energy malnutrition). Between 5 million and 6 million children die each year from infections such as measles (45%), diarrhoeal diseases (61%), pneumonia (52%) and malaria (57%) that would not have killed them had they been well nourished. Micronutrient deficiency diseases such as rickets, beri-beri, pellagra and scurvy also shorten life expectancy. Protein and energy deficiencies lead to weakening of heart muscle as the body burns muscle for fuel, leading to heart attack, arrhythmias or heart failure. Some people simply waste away.

Will it happen to me?

The risk of widespread famine in developed countries is low, but could occur as a result of terrorism, war or natural disaster. Personal malnutrition as a result of anorexia nervosa, wasting diseases or hunger strike are other

DID YOU KNOW?

Every year, hunger and malnutrition kill more people than AIDS, malaria and TB combined. More people die from hunger than in wars.

'Why does hunger persist in a world of plenty? One of the greatest questions of our time, this is also a question of earlier times ... The history of hunger is embedded in the history of plenty.' S. Millman and R.W. Kates, 1990

possibilities. If you are admitted to hospital, your chance of having or developing malnutrition increases.

What to look for

This was best described by anthropologist Audrey Richards in 1932, in her book *Hunger and Work in a Savage Tribe*:

> *Hunger leads first to the concentration of the whole energy of the body to the problem of getting food. Every thought and emotion of the hungry is fixed on this one primary need. Failure to obtain sufficient foods gradually lowers the whole vitality of the body.*

What are the chances of survival?

If you have inherited the so-called 'famine survival gene', known as CRTC3, you have a unique ability to slow the rate at which you burn fat, and are in with a good chance of surviving famine. As well as doubling your supply of brown fat cells, which burn calories to generate heat, this thrifty gene also regulates how white fat cells respond to brain signals that control energy expenditure. Unfortunately, during times of plenty, your genetic inheritance makes you a sitting duck for obesity (see page 169).

HOW TO AVOID IT

Difficult. The World Food Summit of 1996 pledged to halve the number of undernourished people (from 824 million in 1992 to 412 million) by 2015. In 2009, the number had climbed to 1.02 billion people. By 2010 it had fallen, but only to 1 billion – the first decline for 15 years. So not much to celebrate, really.

36

Fire and smoke inhalation

Burning to death is not a good way to go, which is probably why it was the medieval punishment of choice for witches, heretics and scoundrels. These days, victims of fire are more likely to die from smoke inhalation than from burns.

How common is it?

Burns are the fourth most common form of trauma worldwide (after land traffic accidents, falls and homicide). Every year, almost 11 million burn- or fire-related injuries are severe enough to require medical attention, and 310,000 people die as a result.

Who dies?

The very young and those over 60 years are most likely to succumb, and 70% of burns are in children. Infants in Africa are three times more likely to be affected than infants in other parts of the world. More females are affected than males.

Where?

Low- or middle-income countries are the locale for 90% of burns, which usually occur in a domestic setting (kitchen and bathroom); men are more likely to experience burn injuries in work or outdoor locations.

When?

Especially common during cold, dry months.

Why?

Many fires result from inappropriate use of petrol and other accelerants; 80% of burns in children occur while they are unsupervised.

Many who are consumed by flames will have died first from the effects of smoke and superheated fumes, which can contain ammonia, carbon monoxide (see page 55), carbon dioxide, hydrochloric acid, hydrogen cyanide, hydrogen sulphide, sulphur dioxide and other toxins.

Why does it kill?

Smoke inhalation is associated with lack of oxygen and poisoning from toxins such as carbon monoxide and hydrogen cyanide. Cyanide fumes (released from burning wool, silk, cotton, paper, plastics and other polymers) kill quickly by blocking an enzyme (cytochrome C oxidase) needed for the production of energy in cells. Coma, seizures, apnoea (cessation of breathing) and cardiac arrest result. Burning causes tissue damage when skin is heated above 49 °C (120 °F) . If second- or third-degree burns cover more than 10% (children) or 15% (adults) of the body, fluid loss and tissue damage can trigger life-threatening clinical shock (see page 210). Burns, even superficial ones, can become infected with toxigenic strains of *Staphylococcus aureus* to cause toxic shock syndrome, especially in children (see page 211).

Will it happen to me?

If you are careless with fire, matches and accelerants, then yes. Burns can also result from accidents with boiling liquid or hot vapour (scalds), electrical circuits and chemicals.

What to look for

- First-degree burn: only the top layer of skin is injured; reddening and pain occurs. Rapid healing follows. Dead cells often peel after a few days. Sunburn is an example.
- Second-degree burn: cells in the deeper layers of the skin are destroyed and a blister forms. Enough live cells remain for regeneration, and the burn usually heals without scarring.
- Third-degree burn: the full thickness of skin is destroyed. Extensive treatment, including skin grafts, may be needed and scarring results.

What are the chances of survival?

Burns treated in a specialist centre have an average survival rate of 95%, but this depends on age, percentage of total body surface affected and the degree of smoke inhalation/toxicity. Three main risk factors that increase the mortality rate of burns have been identified:

- age greater than 60 years
- more than 40% of body surface area burned
- inhalation injury

Depending on how many of these risk factors are present, your chance of survival is as outlined in the table on page 103:

DID YOU KNOW?

The most common cause of cyanide poisoning is smoke inhalation. New protocols may soon be put in place to treat smoke inhalation survivors with a cyanide antidote.

A new technique has just been perfected in which skin stem cells (cells capable of rapid division) are harvested from an undamaged area of the same patient. Then, rather than being grown laboriously in a laboratory (during which time the patient may die from infection), they are diluted in fluid and 'fired' back onto the damaged flesh with a sophisticated spray-gun. The autotransplanted cells are then fed with a nutrient dressing providing glucose, amino acids, electrolytes and antibiotics, to heal the area within days. Scarring is minimal.

Number of risk factors	*Chance of survival*
None	99.7%
One	97%
Two	67%
Three	10%

HOW TO AVOID IT

- **Smoke detectors save lives – fit at least one on each floor of your home, including children's rooms. Test them regularly, and replace batteries before they run out.**
- **Don't smoke in bed. Or anywhere else in the house, come to that.**
- **Work out an escape plan to evacuate in the case of fire.**
- **Have an all-purpose, charged, regularly maintained fire extinguisher on each floor and know how to use them.**
- **Keep fire lighters and matches out of reach of children. Use screens around fires and heaters.**
- **Ensure furnishings are flame resistant or retardant.**
- **Take special care when cooking, boiling kettles, ironing and running a bath.**
- **Set the maximum temperature on your hot water tank to 49 °C (120 °F).**

Flesh-eating disease and superbugs

37

Superbugs appear out of the blue to cause an initially minor infection that escalates when the usual antibiotics fail to eradicate it.

How common is it?

One in ten people have MRSA bacteria on their skin but are not ill as a result (yet). Superbugs cause at least 2.5 million infections worldwide each year, and result in at least 172,000 deaths. However, this is a vast underestimate. Hospitals avoid naming a superbug as a cause of death when an alternative explanation is available. As many patients are already seriously ill from another underlying disorder, the cause of death is instead given as organ failure, pneumonia, sepsis, etc. Necrotizing fasciitis affects an estimated 15,000 people each year, of whom at least 3000 will die.

Who dies?

Mostly very young children, elderly people, those with pre-existing diseases such as poorly controlled diabetes, HIV or cancer, and intravenous drug abusers.

Where?

85% of infections are acquired in hospital after being admitted for another reason; infection has also been acquired from shared locker rooms and gyms.

When?

After admission to hospital for another reason.

Why?

Reduced patient immunity, increased resistance and virulence in the superbug.

The most-feared of these is undoubtedly the 'flesh-eating disease', necrotizing fasciitis. Notable superbugs include toxin-producing strains of Group A *Streptococcus pyogenes*, methicillin-resistant *Staphylococcus aureus* (MRSA), vancomycin-intermediate *Staphylococcus aureus* (VISA) and vancomycin-resistant *Enterococcus* (VRE). These superbugs are found in many, if not most, hospitals. Recently, a new bacterial supergene, NDM-1 (New Delhi metallobeta-lactamase), was identified; it loves nothing more than to jump from one bacterial species to another. This gene tells bacteria how to produce an enzyme that dissolves multiple antibiotics, and is the shape of infections to come.

Why does it kill?

Uncontrolled spread of infection leads to overwhelming sepsis (see page 208), organ failure and circulatory collapse.

Will it happen to me?

If you are admitted to hospital for any reason, the risk of acquiring a superbug is high. Many people harbour a superbug (for example, in the nose) without ill effects. If a superbug colonizes a wound, however, problems arise.

What to look for

Tenderness, redness, soreness, heat, swelling and pus that do not resolve with the usual antibiotics.

What are the chances of survival?

Less than 20% without treatment. Usually, though, an obscure antibiotic can be found against which the bug is not so super. Necrotizing fasciitis is treated by surgical removal of dead (necrotic) flesh and a combination of antibiotics in the hope of finding one that works.

HOW TO AVOID IT

- Good hygiene is vital, especially in hospital.
- Antibiotic resistance is linked with inappropriate overuse of antibiotics and not finishing the course. Do not demand them for every minor sore throat or viral illness. If they are necessary, take them as prescribed for the correct length of time.

Genetic conditions 38

Our genes have a lot to answer for. Estimates of the number we possess have varied wildly over the past few years up to as many as 150,000.

How common is it?

Over 6000 single-gene disorders are known, affecting at least 1 in every 200 births. An estimated 7.6 million children have a significant genetic disease or congenital malformation; many are fatal before birth. Every baby is born with an inherited probability of acquiring certain common diseases in later life, such as heart disease, diabetes, obesity and cancer. Rheumatoid arthritis is cited as the cause of 26,000 deaths per year.

Who dies?

Infants, children and young to middle-aged adults.

Where?

Everywhere, but 90% of deaths occur in low- to middle-income countries, where medical treatments are not widely available.

When?

At any time.

Why?

Bad luck, consanguineous marriage (especially marriage between cousins, which increases the chance of passing on two identical copies of a faulty gene) and maternal age over 35 years (raising the risk of chromosomal abnormalities as an ageing egg divides).

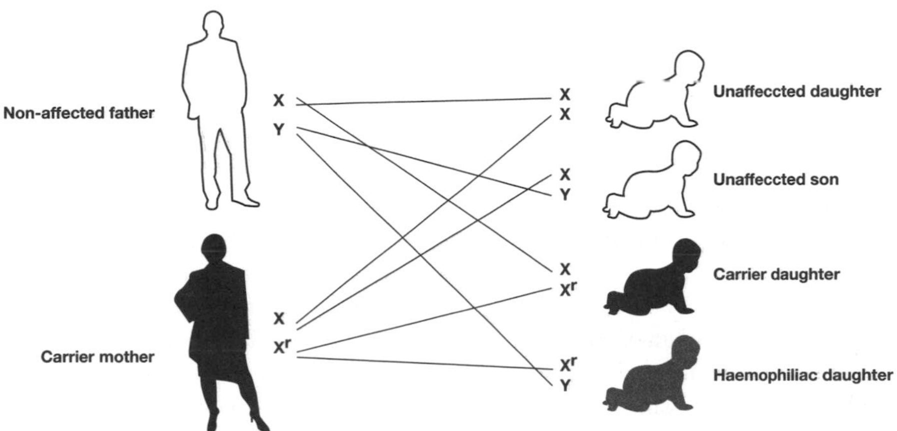

Recent analysis reveals that the true number of genes that actually code for proteins rather than gobbledegook is nearer 20,500. This is similar in number to the 20,000 found in a microscopic roundworm (*C. elegans*) and not even double that found in the common fruit fly (14,000). Anxieties induced by this paradox are only partly assuaged by suggestions that it is quality, rather than quantity, that counts. Human proteins are capable of 10 times more interactions than seen in fruit flies, and 20 times more interactions than those found in single-celled yeast as it converts grape juice into wine.

Your genes are stored along 46 paired molecules of deoxyribonucleic acid (DNA) called chromosomes. You inherited 23 chromosomes from your mother and 23 from your father.

Each chromosome consists of two paired chains of nucleotides, which coil round each other to form a long, double helix (the shape of a 'spiral' staircase). There are only four different types of nucleotide: adenine (A), thymine (T), cytosine (C) or guanine (G). These pair up across the spiral like the rungs of a ladder. Importantly, A always pairs with T, and C always pairs with G. This pairing allows the helix to be unzipped and copied exactly (when things go according to plan).

Your DNA contains 3 billion nucleotides, which provide the code needed for cells to

DID YOU KNOW?

The genes within each of your cells are identical to those of all your other cells, but different genes are switched on or off, so each cell makes different proteins. That's why liver cells, skin cells, muscle cells and fat cells are so different from each other.

make proteins. This code depends on the order in which the nucleotides occur along one strand of the DNA helix. Each run of three nucleotides – called a triplet – acts as the code for a particular amino acid. This code dictates the order in which amino acids are added when making a protein chain.

A gene is a stretch of DNA that provides all the coding needed to make a single protein. Each gene exists in many different forms within the population (owing to the exact order of its A, T, C and G nucleotides) but you inherit only two copies of each gene – one from your mother and one from your father. In some cases, these two copies might be identical.

Some of your genes determine visible features, such as your skin, hair and eye colour. Others determine how your metabolism functions, whether you are at risk of certain diseases, and how your body responds to different infections and drugs. So, although everyone inherits the same number and type of genes, the subtle differences within them make each person unique from the other 6.9 billion people on this planet.

Genetically programmed diseases can arise when mistakes are made during gene-copying. These can involve the insertion, deletion, replacement or transposition of a whole chromosome, a section of a chromosome, or just one or more nucleotides.

The most common gene mutations, accounting for 90% of all human genetic variation, are single-nucleotide polymorphisms or SNPs (pronounced 'snips'). These one-letter changes in the normal genetic code occur when a single nucleotide (A, T, C or G) in the DNA sequence is changed.

Some dominant diseases	*Some recessive diseases*	*Some dominant diseases*	*Some recessive diseases*
Haemochromatosis	Sickle-cell anaemia	**Myotonic dystrophy**	Autosomal recessive polycystic kidneys
Huntington's disease	Haemophilia	**Achondroplasia**	Fanconi anaemia
Neurofibromatosis	Cystic fibrosis	**Acute intermittent porphyria**	Xeroderma pigmentosum
Marfan syndrome	Duchenne muscular dystrophy	**Von Willebrand disease**	Thalassaemia
Tuberous sclerosis	Spinal muscular atrophy	**Hereditary haemorrhagic telangiectasia**	Kartagener's syndrome
Retinoblastoma	Phenylketonuria	**Familial hypercholesterolaemia**	Pyruvate dehydrogenase deficiency

Over 5 million SNPs have been identified. Most are benign, and have no effect on the protein coded for by each gene, but a few cause crucial changes, so that, for example, an enzyme folds into a different three-dimensional shape and no longer works properly.

Genetic diseases are usually grouped into those associated with single genes (e.g. cystic fibrosis) and those associated with chromosomal disorders (e.g. Down's syndrome).

Whether the disease occurs or not depends on whether the faulty gene is dominant or recessive. A dominant gene is one that always produces its effect, even when inherited from only one parent (e.g. the gene for brown eyes). A disease caused by such a gene is then called a dominant disease. A recessive gene is one whose effects are seen only if you inherit two copies of the gene – one from each parent (e.g. the gene for blue eyes). A disease caused by such a gene is then called a recessive disease.

Also, some genes are carried on the Y-chromosome, one of the two sex chromosomes (the other being the X-chromosome). The Y-chromosome occurs only in men, paired with an X-chromosome. Women have two paired X-chromosomes. Faults in genes on the X-chromosome mainly affect men because they don't have another X-chromosome to mask its effect.

Why does it kill?

Genetic abnormalities can affect any body function, and may kill from liver disease (haemochromatosis), haemorrhage (haemophilia), respiratory infections (cystic fibrosis) or an increased risk of malnutrition, cancer, diabetes, heart disease or infection.

Will it happen to me?

Everyone is at risk; just about every disease involves interactions between the genes you have inherited and the environment to which they are exposed. For example, breast cancer has been linked with certain genes found on chromosomes 6, 11, 13, 14, 15, 17 and 22. Our knowledge of risk increases every day as scientists identify new genetic bases for common conditions.

What to look for

Long-lived, healthy parents. If you are feeling brave and can cope with the results, genetic testing is increasingly available. (And if the results are favourable, you can go on to look for low insurance premiums.)

What are the chances of survival?

This depends on the particular genome you have inherited.

HOW TO AVOID IT

You have no control over how your parents' genes were shuffled and redealt at the time of your conception. Scientists may, however, be able to coax more advantageous patterns from those you have inherited in the not-too-distant future.

Gunshot wound 39

The world possesses at least 900 million firearms, of which 75% are owned by civilians rather than the military. One-third of these civilians live in the United States. Firearms are the weapon of choice for those with either homicidal or suicidal intent: 60% of murders involve a gunshot wound.

How common is it?
Every year, 360,000 homicides and 330,000 suicides are carried out using a firearm; in addition, 184,000 people are killed by gunshot wounds during armed conflicts (see page 257).

Who dies?
Anyone, but males are most at risk.

Where?
Colombia (89% of homicides involve a gun), Montenegro (85%), Yemen (80%), United States (70%), Brazil (69%).

When?
Ammunition propelled from a firearm enters the body.

Why?
Haemorrhage, internal bleeding, catastrophic damage to vital organs such as the heart, lungs or brain.

Among suicidal males, the use of a gun ranges from 0.2% in Japan to 60% in the United States. Women tend to prefer 'cleaner' methods such as poisoning and are half as likely to choose a gunshot death. One in five gunshot wounds is accidental, however.

Why does it kill?

Immediate causes of death include damage to vital organs (heart, lungs, brain and spinal cord), haemorrhage, respiratory failure, heart failure and brain death. Delayed death can result from multiple organ failure and infection.

Will it happen to me?

The lifetime chance of being killed by a firearm is 1 in 325 in the United States, where gun ownership is common.

What to look for

Although a smoking gun is a dead giveaway, a penetrating wound is typically surrounded by red-brown skin and may seem unusually small and neat (due to retraction of elastic skin) with minimal bleeding. If the bullet does not remain inside the body, the exit wound is usually larger, often bleeding profusely.

What are the chances of survival?

It depends on who was aiming, their intention, where you were hit, how many times, the type of firearm and the ammunition used. With rapid medical attention, 5% of people will survive a bullet in the head, 15% will survive a bullet in the heart, while 85% can hope to survive a bullet in the abdomen.

DID YOU KNOW?

Only 1 gun in 10 is registered with the appropriate authorities.

HOW TO AVOID IT

- **Keep the gun unloaded until ready to use.**
- **Keep your gun pointed in a safe direction.**
- **Keep your finger off the trigger until ready to shoot.**
- **Know how to use the gun safely.**
- **Store guns securely.**

Hanging

Hanging is a form of strangulation that kills by taking advantage of gravity and the anatomical vulnerability of the neck.

How common is it?

Each year 350,500 people commit suicide by hanging, and the prevalence is increasing; in addition, 5500 accidental hangings occur.

Who dies?

Young children (accident) and young males (suicide, auto-eroticism). Among men who do not have access to guns, hanging is the most common method of suicide, and the second most common in women (after poisoning or drug overdose).

Where?

On the end of a rope or other ligature, usually in the person's own home; 10% of hangings occur in hospital, prison and police custody.

When?

After passing a ligature (rope, belt, flex) around a fixed point (beam, banister, hook, door knob, pipe, cell bar, sink, toilet, tree branch) and jumping from a chair, table or ladder with a noose around the neck. One in two hanging suicides is found freely suspended (feet off the ground), but a similar number manage to hang themselves while standing with both feet on the ground (with the ligature typically supporting 65% of their weight), kneeling, sitting or lying down.

Why?

Failure to solve problems and/or depression; accidents when playing with ropes, swings, scarves etc.

A surprising number of countries still retain hanging as a legal form of capital punishment, and it remains the second most widely used form of state execution. In 2010, for example, six countries (Bangladesh, Egypt, Iran, Iraq, Japan and the Sudan) hanged at least 233 men and 5 women between them as retribution for convicted crimes. Elsewhere, hangings are due to homicide, suicide, auto-eroticism or accident.

Why does it kill?

Sudden constriction of the neck and throat leads to death because blood flow is cut off to the brain (cerebral anoxia) by a vagal nerve reflex that stops the heart (cardiac arrest), and/or because the neck is broken, damaging the spinal cord. Cutting off the air supply (see page 32) is thought to play a lesser role.

Will it happen to me?

Accidental hanging is always a possibility for those who use rope swings, and for those practising strangulation for sexual pleasure. In some countries, the latter may automatically attract a hanging sentence too. Overall, the risk of dying within the next year by hanging or strangulation has been estimated at 1 in 2,165,000, but the risk of dying from self-hanging is 1 in 44,600.

What to look for

Hanging leaves an inverted V-shaped bruise on the neck, as opposed to homicidal strangulation with a ligature, which leaves a straight-line bruise.

What are the chances of survival?

Attempted suicide by hanging is successful in 70% to 80% of cases as, unlike taking an overdose, there is little opportunity to change your mind – death rapidly occurs after suspension. Of those who are found and reach hospital alive, 90% survive, but death may result from bronchopneumonia, pulmonary oedema and adult respiratory distress syndrome. Very occasionally, victims of accidental hanging have been resuscitated after being found dead, but it is wise to assume the worst.

HOW TO AVOID IT

- **Do not allow children to play on rope swings.**
- **Do not commit a crime in countries that still use hanging as a death sentence.**
- **Never leave a suicidal person alone for a second, or they may hang themselves with a sheet, clothing, belt, shoelaces, electric cords ...**

Heart attack

41

A heart attack occurs when heart cells die from lack of blood – coronary artery disease. (Heart failure occurs when the blood supply to the heart is fine, but the muscle is weak and flabby and unable to pump properly; this can follow as a complication of a heart attack.)

How common is it?
Heart attack is the number one killer in the Western world; coronary heart disease kills 3.8 million men and 3.4 million women worldwide each year, meaning that 1 in 3 people die in this way.

Who dies?
Mostly men over the age of 45, and women over the age of 55.

Where?
Usually in bed, on the toilet, or following unusual exertion.

When?
Between 6 a.m. and noon; the risk is highest during dreaming sleep, and during the first 3 hours after waking; the incidence also spikes during cold winter months.

Why?
Spasm or blockage of coronary arteries can be brought on by stress, a sudden shock, bursts of physical activity or obstruction by a blood clot.

Every year, an estimated 32 million heart attacks occur worldwide, of which 7.2 million are fatal. The 'Hollywood heart attack', in which a victim grimaces and clutches his chest, is less common in real life. Often, a heart attack is heralded by feelings of fatigue, indigestion, chest discomfort (rather than pain) and an urgent need to empty the bowels. As a result, many people who die from a heart attack are found slumped on the toilet. Almost as many simply drop to the ground, their imminent death unannounced.

Why does it kill?

The heart is the most important organ in the body. You can survive with very little brain function, but as soon as enough heart cells die to disrupt electrical conduction, the heart stops pumping, blood flow round the body ceases and death soon follows. Vigilant medics may re-establish a normal heart rhythm with a hard blow, drugs and/ or a controlled electric shock. While your heart decides whether or not to respond, artificial respiration and chest compression are vital to pump oxygenated blood around your body.

Will it happen to me?

Your risk of a heart attack is as high as 1 in 3. The chance increases with the more risk factors you accumulate, such as:

- family history (mum having a heart attack before age 60 or dad before age 45)
- smoking
- sedentary lifestyle
- poorly controlled high blood pressure
- poorly controlled diabetes
- elevated LDL-cholesterol levels
- high stress

If you tick every box, then you may want to discuss urgent preventive measures with your doctor. The good news is that improving your diet and lifestyle in middle age can seriously prolong your life.

What to look for

A heart attack can be hard to distinguish from heart pain due to angina. Both are due to a lack of oxygen and nutrients reaching heart muscle cells. Angina is usually brought on by exertion and resolves with rest. In contrast, heart attack symptoms can come on at any time, including when sitting down, and often persist despite resting.

DID YOU KNOW?

Although traditionally viewed as a male disease, heart attack kills three times more women than cancers of the breast, ovaries and cervix combined; they just tend to die 10 to 20 years later in life than men, owing to the protective effects of oestrogen before the menopause (an effect that is nullified by smoking or having diabetes).

Symptoms can include:

- breaking out in a cold sweat
- chest discomfort – pressure, fullness, squeezing (like a bear hug), aching, heartburn or indigestion
- discomfort radiating up to the neck, jaw, shoulders and back or down the arms (often the left arm)
- shortness of breath
- dizziness or light-headedness
- a sudden need to open the bowels
- fatigue
- nausea or even vomiting

What are the chances of survival?

The weak link in surviving a heart attack is patient delay in seeking treatment. Between 40% and 75% of victims die before reaching hospital. Spotting the signs of a heart attack quickly can be life-saving as early clot-busting drugs (even a simple aspirin) are vital. If you think you may be having a heart attack:

- call an ambulance and specify that you fear a heart attack
- chew an aspirin
- lie down and try to stay calm

If you survive a heart attack, treat it as a wake-up call. Address any risk factors that can be improved. One in four men and one in three women die within a year of their first heart attack.

HOW TO AVOID IT

You know the essentials. The difficulty is putting them into practice.

- **Stop smoking – smokers are five times more likely to have a heart attack in their 30s and 40s than non-smokers, and three times more likely to have one overall.**
- **Lose any excess weight, especially the 'menopot' around your waist; being overweight increases your risk by 150%, and obesity by at least 200%.**
- **Exercise for 30–60 minutes, every day.**
- **Eat plenty of antioxidant-rich fruit and vegetables (and drink tea).**
- **Eat more oily fish (or take fish oil supplements); just 1 g of long-chain fish oils (EPA and DHA) daily can reduce heart attack risk by as much as 45%, and increase the chance of survival.**
- **Cut back on salt intake.**
- **Have regular health screenings.**
- **Ensure high blood pressure, diabetes and/or cholesterol levels are well controlled.**
- **Limit your alcohol intake.**
- **Reduce stress levels; excess stress increases your blood pressure by an amount equivalent to carrying an extra 20 kg (44 lb) in weight, or gaining an additional 20 years in age, so take regular time out for relaxation.**

Heart failure

42

Heart failure is, technically, a prerequisite for diagnosing any death, but the term is used more broadly to describe an inability of the heart to pump as efficiently as it should.

How common is it?

A quarter of all patients who survive a heart attack develop congestive heart failure (CHF) within the next 10 years. These include 987,000 people dying from hypertensive heart disease every year, and 440,000 people dying from inflammatory heart disease (heart muscle inflammation and cardiomyopathy); the actual number of deaths is significantly higher, however, as data on heart failure is not reliable in developing countries.

Who dies?

Heart failure affects 1% of 50 year olds, 10% of 65 year olds, and 20% of those aged over 85. The average age of death from heart muscle infection (myocarditis) is much younger, at 42 years.

Where?

Usually in bed, often in hospital.

When?

One-third of those newly diagnosed with heart failure die within a year; half die within 5 years.

Why?

The heart muscle gives up even trying to fulfil its pumping role.

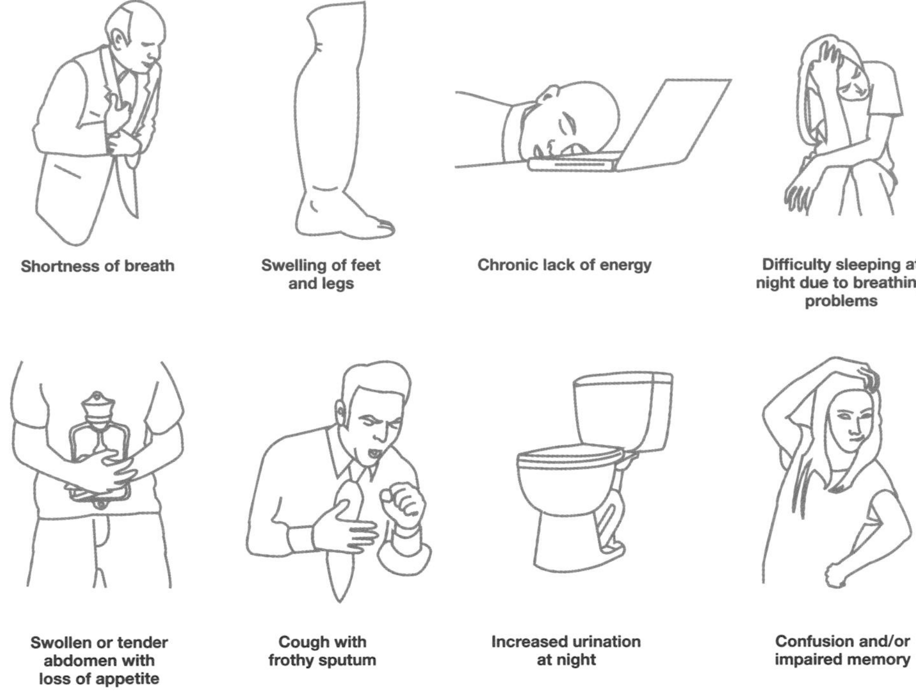

When heart failure occurs, the resulting back-pressure and pooling of blood in the veins causes fluid to leak out into body tissues that become congested.

The left side of the heart pumps oxygen-rich blood from the lungs to the rest of the body. So, in left-heart failure, it is the lungs that become congested with excess fluid (pulmonary oedema), causing shortness of breath. In the case of right-heart failure, the lower body becomes congested leading to swollen ankles (or worse, legs that swell as high as the buttocks). When one side of the heart is affected, the other experiences extra strain and usually fails, too, so left- and right-heart failure tend to occur in pairs, usually described as congestive heart failure (CHF).

Heart failure is a syndrome (collection of symptoms) rather than a diagnosis, and investigations are needed to ascertain the underlying disease. Most cases result from hardening and furring up of the arteries, smoking, high blood pressure, diabetes, heart attack or valvular heart disease (see page 254). Other causes include heart muscle disease (cardiomyopathy), infection (Chagas' disease, influenza, Coxsackie B

DID YOU KNOW?

Traditionally, congestive heart failure with accumulation of fluid in the lower body was known as 'dropsy'.

virus, HIV) and any condition that increases the workload of the heart, such as severe anaemia, overactive thyroid, abnormal heart rhythm and obesity. Right-sided heart failure can also result from long-standing lung disease, such as chronic bronchitis and emphysema.

Someone with congestive heart failure is four to eight times more likely to die at any age than someone without heart failure.

Why does it kill?

Half die suddenly from an irregular heart rhythm (arrhythmia). Other causes of death include heart attack, stroke, respiratory failure and sleep apnoea.

Will it happen to me?

Your risk is 1 in 100 if you are below the age of 50, 1 in 10 if you are 65, and 1 in 5 if you are 85 or over. If you suffer from shortness of breath (during exercise or at rest), fatigue, poor circulation, puffy extremities and weight gain owing to fluid retention, and your level of physical activity is limited by shortness of breath or fatigue, you could already have it.

What to look for

CHF affects quality of life more than most common chronic illnesses, with puffy extremities and shortness of breath limiting physical activities such as sex, walking and even talking. Shortness of breath may be associated with wheezing and sweating. Congestion of the lungs is worse on lying down, with sudden difficulty in breathing, so you may wake at night gasping for breath. Those with CHF typically sleep propped up on several pillows. Heart failure also leads to fatigue, loss of appetite, nausea, poor circulation and weight gain owing to fluid retention.

What are the chances of survival?

Two in three people survive their first year after diagnosis; 50% survive for 5 years. Treatment involves a combination of drugs, including a diuretic to flush excess fluid from the body and an ACE inhibitor to reduce the workload of the heart.

HOW TO AVOID IT

All the usual (boring but essential) advice applies:

- **Maintain a healthy weight.**
- **Limit your alcohol intake to no more than 2 or 3 units per day.**
- **Take regular exercise.**
- **If you smoke, stop before it's too late.**
- **Reduce salt intake by excluding obviously salty foods and not adding salt during cooking or at the table.**

Heat stroke

43

Humans are some of the most adaptable animals on the planet. But if global warming is a real phenomenon, then excessive heat will become an increasingly common cause of death. Heat stroke (hyperthermia) is diagnosed when body temperature rises above 41.1 °C (106 °F).

How common is it?
More than 35,000 people are thought to die from excessive heat every year.

Who dies?
Mostly children under the age of 4 years, and older people aged 70 and over.

Where?
Often tropical climates, but it can occur even in northern countries.

When?
The 'Dog Days' of summer, when temperatures peak above 38 °C (100 °F) and humidity is high.

Why?
Dehydration, overheating, multi-organ dysfunction.

Heat stroke mostly affects the very young, the very elderly, and those with chronic illnesses, who are unable to regulate their body temperature by appropriate sweating. Exertional heat stroke can also occur in otherwise young, fit adults engaged in prolonged, strenuous activity in a hot, humid environment (e.g. athletes, rave dancers).

DID YOU KNOW?

By 2080, heat waves are predicted to become an annual summer event even in temperate climates such as those of Great Britain.

Why does it kill?

Dehydration and heat cause multiple organ failure, including the lungs, liver, kidneys and brain. The most common contributors to death are respiratory failure, raised acid levels, salt imbalances and coma.

Will it happen to me?

If you visit a hot climate during a heat wave and are not acclimatized, then it is a possibility, especially if you have a viral illness, or are dehydrated, obese, or unfit and you overexercise. Unsuitably heavy clothing, overeating, alcohol and taking certain drugs can also reduce your ability to sweat.

What to look for

Heat stroke is usually preceded by heat exhaustion, which is characterized by profuse sweating, tiredness, abdominal and muscle cramps, nausea, headache, shortness of breath and weakness. Fainting and loss of consciousness can also occur. The affected person will feel hot, with dry, flushed skin, rapid shallow breathing and a weak, rapid pulse, and will become confused and disorientated. As body temperature continues to rise, drowsiness is followed by seizures, coma and death if the person is not urgently cooled and treated.

What are the chances of survival?

Without medical treatment, the mortality rate is greater than 80%. Early diagnosis and immediate cooling can increase survival rates to 90%.

HOW TO AVOID IT

- **Acclimatize yourself to hot weather slowly by spending gradually longer periods of time in the heat, before returning to cooler shade – full acclimatization can take up to 3 weeks.**
- **Stay in the shade as much as possible.**
- **Never fall asleep in the sun.**
- **Avoid strenuous exercise, wear loose, lightweight clothes and drink plenty of fluids.**
- **Cool off in a shower when possible.**
- **Seek advice from a pharmacist about whether you need salt tablets.**
- **Eat a light diet and avoid alcohol.**

Hepatitis 44

Hepatitis is an inflammation of the liver. Some deaths from hepatitis are due to alcohol (see page 13), toxins or drugs, but the majority result from a viral infection.

How common is it?

Hepatitis B causes 600,000 deaths per year and hepatitis C kills more than 350,000 people annually. Between them, all the hepatitis viruses kill over a million people yearly – 3% of deaths worldwide.

Who dies?

Those most at risk of hepatitis B, C and D include children, healthcare workers, travellers abroad, drug injectors and people with risky sexual practices.

Where?

Hepatitis viruses are found worldwide; HBV is endemic in Asia, especially China, where most people encounter the virus during childhood, and 10% of the adult population are chronically infected; HBV vaccination has reduced carrier rates to less than 1% in some areas.

When?

All hepatitis viruses can kill during the acute infection, which develops 15–180 days after exposure; deaths through HBV, HCV and HDV more commonly occur 5–30 years later, from liver disease.

Why?

From loss of liver function, which is vital for generating heat, processing nutrients and wastes, maintaining glucose levels, making proteins and clearing toxins from the body.

Five main hepatitis viruses are recognized, named simply A, B, C, D and E. No doubt others are evolving as you read.

Hepatitis A and E are transmitted by the faecal–oral route (stool to mouth) via person-to-person contact or contaminated food or water. Hepatitis B, C and D are passed on through contact with infected body fluids: from blood transfusions; or sharing of toothbrushes, razors or sex toys; from unsafe sex and unsafe injections; or from mother to baby at birth.

Hepatitis A (HAV) causes at least 1.5 million recognized infections per year, and perhaps as many as a hundred times more subclinical infections. It is usually relatively benign, but 1 in 100 cases progresses to 'fulminant' (sudden and severe) hepatitis with severe liver impairment. Mortality rate is 1 per 250 of those who develop acute symptoms, but this rises to 1 in 57 cases in the over-50 age group.

Hepatitis B (HBV) is the biggest killer. More than 2 billion people have been infected worldwide – one-third of the global population. One in 100 people develop fulminant hepatic necrosis and will die unless liver transplantation is available. Of those that survive acute infection, at least 17.5% – that's 350 million people – fail to clear the virus and remain chronically infected. This most commonly occurs with infants or children. These figures are heartbreaking, as HBV is 95% preventable with vaccination.

Hepatitis C (HCV) has infected 3% of the world's population – around 210 million people. Eight out of ten are not diagnosed, but may have persistent symptoms such as fatigue. It does not usually cause acute fulminant hepatitis, but it mutates so quickly within the body that the immune system finds it difficult to recognize and spontaneous elimination of the infection is rare; no vaccine is currently available. As a result, 80% progress to chronic infection and remain infectious. There are 4 million carriers in Europe alone.

Hepatitis D (HDV) infects more than 10 million people worldwide, of whom 20% will die as a result of their infection. This is despite the fact that it is a 'defective' virus – it can replicate only if passed on together with its partner, hepatitis B virus. The two together wreak unusual havoc, so that acute fulminant hepatitis is 10 times more common than with HBV alone. It has a mortality rate of 80%. Of those that progress to chronic hepatitis D infection (5%), the overall mortality rate from cirrhosis and liver cancer is 10 times higher than for HBV on its own.

Hepatitis E (HEV) was recognized only in 1980, but has infected as many as 1 in 5 of the world's population. The mortality rate is similar to that of HAV (1 in 250) but rises to 1 in 4 during pregnancy.

Why does it kill?

Acute hepatitis can cause acute liver failure (fulminant hepatic necrosis) when as many as 90% of liver cells die. A buildup of toxins and wastes affects brain function (hepatic encephalopathy with coma), while lack of blood-clotting proteins can cause haemorrhage. If persistent infection develops, between 1 in 4 and 1 in 5 will eventually die from progressive liver damage

AM I NUMBER 12?

leading to cirrhosis (see page 150) or liver cancer in later life. Worldwide, hepatitis viruses account for 57% of liver cirrhosis and 78% of primary liver cancers; as a result, liver cancer is among the top three causes of cancer death in Asia.

Will it happen to me?

If you are not vaccinated against hepatitis A or B, then it remains a possibility, especially if you travel to endemic areas. One in 12 people – 500 million – live with chronic viral hepatitis B or C. Not all of them are aware of their condition. One could easily infect you if you do not take sensible precautions.

What to look for

Fever, nausea, vomiting, extreme fatigue and pain in the upper right quadrant of the abdomen. Jaundice causes yellowing of the skin and eyes, dark urine and pale stools.

If your skin turns yellow but the whites of your eyes stay crystal clear, and you feel well, you probably do not have jaundice. Skin discoloration can be caused by eating too many carrots – and cheap tanning products.

What are the chances of survival?

There is no specific treatment for acute hepatitis. Nine out of 10 adults who develop viral hepatitis recover. Antiviral drugs can suppress chronic infection in HBV and HPC, but these are expensive and not readily available in developing countries.

HOW TO AVOID IT

- **Maintain good hygiene and sanitation (hepatitis A, E).**
- **Get vaccinated if you are at risk (hepatitis A, B).**
- **Keep cuts and skin lesions covered (hepatitis B, C and D).**
- **Practise safer sex and never share needles if injecting drugs (hepatitis B, C and D).**
- **Avoid dodgy tattoos and needle stick injuries (hepatitis B, C and D).**
- **Avoid contact with infected clothing contaminated with vomit or faeces (hepatitis A, B, C, D and E).**

Emergency protection against hepatitis B infection is available. If an unprotected individual is exposed to risk of infection (e.g. needle stick injury), the routine procedure is to:

- **Take blood and test for pre-existing protective levels of hepatitis B antibodies.**
- **Give a first dose of hepatitis B vaccine.**
- **Give short-term protection with an injection of specific hepatitis B antibody (immunoglobulin).**

45 Homicide

Homicide is the act of killing another person. Some cases are considered justified, for example, in self-defence. Others are premeditated and classed as murder.

How common is it?

Every year, an astonishing 1.6 million people lose their lives to acts of human violence, of which 525,000 are considered murder – that's roughly one life taken by another person every 60 seconds worldwide. Interpersonal violence is the leading cause of death in people aged 15–44 years, accounting for 14% of male deaths and 7% of female deaths in this age group.

Who dies?

Men are twice as likely as women to die a violent death; 75% of murder victims are male.

Where?

Anywhere that personal disputes are resolved by violence; the death rate in the Americas is nine times higher than in the Western Pacific.

When?

One in two murders is committed after consuming alcohol or drugs, or for money to fuel these habits.

Why?

Self-defence, uncontrolled anger, jealousy, crimes of passion, cold calculating homicide for gain.

Method of murder	*Incidence*	*Method of murder*	*Incidence*
Shooting (see page 110)	32%	**Suffocation (see page 32)**	4%
Stabbing	28%	**Narcotic drugs**	1%
Beating (hands, feet, fists)	12%	**Fire (see page 101)**	1%
Blunt objects (bats, clubs, hammers)	10%	**Drowning (see page 88)**	1%
Strangulation	10%	**Other methods: poisoning (see page 192), neglect, exposure to cold, tampering with brakes, cannibalism**	1%

Where an unlawful killing does not involve malice or intent, or where there are mitigating circumstances such as mental illness, it may be downgraded to manslaughter.

In each country, the most popular method of homicide is either shooting or stabbing. In the USA, where one in two households has one or more guns, a firearm is 175 times more likely to be used in a homicide than in the UK, where only 5% of households have access to a gun. In contrast, sharp knives are widely available.

Why does it kill?

Shooting, stabbing and bludgeoning kill by damaging vital organs and internal bleeding. Strangulation can kill by cutting off blood flow to the brain (cerebral anoxia), by a vagal nerve reflex that stops the heart (cardiac arrest) and by cutting off air supply (see page 32).

Will it happen to me?

If you upset someone enough, possess something they want badly, or are just in the wrong place at the wrong time, then yes.

What to look for

Situations that would lead to confrontations.

What are the chances of survival?

Homicide, by definition, is non-survivable. Prevention is your best bet. Don't upset anyone, take self-defence classes.

HOW TO AVOID IT

- **Stay in well-lit areas where there are lots of other people.**
- **Keep valuables like jewellery, mobile phones and music players out of sight.**
- **If caught in a mugging, try to stay calm and think logically. Comply with the mugger's demands in a neutral, non-confrontational manner – you can always block your credit card and phone later, after you survive the encounter.**

Hypothermia 46

Using the igloo principle helps native Inuits survive temperatures of –40 °C (–40 °F) in relative comfort.

How common is it?

Most deaths from hypothermia are undiagnosed (it is not unexpected to find that a dead body is cold) and are attributed to heart attack instead; reported numbers are the tip of the iceberg. People in countries with mild climates are less prepared for cold weather. Countries such as Ireland experience a 30% increase in deaths during a cold winter, compared with just 2% in Scandinavia. Hypothermia is recognized as contributing to 30,000 deaths per year in the UK, compared with only 700 deaths in the USA.

Who dies?

Mostly the very young, very old, frail or malnourished, or trauma patients, as well as those who travel to frozen wildernesses such as the Arctic or Antarctic. A study in Ireland found that men were 30% more likely to die from hypothermia than women, and that single men and single women were 6.5 and 4 times more at risk, respectively, than married men or women. Snuggling up and sharing body heat is of paramount importance.

Where?

Temperate climates such as the UK, USA and Canada.

When?

Cold spells, especially in winter or if under the influence of alcohol/drugs.

Why?

Primary hypothermia results from environmental exposure; secondary hypothermia is associated with medical illnesses such as hypothyroidism, severe malnutrition and MS. Poverty is often a factor.

Sleeping on or under the ice is not recommended for those who are less well prepared, however. Your body temperature is normally tightly regulated within the range of 36.5–37.5 °C (97.7–99.5 °F). Hypothermia occurs when body temperature drops below 35 °C (95 °F). Hypothermia is sometimes called a 'silent killer' as many victims are unaware they are at risk. Older people, in particular, are more sensitive to the effects of falling temperature but are less likely to realize that they are cold. The body's metabolic rate slows by 10% for every degree Centigrade fall in temperature. This effect may be used therapeutically to slow oxygen requirements during medical procedures such as heart transplant, and to reduce risk of death and disability in babies deprived of oxygen at birth.

Why does it kill?

Metabolic slowdown leads to organ failure, with cardiac arrhythmias, low blood pressure, slowed brain function, pulmonary oedema (fluid in the lungs), pneumonia, metabolic acidosis, respiratory failure and cardiac arrest. At a brain temperature of 20 °C (68 °F), an electroencephalogram (EEG) may be consistent with brain death (see page 44). Circulatory collapse to peripheries can lead to frostbite (formation of ice crystals in tissues), gangrene and sepsis. The incidence of heart attack always peaks during cold weather.

Will it happen to me?

Not if you wrap up warm and take sensible precautions.

What to look for

Muscle stiffness, shivering (though this response may be absent in elderly people), cold skin with a blue tinge (as the body diverts warm blood centrally), poor coordination, confusion, apathy, slowed breathing and heart rate, followed by coma.

What are the chances of survival?

Mild hypothermia (body temperature of 32–35 °C / 90–95 °F) is usually survivable. Moderate hypothermia (28–32 °C/82–90 °F) leads to death in 21% of cases. Severe hypothermia (less than 28 °C/82 °F) kills in at least 40% of cases and if prolonged is invariably fatal.

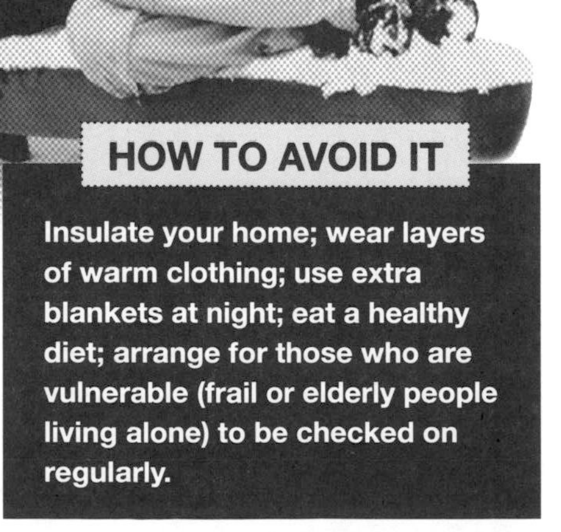

HOW TO AVOID IT

Insulate your home; wear layers of warm clothing; use extra blankets at night; eat a healthy diet; arrange for those who are vulnerable (frail or elderly people living alone) to be checked on regularly.

Iatrogenesis 47

One of the basic tenets of medicine is *primum non nocere*, Latin for 'first do no harm'. Basically, this admonishes doctors not to jump in with a scalpel or drug if there is a risk of worsening rather than improving the patient's condition. An iatrogenic death (from the Greek *iatros*, meaning 'healer') is essentially one that is physician-induced.

How common is it?

More frequent than most doctors like to admit – only 10% to 20% of serious events are reported, but claims that iatrogenesis is a leading cause of death worldwide usually reflect prejudice rather than a regard for the facts. Although it is undoubtedly the case that people who die are often under the care of a physician or surgeon, that is usually because they are already seriously ill.

Who dies?

Medical patients.

Where?

Often in hospital.

When?

After a medical intervention that did not go well.

Why?

An attempt to help gone wrong.

'Doctors are men who prescribe medicines of which they know little, to cure diseases of which they know less, in human beings of whom they know nothing.' Voltaire

The fact that doctors describe themselves as 'practising' medicine may not inspire confidence – especially as there is potential for the unscrupulous to bury their mistakes. With some notable exceptions (such as the English doctor Harold Shipman, convicted of murdering 15 patients and widely thought to be responsible for murdering hundreds more), most such mistakes are accidental, rather than deliberate. The use of inappropriate treatments, such as bloodletting, is a less common cause of iatrogenic death in these days of obsessively evidence-based medicine.

Why does it kill?

Lethal medical errors involve misprescribing (wrong drug, wrong dose, wrong combination, wrong patient), misdiagnoses, carrying out unnecessary procedures and negligence (inadequate assessment, failure to request necessary tests, monitor the patient or check test results). Other unexpected medical causes of death include the pitfalls of surgery (see page 231) and plain old bad luck (including anaphylactic reactions – see page 19 – and acquisition of a superbug – see page 104).

Will it happen to me?

It is generally accepted that medical errors of some kind affect 1 in 10 patients, but most are non-lethal. If you are admitted to hospital, there is a 1% to 2% chance of iatrogenesis hastening your demise. The most dangerous time to be admitted to hospital is when newly qualified doctors start their rotations, traditionally on February 1 and August 1 each year – though these dates are becoming more flexible.

What to look for

Health problems that get worse rather than better.

What are the chances of survival?

If the doctor recognizes his or her error in time, the chances of putting it right are relatively good.

HOW TO AVOID IT

Choose your physician carefully.

Influenza 48

The great influenza pandemic of 1918 killed more than 40 million people in just 2 years; some estimates put the death toll as high as 100 million.

How common is it?

Normal seasonal flu kills around 1 in 1000 of those infected. During a virulent pandemic, 50% of people may be infected, of whom 2% to 10% may die; with bird flu, the human mortality rate approaches 60%, but infection is rare.

Who dies?

Typically the very young, the very old and those with pre-existing health problems, such as diabetes, immunosuppression, kidney failure, chronic lung disease or heart disease.

Where?

In bed, often in hospital.

When?

Seasonal flu is most prevalent during the winter months.

Why?

Exposure to a mutated, particularly virulent strain of Influenzavirus A (or occasionally B) .

Known as Spanish flu, the 1918 flu was unusually severe, causing bleeding from the ears, nose and intestines, with some people dying from haemorrhage rather than the more usual influenza complications. Up to 1 in 5 of those infected died, most of whom were previously fit young adults.

Influenza viruses are among the most primitive life forms on the planet, and their replication is unsophisticated. They lack the proof-reading enzymes needed to correct errors in gene copying (transcription) and, as a result, newly formed viruses frequently contain mutations. In fact, swarms of flu viruses contain so many closely related mutants that scientists refer to them as a 'quasi-species' rather than a true biological species, which, by definition, must share a more or less distinctive form. This biodiversity allows influenza viruses to adapt rapidly to changing host environments, with new, more virulent subtypes quickly arising when the host's nutritional status is poor.

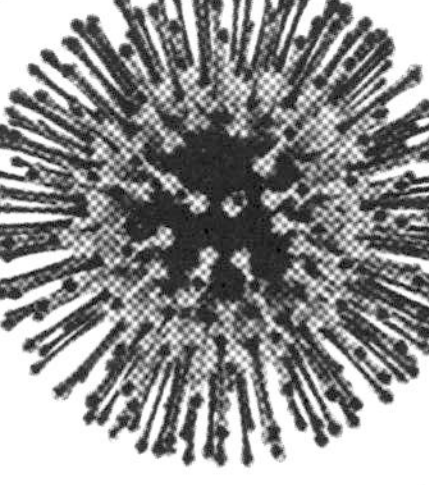

Flu virus

Lack of selenium is a 'driving force' for viral mutations. Viruses infecting a selenium-deficient host are more likely to mutate, become virulent, and cause more severe symptoms for longer. This may explain why so many new pathogenic influenza viruses emerge from Asia, where selenium intakes are among the lowest in the world.

Two strains of Influenzavirus mainly affect human beings: types A and B, of which A tends to be the more severe.

Why does it kill?

For most healthy people, influenza is an unpleasant experience but not usually life-threatening. When lethal complications occur, death may result from:

- pneumonia
- inflammation of heart muscle (myocarditis)
- inflammation of the outer heart lining (pericarditis)
- excessive fever (hyperpyrexia)
- inflammation of the brain (encephalitis)
- toxic shock syndrome (owing to secondary infection with toxin-producing strains of the bacterium *Staphylococcus aureus*)
- worsening of previous disease (e.g. lung problems, diabetes)

Over the years, the rate of spread of influenza infection has increased thanks to air travel, but the number of deaths has decreased due to vaccination and antiviral drugs such as amantadine, oseltamivir and zanamivir.

Eleven outbreaks of so-called bird flu (H5N1) occurred in 2008, causing widespread concern, but person-to-person spread has been low. By the end of 2010, only 510 human cases had been reported, of whom 303 died.

Will it happen to me?

Some people are more at risk of lethal influenza complications than others. These include infants under the age of 2, those over 70 years of age, and those with:

- chronic lung disease, including asthma, bronchitis and emphysema
- heart disease

Death toll of flu pandemics

Pandemic	*Year*	*Estimated deaths*	*Influenza A strain*
Russian flu	1889–90	1 million	H2N2
Spanish flu	1918–19	40 million+	H1N1
Asian flu	1957–8	2 million	H2N2
Hong Kong flu	1968–9	1 million	H3N2
Swine flu	2009–10	18,000	H1N1/09

- kidney failure
- hormone problems, such as diabetes
- low immunity owing to drugs (e.g. steroid tablets) or disease (e.g. cancer)

Annual flu vaccination for at-risk groups helps to protect against influenza infection. Where symptoms do occur, the risk of complications is also significantly reduced if the person has been vaccinated.

What to look for

Symptoms are initially similar to a common cold but get significantly worse, with chills, fever, fatigue and widespread muscle-ache. All you will want to do is lie down without moving – even going to the toilet is exhausting. You know you have the flu rather than a cold if you would be unwilling to get out of bed even to buy the winning lottery ticket. If flu-like symptoms develop in the very young or elderly, or in someone with pre-existing lung, kidney, heart or other serious medical problems, contact a doctor straight away. Seek immediate medical advice if you develop chest pain, severe headache or difficulty in breathing.

What are the chances of survival?

Antiviral drugs may shorten the duration of flu symptoms and reduce the risk of complications in vulnerable groups.

In those most at risk, flu vaccination can:

- reduce the risk of flu infection by 30%
- reduce the risk of bronchopneumonia and other complications by 90%
- reduce the risk of admission to hospital by 70%
- reduce the risk of death from flu by 70%

HOW TO AVOID IT

- **Consider vaccination.**
- **Boost your natural immunity to reduce the risk of overwhelming flu infection by eating a healthy diet, and exercise regularly for good cardiovascular fitness.**
- **Avoid those who spread disease by coughing and sneezing.**
- **Use antiviral tissues, wash your hands regularly and try to avoid touching your face, mouth, nose and eyes with your hands.**

Jugular vein/ carotid artery constriction

49

'Going for the jugular' is a popular ruse in martial arts films, where hapless guards collapse, immobile, to the ground after a brief grip to one side of their neck. Known as the Death Touch or Vulcan Nerve Pinch, this supposedly stimulates pressure points to cause instant loss of consciousness.

How common is it?

Possibly one or two 'accidental' deaths per year.

Who dies?

Mostly young, aggressive males.

Where?

In situations where they need subduing.

When?

After a disagreement, violent run-in with the law, or occasionally during a close-contact sport such as martial arts or wrestling.

Why?

Overzealous, prolonged application of a choke hold.

DID YOU KNOW?

The oriental art of Dim Mak is said to focus on pressure points that induce instant or delayed death. However, it seems to have originated in Kung Fu novels from the 1950s.

What to look for

Bruising or marks on both sides of the neck. Don't try it at home.

What are the chances of survival?

Pretty high.

While pressure over the jugular notch, brachial plexus or vagus nerve might feasibly trigger a neurocardiogenic syncope (the medical name for a faint), this is best left in the realm of fiction.

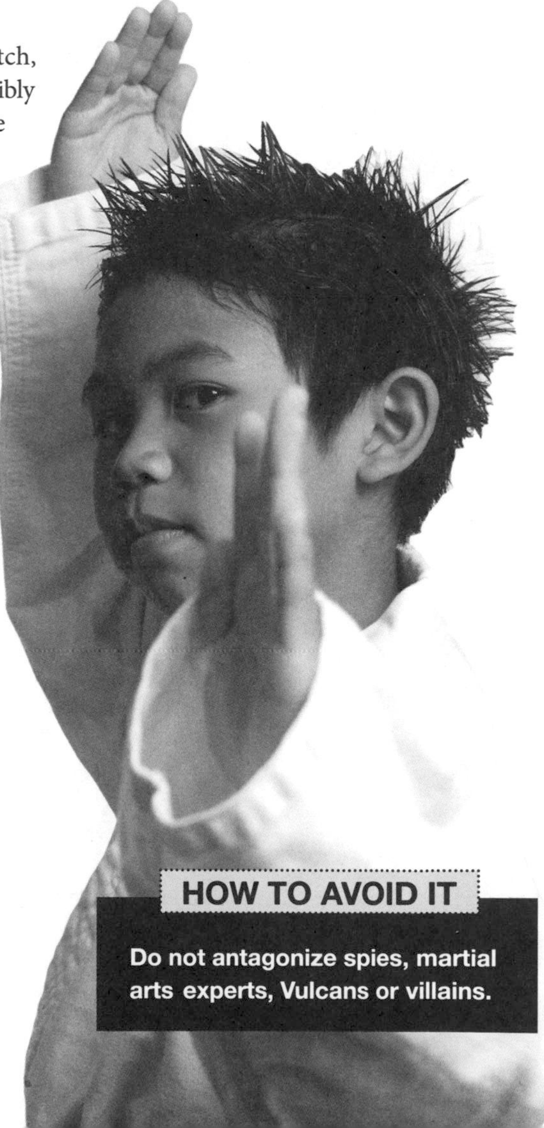

Choke manoeuvres such as The Sleeper, Carotid Restraint, Blood Choke or Stranglehold (allegedly used by spies and villains) restrict blood flow through the carotid artery and jugular veins on both sides of the neck. Victims lose consciousness within 10–20 seconds as a result of cerebral hypoxia. If pressure is removed immediately, they may live. If sustained for more than a few minutes, brain damage or death will result. This is different from strangulation (see page 32), in which pressure is also applied to the airway.

Why does it kill?

Lack of oxygen to the brain.

Will it happen to me?

Unlikely.

HOW TO AVOID IT

Do not antagonize spies, martial arts experts, Vulcans or villains.

Kidney failure 50

The kidney is now the most sought-after organ for transplantation. This reflects the current world epidemic of kidney failure, and the fact that, as we each have two, there is a temptation to donate a 'spare' for love. Or for money.

How common is it?

1% of patients admitted to hospital have acute kidney failure, while 3% of the global population have some degree of chronic kidney failure – over 200 million people. One million enter end-stage kidney failure every year, and over 1.5 million are on dialysis; over 66,000 kidney transplants occur each year – a further 594,000 need one. Kidney failure is the ninth-leading cause of death in developed countries.

Who dies?

Mostly people with poorly controlled diabetes; males are at slightly higher risk.

Where?

60% die in hospital.

When?

Your kidneys fail to filter blood or concentrate urine appropriately.

Why?

Lack of availability of kidneys for transplantation.

The kidneys are two bean-shaped organs at the back of the abdomen. They play a vital role in regulating blood salt levels, blood pressure and blood acidity.

Each kidney contains around a million filtration units called nephrons. When blood is forced through under pressure, water and soluble wastes take the route of least resistance, squirting through sieve-like holes into tubes that loop deeper into the kidney. Filtered fluids are usually protein-free and pass through a series of drains that reabsorb variable amounts of salt and water. Filtered nutrients such as glucose are reclaimed (up to a limit), and body acidity is finely tuned by tinkering with the reabsorption of bicarbonate and the excretion of protons. The final product – concentrated urine – then trickles down the ureters into the bladder and is stored for your next bathroom break. The kidneys also produce hormones (erythropoietin, renin) and activate vitamin D.

Kidney failure can come on suddenly (acute) or slowly (chronic). Acute kidney failure (now often called acute kidney injury) can accompany severe dehydration, sepsis, haemorrhage, heart attack and other causes of shock (see page 210), sudden lack of blood flow (aortic aneurysm, inflammation from infection or autoimmune attack) or obstruction to urinary outflow (kidney stones, tumour, prostatism), or occur as a side effect of nonsteroidal anti-inflammatory drugs (NSAIDs).
Between 1 in 10 and 1 in 5 people with diabetes will die from chronic kidney failure, making it the main underlying cause of this disorder. As more than 246 million people currently live with diabetes, and the number is expected to double by 2030, a massive problem is waiting in the wings. Other causes include high blood pressure, infection/inflammation (glomerulonephritis), autoimmune kidney disease and polycystic kidneys.

The kidneys filter over 7 litres (15 pints) of blood every hour; this high volume is necessary because wastes such as urea are present in relatively low concentrations. Most filtrate is reabsorbed – only around 0.5 ml is sent to the bladder per minute.

Why does it kill?

Kidney failure can cause a buildup of fluid, salts, acid and urea in the body, all of which are potentially lethal in their own right. Electrolyte imbalances, especially raised potassium levels, can cause cardiac arrest. High blood pressure can cause stroke.

Will it happen to me?

If you are ever admitted to hospital you will have a 1 in 100 chance of experiencing acute kidney failure. If you have diabetes that is not well controlled, your risk of experiencing kidney failure is at least 1 in 10.

Country	Number of people battling some form of kidney disease	Country	Number of people battling some form of kidney disease	Country	Number of people battling some form of kidney disease
China	35,400,000	**Japan**	3,475,000	**France**	1,644,000
India	29,000,000	**Mexico**	2,860,000	**UK**	1,640,000
USA	7,990,000	**Philippines**	2,347,000	**Congo**	1,587,000
Indonesia	6,500,000	**Germany**	2,243,000	**Italy**	1,580,000
Brazil	5,010,000	**Egypt**	2,071,000	**South Korea**	1,313,000
Pakistan	4,340,000	**Ethiopia**	1,941,000	**South Africa**	1,210,000
Russia	3,920,000	**Turkey**	1,875,000		
Bangladesh	3,850,000	**Iran**	1,837,000		

What to look for

Progressive kidney failure often causes no symptoms until it's too late. You may experience itching, lethargy, weakness, loss of appetite, shortness of breath, swelling, high blood pressure, confusion and coma.

What are the chances of survival?

Kidney failure has a mortality rate from 50% to 90% depending on the underlying cause. Once you reach end-stage kidney disease, your life expectancy is shortened, with mortality rates at any age up to six times higher than for the general population. At age 60, for example, a healthy person can expect to live until the age of 80. For someone of that age starting haemodialysis, average life expectancy is only 4 years, taking them to 64. If you have access to a kidney for transplant, 2-year survival rates are better than 90%. In general, survival is greatest with a living donor. Five-year survival rates are 80% with cadaver donation and 90% with a living donation. Ten-year survival rates are 59% with a cadaver donor and 78% with a living donation. Family members who share similar genes are the best donors, as this reduces the chance of rejection. A global trade in kidneys has also arisen in which living donors from poor nations are paid to donate a healthy organ. This is widely criticized for obvious ethical reasons.

HOW TO AVOID IT

- **Have regular checkups to assess glucose levels, blood pressure and kidney function.**
- **If you have diabetes or hypertension, take medication to ensure the condition is well controlled.**
- **Increasing evidence suggests that an ACE inhibitor drug (which lowers blood pressure) may protect against diabetic kidney disease.**

Land transport accidents 51

The 'infernal' combustion engine is responsible for 3560 deaths on the world's roads every day. Yet, in theory, none of these deaths would occur if every road user took some common sense precautions.

How common is it?

Road traffic collisions kill 1.3 million people per year – similar in number to all the communicable diseases combined. Another 50 million or more are also injured or disabled on the roads every year.

Who dies?

Previously fit and well young people aged 15–44, in whom it is the leading cause of death. Among teenagers, road deaths account for 40% of mortality. Overall, half of victims are pedestrians, cyclists or motorcyclists.

Where?

90% of fatalities occur in low- and middle-income countries, despite hosting only half the world's vehicles.

When?

Often after speeding, taking alcohol or drugs, when lacking in sleep or experiencing road rage.

Why?

Rushing, aggression, ignorance, tiredness and lapse of concentration or judgement kill far more people than mechanical failure or dangerous road conditions.

Unless immediate action is taken, the WHO estimates that the number of human road-accident victims will almost double to 2.4 million per year by the year 2030, which will elevate road traffic injuries to the fifth-leading cause of death overall, from its current position around number 9.

Why does it kill?

The kinetic energy of a vehicle is transmitted to your body in proportion to the square of the speed at impact. That's a complicated way of saying a vehicle is bigger, harder and heavier than you. Head injury, internal bleeding and other serious traumas result.

Will it happen to me?

Your annual risk of being killed in a road collision is around 1 in 5000 if you live in a country with proper road safety legislation. If you drive a sports car, make that 1 in 2500 or less. But statistics mean nothing when you are up against an idiot on the road.

What to look for

The Highway Code. Buy one and read it – even if you don't drive. Its rules apply to pedestrians, horse-riders and cyclists as well as drivers and motorcyclists.

What are the chances of survival?

If you are travelling in a car, your chance of dying, if you crash, doubles for every 10 miles/16 km per hour increase in speed above 50 mph or 80 km/hr. If you are a pedestrian and are hit by a car, your risk of death depends on the speed of the car:

Speed of car	*Your chance of living*
20 mph or 32 km/h	95%
30 mph or 48 km/h	60%
40 mph or 64 km/h	20%
50 mph or 80 km/ph or more	between 0 and 15%

HOW TO AVOID IT

- **If walking at night, carry a torch and wear high-visibility clothing.**
- **Wear a helmet on a bike.**
- **Drive defensively – assume all other road users are bad drivers and you won't be far wrong.**
- **Minimize distractions – don't read a map or use the phone when driving!**
- **Always use a seat belt and, where appropriate, a child seat.**
- **Don't drink and drive.**
- **Don't exceed speed limits.**
- **Always obey traffic signs.**
- **Maintain your vehicle properly. Check tyre pressures.**
- **Keep checking your mirrors.**
- **Leave a safe distance between your car and others.**
- **Intersections are the scenes of most accidents – proceed with caution. Above all, be courteous.**

Leishmaniasis

52

Like Chagas' disease and sleeping sickness, leishmaniasis is caused by a single-celled parasitic protozoan – in this case transmitted by sandflies.

How common is it?

Leishmaniasis threatens 350 million people in 88 countries. Between 12 million and 20 million people are currently affected and an estimated 2 million new cases occur every year (1.5 cutaneous forms, 500,000 visceral forms) with between 80,000 and 200,000 deaths annually. Epidemics are frequent.

Who dies?

Impoverished people living in unhygienic conditions, especially those with concurrent HIV infection; males are more commonly affected than females, owing to increased exposure to sandflies, and are twice as likely to develop visceral leishmaniasis. *Leishmania infantum* mainly affects young children.

Where?

Of visceral forms, 90% occur in Bangladesh, Brazil, India, Nepal and Sudan; 90% of mucocutaneous forms occur in Bolivia, Brazil and Peru; 90% of cutaneous forms occur in Afghanistan, Brazil, Iran, Peru, Saudi Arabia and Syria.

When?

Within 2 years of developing visceral leishmaniasis.

Why?

Poverty, malnutrition, low immunity, human migration, deforestation, urbanization with poor sanitation, and lack of medical diagnosis/treatment.

In this case, the culprit, *Leishmania*, comes in 20 different species, with names such as *L. mexicana*, *L. amazonensis*, *L. venezuelensis*, *L. braziliensis* and *L. aethiopica*, giving a clue to their distribution. *Leishmania* are spread by at least 30 different species of phlebotomine sandflies, which breed in the bark of forest trees, caves, ruined buildings, cracks in brick houses, rubbish tips and the burrows of small rodents. Avoid such sites as leishmaniasis is notoriously difficult to treat. The parasite creates a blockage in the oesophagus of an infected sandfly, causing it to 'cough' and clear its throat just before it feeds. Expelled *Leishmania* on your skin then enter your body as the sandfly bites.

Four main patterns occur. In the most benign (cutaneous form), skin ulcers develop on exposed areas such as the face, arms and legs, which may heal to leave scars after 2–10 months. More disfiguring lumps can resemble lepromatous leprosy (diffuse cutaneous form), or the disease can attack and progressively destroy the mucous membranes of the nose, mouth and throat (mucocutaneous form). The most lethal type, visceral leishmaniasis, occurs when the parasites invade the spleen and liver. Known in Asia as kala-azar, meaning 'black fever,' individuals with light-coloured skin acquire a darker, greyish tone on the face and hands.

Why does it kill?

Death occurs from secondary infection of ulcers leading to sepsis. Swelling of the spleen and liver can kill through rupture (from trauma) or anaemia. Deformity and scarring cause social stigma, which can even lead to suicide or murder. Co-infection with HIV is an emerging threat, although some anti-HIV drugs may slow parasite growth.

Will it happen to me?

If you are bitten by an infected sandfly, yes.

What to look for

Cutaneous forms: up to 200 boils, pustules and deep skin ulcers, each measuring 1 cm (0.5 in) to 4 cm (1.5 in) or more across, can erupt. Mucocutaneous forms: swelling and distortion of the nose, mouth and face. Visceral forms: fever, weight loss and distension of the abdomen that mimics advanced pregnancy. Pale skin may acquire a grey tone.

What are the chances of survival?

Visceral leishmaniasis is 100% fatal if not treated. Treatment with antimony-based drugs or liposomal formulations of amphotericin B (expensive) reduces fatalities to 10%.

HOW TO AVOID IT

No vaccines are yet available but genomic sequencing of the parasite is gearing towards this. Avoid endemic areas. If you must visit, take insect repellents and sleep under an insecticide-impregnated net. Fly swats are unlikely to help as the tiny sandfly vectors are only 2–3 mm (about a tenth of an inch) long and difficult to spot as they home in. Avoid being treated with blood products.

Leprosy 53

Also known as Hansen's disease, leprosy is caused by *Mycobacterium leprae*, a close relative to the bacterium that causes tuberculosis.

How common is it?

Around 249,000 people a year have newly diagnosed leprosy – one person every 2 minutes. Annually, leprosy contributes to 6000 premature deaths worldwide, but under-reporting is rife, owing to the stigma of disease. Thirty per cent of those treated are left with irreversible disabilities.

Who dies?

Young, blind leprosy patients are 4.8 times more likely to die than non-blind patients.

Where?

India, Brazil and Indonesia account for 77% of new cases.

When?

Often many years after infection.

Why?

Damage to eyesight and loss of sensation lead to accident and injury.

WHO region	*New cases per year*
Africa	28,800
Americas	41,900
East Mediterranean	3900
South-East Asia	168,500
Western Pacific	5900
Total for World	249,000

The development of an effective multidrug treatment for leprosy, taken as a 6- to 12-month course, means this disease should no longer kill anyone – especially as the WHO provides treatment free of charge to all diagnosed patients. Unfortunately, leprosy elimination remains a dream. Although it is rarely considered a lethal disease, the mortality rate of people with leprosy is between two and four times greater than for similar people in the general population.

Why does it kill?

Mycobacterium leprae infiltrates and thickens mucous membranes, skin and nervous tissues. Numbness leads to recurrent damage, especially to eyes, hands and feet, and to painless injuries (burns, wounds) that can lead to sepsis or gangrene. Blindness increases the chance of a fatal accident, especially in countries where safety legislation and traffic control are not priorities. Some victims are killed by their family to avoid social stigma.

Will it happen to me?

Mycobacterium leprae is not highly infectious, and only 1 in 10 people are genetically susceptible. Peak diagnosis is between the ages of 10 and 20 years. Spread, via droplets from the nose and mouth, usually requires close, frequent family contact with someone who has untreated leprosy. HIV infection increases susceptibility.

What to look for

Symptoms appear around 5 years after infection, but can incubate for 20 years. First signs are numb skin patches with loss of sensation in the fingers and toes. Thickening of skin with nodules can also occur.

What are the chances of survival?

With treatment, the cure rate is 100%.

HOW TO AVOID IT

Prophylaxis with a single dose of rifampicin can protect against infection in 57% of individuals who have had close contact with a newly diagnosed patient.

BCG vaccine (used against tuberculosis) may protect in 1 in 4 cases. If you have visited an endemic area in the past, report any numb skin patches or lesions.

54

Leukaemia

Leukaemia is a cancer of the white blood cells and bone marrow. Nine out of ten cases are diagnosed in adults, but it accounts for 30% of childhood malignancies.

How common is it?

Every year, around 350,000 people worldwide are diagnosed with leukaemia, and more than 250,000 die as a result. It is the most common cancer diagnosed in children under the age of 15 years, but around the tenth most common cancer in males and females in developed countries.

Who dies?

Four out of five deaths are in people over the age of 60; males are more susceptible than females (57% versus 43%).

Where?

The countries with the highest incidence of leukaemia per head of population are: Denmark, Luxembourg, Italy, Belgium, France, Croatia, Latvia, Germany, New Zealand and Australia.

When?

Some studies suggest that diagnoses and deaths are slightly more common during winter months, and in winter-born children.

Why?

Overproduction of white blood cells in the bone marrow.

Type of leukaemia	*% of cases*	*Five-year survival rates in developed countries*
Chronic lymphocytic leukaemia (CLL)	35%	75%
Acute myeloid leukaemia (AML)	30%	40%
Acute lymphoblastic leukaemia (ALL)	70% (child) 10% (adult)	85% (child) 50% (adult)
Chronic myeloid leukaemia (CML)	11%	90%

Why does it kill?

Abnormal leukaemia cells overwhelm the bone marrow and circulation, so that the numbers of red blood cells, other white cells and platelet cells plummet. This leads to anaemia, reduced resistance to infection and abnormal blood clotting. Abnormal cells can also invade the liver, spleen and other organs. Death is usually a result of infection (pneumonia, sepsis), haemorrhage or organ failure, especially of the kidneys.

Will it happen to me?

Recognized risk factors include smoking, exposure to ionizing radiation, occupational exposure to benzene, and receiving radiation or chemotherapy to treat other cancers. There appears to be an association between exposure to electromagnetic fields and childhood leukaemia. Adult T-cell leukaemia–lymphoma (ATL) is linked with a viral infection.

What to look for

Acute leukaemia may cause easy bruising or bleeding, paleness, easy fatigue, recurrent minor infections (e.g. sore throat) and poor wound healing. Chronic leukaemia often causes few symptoms and is diagnosed during routine blood-screening tests.

What are the chances of survival?

Improved treatments mean that survival rates have tripled in the past 30 years. In developed countries, leukaemia is an increasingly survivable disease. In developed countries, overall 5-year survival rates are 40%, compared with just 15% in developing countries.

The table above gives 5-year survival rates for four of the most common types of leukaemia. Other rarer forms also occur.

HOW TO AVOID IT

Most people have no obvious risk factors and there is no known way to reduce your risk, except by not smoking and avoiding obvious exposure to ionizing radiation or benzene.

Listeriosis 55

***Listeria monocytogenes* is an important bacterium to avoid when you are pregnant or otherwise immunocompromised. Unfortunately, this is easier said than done. The pathogen is widely present in the soil and foods, especially dairy and ready-to-eat meat and fish products. It can also be acquired through contact with infected live animals.**

How common is it?
An estimated 66,650 cases of invasive listeriosis occur each year, with around 20,000 deaths. Neonatal deaths and miscarriages are counted separately.

Who dies?
Immunocompromised people (70%); an estimated 30% of cases occur in pregnant women, of which 1 in 5 results in miscarriage or neonatal death.

Where?
Despite a worldwide presence, most cases are diagnosed and reported only in Western countries.

When?
Symptoms develop up to 6 weeks after exposure.

Why?
Rapid cellular invasion within immunocompromised hosts.

Once ingested, *Listeria* attaches to intestinal lining cells and uses a cellular password to gain entry. After reproducing, it causes portions of the cell membrane to bulge outwards, forming structures known as listeriopods. These protuberances are engulfed by adjacent cells, allowing the bacterium to pass from one body cell to another by direct transfer, cleverly avoiding host antibodies and other immune mechanisms. Even so, most people only develop non-invasive, self-limiting gastroenteritis (vomiting, diarrhoea), which is dismissed as a 'tummy bug'. However, for those who are pregnant or debilitated by another illness (HIV, cancer), it's another story. These conditions increase the risk of invasive listeriosis 17-fold.

Listeria *bacteria*

Why does it kill?

If immunity is reduced, *Listeria* quickly disseminates to cause sepsis, pneumonia and meningitis. During pregnancy, it can cause miscarriage, pre-term birth, stillbirth and neonatal death.

Will it happen to me?

If you feel unwell and have recently eaten contaminated meat, cheese or even salads, it is a possibility if you are pregnant or have reduced immunity. High-dose antibiotics (penicillins, chloramphenicol, tetracyclines) are effective when listeriosis is treated early.

What to look for

A flu-like illness with low-grade fever, sore throat, vomiting and diarrhoea that rapidly worsens.

What are the chances of survival?

If you develop invasive listeriosis, the mortality rate is 30%.

HOW TO AVOID IT

If you are pregnant or immunocompromised, avoid foods with a high *Listeria* risk, such as:

- ripened soft cheeses
- blue-veined cheeses
- goat or sheep cheeses
- any unpasteurized soft and cream cheese
- undercooked meat and seafood
- cook-chill meals and ready-to-eat poultry unless thoroughly reheated
- all types of pâté
- ready-prepared coleslaw and salads
- unpasteurized dairy products
- all foods past their 'best before' date
- rolls and sandwiches containing any of the above

Wash raw vegetables; cook or reheat foods thoroughly.

56
Liver failure

Your liver is a very forgiving organ. Exposed to dietary excesses and environmental toxins on a daily basis, it struggles on without complaint. Even when surgeons remove 75% of a liver lobe, it usually tries to grow back.

How common is it?

Liver failure due to cirrhosis kills 772,000 people per year; viral hepatitis kills over 1 million annually; an additional 1,031,000 deaths result from auto-immune and other causes of hepatitis. Over 21,000 liver transplants are carried out globally each year.

Who dies?

Different subsets of genes are expressed in male and female livers, and women are more susceptible to liver failure than men; liver graft quality is also better from a male donor. Patients younger than 10 years or older than 40 years tend to fare worse than those in between.

Where?

Everywhere, but especially in Asia where hepatitis B is rife.

When?

After acute or chronic exposure to liver toxins.

Why?

Inability of modern medicine to invent an artificial liver.

Tethered in the upper right-hand side of your abdomen, your liver fulfils a number of vital functions, without which you would soon die.

Liver failure can result from a number of different problems, each of which kills at least 80% of your liver cells. Acute liver failure comes on rapidly and can result from chemical poisons (paracetamol, carbon tetrachloride, vinyl chloride, ethylene glycol, death-cap mushrooms, certain painkillers), viral infections (yellow fever, hepatitis B), acute fatty liver of pregnancy, auto-immune hepatitis, Reye's syndrome (linked with use of aspirin in children) and Wilson's disease (a hereditary inability to handle copper).

Chronic liver failure occurs when liver cells are replaced by scar tissue (fibrosis) and regenerative nodules. This can result from alcoholic cirrhosis (see page 14), chronic viral infections (hepatitis B, C), auto-immune disease (primary biliary cirrhosis, primary sclerosing cholangitis) and haemochromatosis (a hereditary overabsorption of iron).

Many cases are of unknown origin and described as 'idiopathic'.

Your liver:

- makes bile, a green-yellow liquid that emulsifies fats to aid digestion
- breaks down haemoglobin to produce bile pigments (bilirubin and biliverdin)
- converts dietary fats into triglycerides and cholesterol
- makes proteins (e.g. albumin, globulin, blood-clotting proteins)
- converts ammonia, a waste product of protein metabolism, into urea
- makes glucose
- stores excess glucose as glycogen – a starchy emergency fuel that keeps you alive during your overnight fast
- stores fat-soluble vitamins (A, D, E and K plus vitamin B12) and some minerals (e.g. iron and copper)
- generates heat to warm passing blood
- detoxifies poisons (e.g. alcohol)
- helps to regulate blood-cell formation and destruction
- acts as an immune 'sieve', filtering out antigens absorbed from the intestines

Why does it kill?

A buildup of toxins (ammonia, acetone, thiols) poisons the brain (hepatic encephalopathy), leading to coma and death. Toxins, fluid retention, salt imbalances and changes in blood flow can also cause kidney failure (hepatorenal syndrome) or heart attack. Widespread inflammation promotes sepsis and multi-organ failure. Death can also result from reduced glucose levels (hypoglycaemia) and lack of blood-clotting proteins (haemorrhage). In fact, liver failure diagnosis is partly based on having a blood-clotting time that is 50% slower than normal.

DID YOU KNOW?

Liver spots – flat, brown patches of pigmentation on sun-exposed parts of the body – are due to sun damage (solar lentigo) and are nothing to do with liver function.

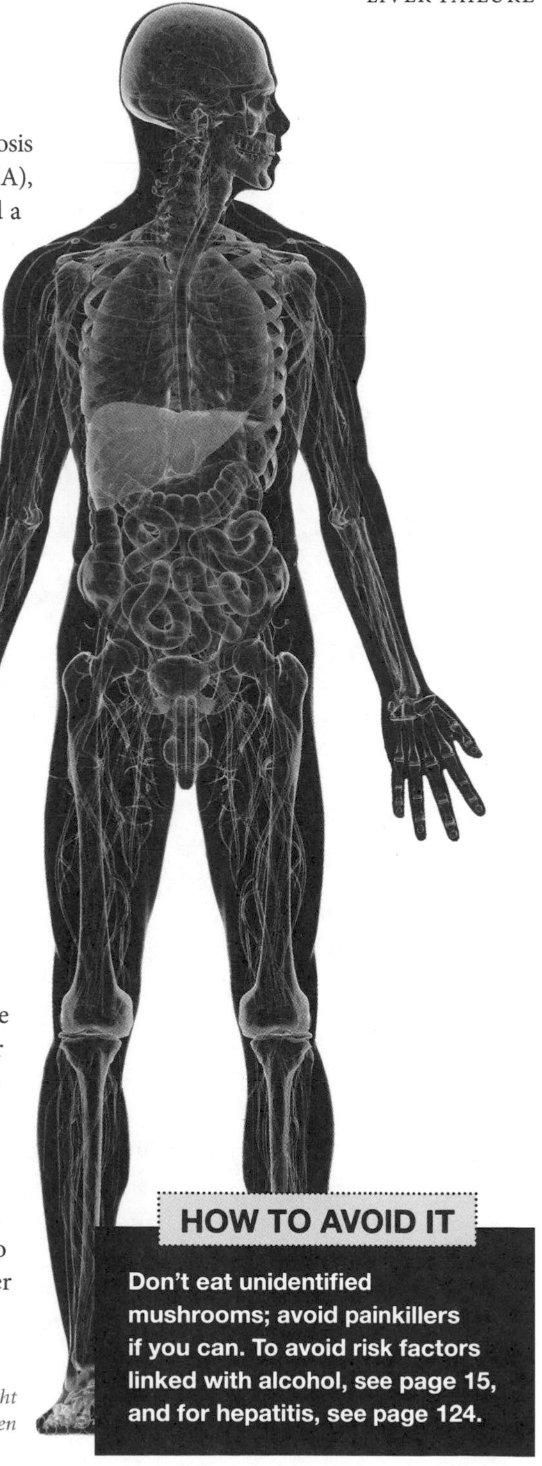

Will it happen to me?

Your lifetime risk of developing liver cirrhosis or failure is 1 in 109 (UK), 1 in 136 (USA), 1 in 86 (Europe), 1 in 35 (Ukraine) and a hefty 1 in 12 if you live in Moldova. Your annual risk of dying from liver failure is somewhere between 1 in 955 (Moldova) and 1 in 10,753 (USA).

What to look for

Acute liver failure: tenderness or pain in the upper right abdomen; jaundice (yellow whites of the eye and skin) and easy bruising or bleeding. The so-called stigmata of chronic liver disease can include red spider-like thread veins on the skin of the upper trunk, red palms, gynaecomastia (enlarged breasts in males), flapping tremor of the hands, and ascites (fluid accumulation in the abdominal cavity).

What are the chances of survival?

Unlike your heart and kidneys, there are no machines capable of taking over liver function. 'Mild' liver failure (if there is such a thing) may slowly recover with general life support and excellent medical care to avert or treat complications once the original problem is removed. Survival rates for liver failure are 20% to 50% at best, unless salvaged with a liver transplant (survival rate of 65%).

The liver is in the upper right hand side of the abdomen

HOW TO AVOID IT

Don't eat unidentified mushrooms; avoid painkillers if you can. To avoid risk factors linked with alcohol, see page 15, and for hepatitis, see page 124.

57 Lymphoma

Lymphoma is a group of cancers that affect immune cells known as lymphocytes. These come in a variety of forms, with different surface markers and different patterns of activity.

How common is it?

An estimated 222,000 people die from lymphoma each year; it is the seventh most common cancer worldwide, and the 12th-leading cause of cancer deaths.

Who dies?

Mostly older patients; males are one and a half times more likely to be affected than females.

Where?

Highest death rates are recorded in the Yemen, Lebanon, Ethiopia, Saudi Arabia, United Arab Emirates, Russian Federation and Pakistan. Japan has one of the lowest rates.

When?

In those who do not achieve a cure, lymphomas have a survival period of 5–10 years.

Why?

An unhappy confluence of gene translocations, environmental factors (pesticides, herbicides, solvents such as benzene) and certain infections.

Because of these variations, more than 30 subtypes of lymphoma can occur when one of these cells multiplies uncontrollably in a bid to take over the bone marrow, lymphatic system and nearby organs. To simplify things, lymphomas are divided into two main groups: Hodgkin's lymphoma (HL, of which there are five types) and the rest (non-Hodgkin's lymphoma, or NHL, of which there are 30 types). All cause similar symptoms and signs, but are based on the type of cell seen under a microscope. These classifications aren't just academic niceties: their importance lies in the fact that different types of lymphocyte respond to different treatments and have different success rates in terms of cure.

Lymphocytes make up around 40% of circulating white blood cells. The three main types are:

B-lymphocytes (20% of total; derived from the bone marrow) make antibodies. There are many different strains, each of which makes one specific antibody. They patrol the body in an inactive form known as B memory cells. As soon as these encounter the foreign protein against which their antibody is directed, they become active and produce large numbers of their single, specific antibody. Their activity is regulated by T-lymphocytes, which act like supervisors to control, encourage or inhibit their various activities.

T-lymphocytes (70% of total; derived from the thymus) exist in several different forms:

- T-helper cells interact with B-lymphocytes to trigger antibody production.
- T-suppressor cells bring antibody production to a halt when infection is beaten.
- T-cytotoxic (killer) cells attack normal or abnormal body cells, tending to survive their attack and go on to kill other targets.
- T-hypersensitivity cells are involved in cell-mediated, delayed allergic reactions such as those involved in eczema. Allergic reactions take over 12 hours to develop.
- T-cytotoxic cells may be drafted in to help as well.

Natural Killer (NK) cells (10% of total lymphocytes) are mainly concerned with killing abnormal body cells that are infected with a virus or are cancerous. They provide an important first line of defence while the more specific T- and B-lymphocytes power up. Rather like a kamikaze pilot, NK cells tend to get overexcited and die during attack.

DID YOU KNOW?

- **Certain viruses increase the risk of developing lymphoma by infecting lymphocytes and overstimulating their production: HIV, Epstein-Barr virus, hepatitis B virus, hepatitis C virus, human T-cell leukaemia virus type 1, Kaposi sarcoma-associated herpesvirus.**
- **Black hair dye has been linked with non-Hodgkin's lymphoma.**

Why does it kill?

One-third of patients die from overwhelming infection or sepsis as a result of reduced immunity. Other causes of death include haemorrhage and respiratory failure from infiltration of the lungs.

Will it happen to me?

Your risk of developing lymphoma is around 1 in 448 for males, and 1 in 596 for women.

What to look for

Painless swelling of lymph nodes in the neck, armpit or groin. These may press against blood vessels, lymph vessels or nerves to cause limb swelling, numbness or tingling. Enlargement of the spleen can cause abdominal discomfort. Other symptoms that can occur include fever, chills, night sweats, weight loss, lack of energy and itching.

What are the chances of survival?

The prognosis depends on your type of lymphoma and how far it has spread before diagnosis. Stage I (early) affects a single lymph node region or organ; Stage II (locally advanced) involves two or more lymph node regions or organs on the same side of the diaphragm; Stage III (advanced) affects two or more lymph node regions or organs on opposite sides of the diaphragm; Stage IV disease is widespread or disseminated. Treatments involve combinations of chemotherapy, biological therapy (targeted antibodies, stem cell transplantation) and radiotherapy. HL is one of the most curable cancers with 5-year survival rates of: 90% for children and for adults with Stage I or Stage II; 84% (adults, Stage III); and 65% (adults, Stage IV). Prognosis for NHL is also improving, with a 5-year survival rate of 63% for adults and up to 90% for children. Many live in stable remission in which the disease is fully controlled.

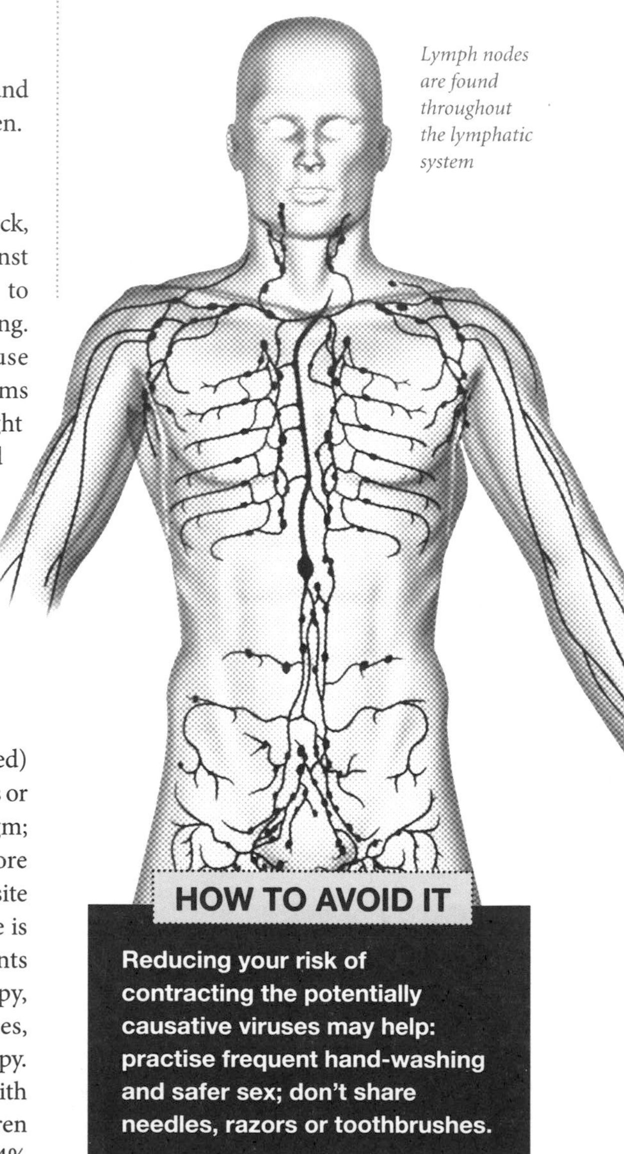

Lymph nodes are found throughout the lymphatic system

HOW TO AVOID IT

Reducing your risk of contracting the potentially causative viruses may help: practise frequent hand-washing and safer sex; don't share needles, razors or toothbrushes.

Mad cow disease 58

Bovine spongiform encephalopathy, or BSE, is a disease of cattle transmitted by an unsophisticated, self-replicating protein, or prion, that doesn't even contain any genes. Yet, it can cause CJD or vCJD in people, a fatal neurological disorder.

How common is it?

CJD affects one in a million people; testing of stored appendix tissue samples suggests vCJD could have a prevalence as high as 1 in 20,000 in the UK, at least in the age group tested. However, fewer than 250 have been diagnosed worldwide, suggesting that most cases show no symptoms. It is thought that only people with a certain genotype are susceptible. Almost all victims have one thing in common – they carry a gene variant called MM.

Who dies?

Those with CJD are aged 65 on average; those with vCJD have an average age of 29.

Where?

Mostly in the UK, as a result of an outbreak of BSE in cattle in the 1980s, if figures are to be believed; this is probably because of a high degree of monitoring.

When?

Classic CJD kills within 5 months of symptoms developing; vCJD kills within 14 months.

Why?

Widespread death of brain cells.

Somehow, the prion manages to replicate, punching holes in the brain, which starts to resemble a Victoria sponge.

Unlike most other proteins, prions aren't denatured and destroyed by freezing, drying, cooking, pasteurization or sterilization. And they have no respect for their place in the food chain. They have learned to jump species and can affect human hosts. They cause symptoms known as variant Creutzfeldt-Jacob disease, or vCJD. This is to differentiate it from 'classic' CJD – a disease with a slow incubation period measured in decades. The average age of classic CJD victims is 65; cases are sporadic and the cause is not really understood.

The swifter-striking vCJD was recognized in 1996. Its victims have an average age of 29. It is vCJD that is thought to have originated as BSE in cattle. It appears to be transmitted by eating prion-infected meat. A few cases are iatrogenic (see page 129) – passed on by contaminated medical equipment, growth hormone extracts or transplants, before the risks were recognized.

Why does it kill?

Loss of brain cells leads to degeneration of body functions, so victims become bedridden and eventually develop respiratory failure, heart failure or an infection such as bronchopneumonia.

Will it happen to me?

Not something you should lose sleep over. If you haven't inherited the mutant gene MM, your risk of vCJD is infinitesimal. Classic CJD is sporadic and completely unpredictable.

What to look for

Early symptoms are psychiatric and include depression or psychosis. Sensory abnormalities, such as thinking your skin feels sticky, occur in half of cases. Progressive unsteadiness, difficulty walking and involuntary movements then develop. Patients become completely immobile and mute by the time of death.

What are the chances of survival?

There is currently no effective treatment.

HOW TO AVOID IT

Not much you can do, really, except possibly become vegetarian. Some bodies suggest that travellers to areas where BSE has occurred may consider either avoiding beef and beef products, or eating only muscle meat rather than brains, burgers or sausages.

However, BSE is recognized solely where there is surveillance and reporting. Countries that claim not to have any BSE may be fooling themselves.

Malaria 59

Malaria is a life-threatening disease caused by one of four strains of single-celled parasite: *Plasmodium falciparum, P. vivax, P. malariae* and *P. ovale*. After spending part of their lifecycle within a female Anopheles mosquito, they transfer to human beings.

How common is it?
Almost half the world's population, comprising 3.3 billion people, is at risk of malaria; in Africa alone, one child dies of malaria every 30 seconds, and between 800,000 and 1 million people succumb annually, including 10,000 pregnant women and 200,000 infants.

Who dies?
Mainly children, pregnant women, those with HIV infection, and non-immune travellers who forget their anti-malaria tablets.

Where?
85% of deaths occur in sub-Saharan Africa, where the Anopheles mosquito is long-lived and has acquired a taste for human rather than animal blood; HIV increases the risks.

When?
Falciparum malaria can kill within 1–3 weeks of infection.

Why?
Lack of mosquito-avoidance procedures and inadequate malaria prophylaxis.

A mosquito becomes infected when feeding on the blood of someone who carries the malaria parasite, then transmits it to other human beings every time it bites.

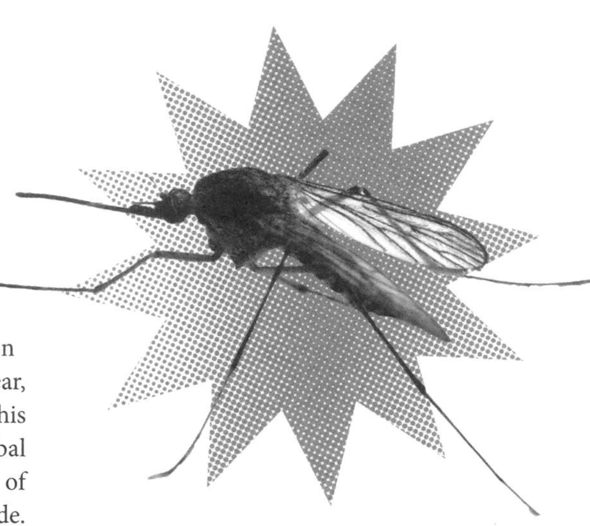

Anopheles mosquito

According to the WHO, 250 million people are infected with malaria each year, and there are nearly 1 million deaths. This can be viewed as a success story – global interventions have halved the number of infections and deaths over the past decade. On the other hand, it is a tragedy as malaria remains both a preventable and a curable disease.

Why does it kill?

Once deposited in the human bloodstream, malaria parasites invade the liver to multiply before entering red blood cells and multiplying further. Infected red cells rupture, producing the typical fever, chills and shakes. Death is most often due to *Plasmodium falciparum*, which can invade the brain to cause drowsiness, convulsions, severe brain damage and coma within hours or days. Severe anaemia, low blood glucose, pulmonary oedema (fluid on the lungs), high acid levels (metabolic acidosis), bleeding, excessive clotting (disseminated intravascular coagulation), kidney failure (sometimes with dark red or black urine) and severe low blood pressure (shock) can also contribute to death.

Will it happen to me?

Undoubtedly, if you visit an endemic area and do not take steps to avoid mosquito bites, or do not take prophylactic medication correctly. Even then, protection is not guaranteed, as drug resistance is a growing problem and may just prolong the incubation period. Most non-immune travellers with falciparum malaria develop symptoms within a month of leaving an endemic area, but there have been reports of falciparum malaria presenting up to 4 years later. The longest reported incubation for *Plasmodium vivax* is 30 years.

What to look for

Symptoms due to rupturing of red blood cells typically appear 6–14 days after an infective bite. Cycles of sudden coldness followed by shaking (rigors), fever and profuse sweating last from 4–6 hours and occur every 1–3 days. The number of parasites and severity of symptoms are amplified 20-fold with each cycle. Symptoms are generally more severe and frequent with *Plasmodium falciparum*. If not treated within 24 hours, *P. falciparum* can progress to severe (or fulminant) malaria with delirium, coma and death. Both *P. vivax* and *P. ovale* can hide in the liver to cause relapses several months or even years after the initial treatment was declared a success.

What are the chances of survival?

Combination therapy with an artemisinin drug, derived from wormwood (artesunate, artemether), and a partner drug (lumefantrine, amodiaquine, mefloquine) is more effective than a single drug, with less likelihood of resistance. The global fatality rate for all types of malaria is 1 in 10. Early diagnosis and treatment in returning travellers with uncomplicated malaria increases the chance of survival to between 96% and 99%. With severe *Plasmodium falciparum*, mortality is greater than 1 in 5, even with intensive medical care. With cerebral malaria there is a 50% to 90% chance of survival with treatment. The deeper the coma, the worse the prognosis. Exchange blood transfusion (in which just about all of the blood is replaced with donor blood) may be life-saving.

HOW TO AVOID IT

Anopheles mosquitoes breed in shallow fresh-water puddles and paddy fields. The only good thing about a drought is that it knocks out mosquitoes before people. Vector control measures involve eradicating breeding-grounds and spraying with insecticides, which can reduce malaria transmission rates from very high to almost zero.

Personal preventive measures involve bite avoidance and taking prophylactic drugs that suppress the blood stage of malaria infection to prevent disease.

- **Like vampires, mosquitoes tend to bite between dusk and dawn.**
- **Obtain the most up-to-date information about the best prophylactic drugs for the endemic area you intend to visit.**
- **Take your anti-malarials exactly as prescribed, for the correct length of time, especially after leaving an endemic area, when many people promptly stop.**
- **Ensure your living space is sprayed with residual insecticides.**
- **Sleep under a long-lasting insecticide-impregnated mosquito net at night, and check it for invaders before tucking the ends in carefully under your mattress.**
- **Cover exposed flesh with long trousers and sleeves, especially from dusk onwards.**
- **A face net with a wide-brimmed hat is a good idea if you will be out and about in the evenings.**
- **Close all windows at dusk unless undamaged mosquito mesh has been fitted.**

Measles 60

Measles is a highly infectious disease caused by a *Morbillivirus* that invades cells in the upper and lower respiratory tracts. The Germans call it English measles, and the English call it rubeola, causing confusion with the relatively benign rubella, which is also known as German measles.

How common is it?

More than 20 million people catch measles every year; in 2008, there were 164,000 measles deaths, equivalent to one every 3 minutes. An estimated 500,000 deaths will occur in 2013 alone.

Who dies?

Mostly unvaccinated children under the age of 5, especially those who are malnourished or have other serious illnesses (e.g. leukaemia, HIV); however, in the West, half of acute measles deaths are in previously healthy, but non-immunized, children.

Where?

95% of measles deaths are in low-income countries in Africa and Asia.

When?

Epidemics occur in 2-year cycles and after national disasters.

Why?

Non-immune exposure to the causative virus.

For those who enjoy access to free immunization, it is easy to forget that measles is a potentially serious disease. Measles vaccine has been available for over 40 years. Between 2000 and 2008, it helped to reduce the global measles death rate by 78%. Even so, it remains a leading cause of childhood death in some parts of the world.

Why does it kill?

Although most people recover from measles, 1 in 15 develops potentially serious complications, including bronchopneumonia (80% of deaths) and seizures. One in 5000 has an inflammation of the brain (encephalitis) and 1 in 10,000 dies as a result. Those who recover have a 20% to 40% chance of some form of brain damage or blindness. One in 100,000 has a rare, persistent brain infection known as subacute sclerosing panencephalitis (SSPE). Death may follow within 3 years, although remissions can occur with treatment.

Will it happen to me?

If you are vaccinated, or had the measles before vaccination was invented, the chances are slim. If you are not vaccinated and travel to an endemic country, you are at risk. Two doses of measles vaccine (usually combined with mumps and rubella protection) are needed to provide immunity. This is because 15% of vaccinated people do not acquire protective levels of antibody after a single dose.

What to look for

Symptoms start 8–14 days after infection, with a fever, runny nose, conjunctivitis, sneezing and coughing. This spreads the virus, which can survive for 2 hours away from the body. Some get diarrhoea and vomiting, too. Before the main rash announces itself, white spots appear on the inner cheek that resemble grains of salt on a red velvet cushion. Known as Koplik's spots, these are pathognomonic of measles (meaning they diagnose it with 100% accuracy) but are fleeting and often missed. A few days after the appearance of Koplik's spots, the classic red rash appears.

What are the chances of survival?

The mortality rate is less than 1 in 1000 in developed countries, but up to 10% in sub-Saharan Africa. There is no specific treatment except good nutrition and fluids. In endemic areas, two doses of vitamin A supplements, 24 hours apart, help to reduce blindness and halve the number of deaths.

HOW TO AVOID IT

Infected people start to spread the virus from 4 days before the onset of rash until 4 days afterwards. Avoid those who are obviously spotty. Ensure you have received vaccination if travelling to endemic countries.

61 Meningitis

The thought of meningitis strikes fear into any parent's heart. Defined as an inflammation of the brain membranes (meninges), it is often accompanied by inflammation of underlying tissue to cause meningoencephalitis.

How common is it?

Bacterial meningitis accounts for 170,000 deaths every year; mortality from viral meningitis is less easy to determine, but is estimated at around 7500 cases worldwide.

Who dies?

The very young, elderly people and those with other diseases, such as HIV, are most vulnerable.

Where?

Sub-Saharan Africa has the highest rate of Group A meningococcal disease; the area stretching from Senegal to Ethiopia is known as the 'meningitis belt'.

When?

Viral meningitis is more common during summer and early autumn; epidemics of meningococcal meningitis occur every 7–14 years.

Why?

Lack of vaccination and natural immunity.

Avoid meningitis like the plague. Of all the strains, though, 'aseptic' viral meningitis is the least harmful. This is the most common type (85%), caused by a variety of non-polio intestinal enteroviruses. Most of those affected make a full recovery, and the mortality rate is less than 1%. Exotic and potentially nastier viral culprits include polio, measles, mumps and herpes, as well as Japanese B, St Louis, Murray Valley and West Nile encephalitis viruses.

Much more worrying is 'septic' bacterial meningitis. At least 1 in 2 cases is fatal if not treated promptly with appropriate antibiotics. Even when treated, the mortality rate is 1 in 10. Of those who survive, 1 in 5 has some degree of brain damage, hearing loss or learning difficulties. Meningococcal meningitis, the most prevalent form, is caused by *Neisseria meningitides*, of which five groups (A, B, C, W135 and X) frequently cause epidemics. Other bacteria that also attack the meninges include *Haemophilus influenzae* type B, and *Streptococcus pneumoniae.*

Rarely, meningitis is caused by assorted fungi, or by *Rickettsia*, *Borrelia* and *Mycobacteria*, especially in those who are immunocompromised. Parasites such as malaria can also infect the brain.

Why does it kill?

Meningitis causes inflammation of nerve roots as they leave the brain and spinal cord. This can affect control of respiration, blood pressure or heart rate. Infection of the brain can cause clotting of cerebral blood vessels and tissue death (cerebral infarction). Swelling increases intracranial pressure and reduces blood flow to cause ischaemic stroke. In severe cases, the brain may herniate through the hole in the base of the skull (foramen magnum) to cause catastrophic brain damage. More commonly, victims succumb to sepsis (see page 208).

Will it happen to me?

Organisms that cause meningitis spread in the same way as colds and flu – from person to person through coughs, sneezes and other respiratory droplets. Everyone is potentially at risk, especially as 1 in 10 people carry *Neisseria meningitidis* up their nose.

What to look for

Fever, severe headache, vomiting, drowsiness and stiff, painful neck movements. Intolerance of light may also occur. Meningococcal meningitis can spill over into the circulation to cause sepsis. Bacterial toxins trigger clotting in small blood vessels (disseminated vascular coagulation) to produce a red blotchy rash that does not

DID YOU KNOW?

The meningococcus (*Neisseria meningitidis*) is a close relative of the gonococcus (*Neisseria gonorrhoeae*) that causes the sexually transmissible infection gonorrhoea.

blanch when you press a glass against the skin. But this rash appears on only 50% of cases, often in a late stage of the disease when diagnosis is too late.

Infants under the age of three may not have obvious headache, neck stiffness or dislike of light. A toddler with meningitis is obviously very ill, however, and usually shows a fever, vomiting and a sudden change in mood or personality (drowsy, clingy, frightened or aggressive). A young baby with meningitis is also obviously very ill, off feeds and irritable or withdrawn and drowsy. The baby may seem floppy or jerky and a seizure may occur. Sometimes the soft spot on the skull – the fontanelle – becomes tense and bulges.

What are the chances of survival?

Meningitis can resemble flu in the early stages and is difficult to diagnose. Symptoms can come on quickly. If you even remotely suspect meningitis, seek immediate medical advice. Don't worry about being alarmist. If a baby or toddler seems ill and unlike their usual self, call your doctor. Even if they have already been checked, call the doctor again if the patient gets worse or you are still not happy for any reason. Stories abound of children being sent home from hospital emergency departments with a missed diagnosis – sometimes on several occasions.

HOW TO AVOID IT

Ensure those at risk (children, travellers, elderly people) are vaccinated against *Haemophilus influenzae* type B (HiB), the pneumococcus, and meningococcal Groups A, C, W and X, as appropriate. Some countries also have a vaccine against local strains of Group B meningococcus.

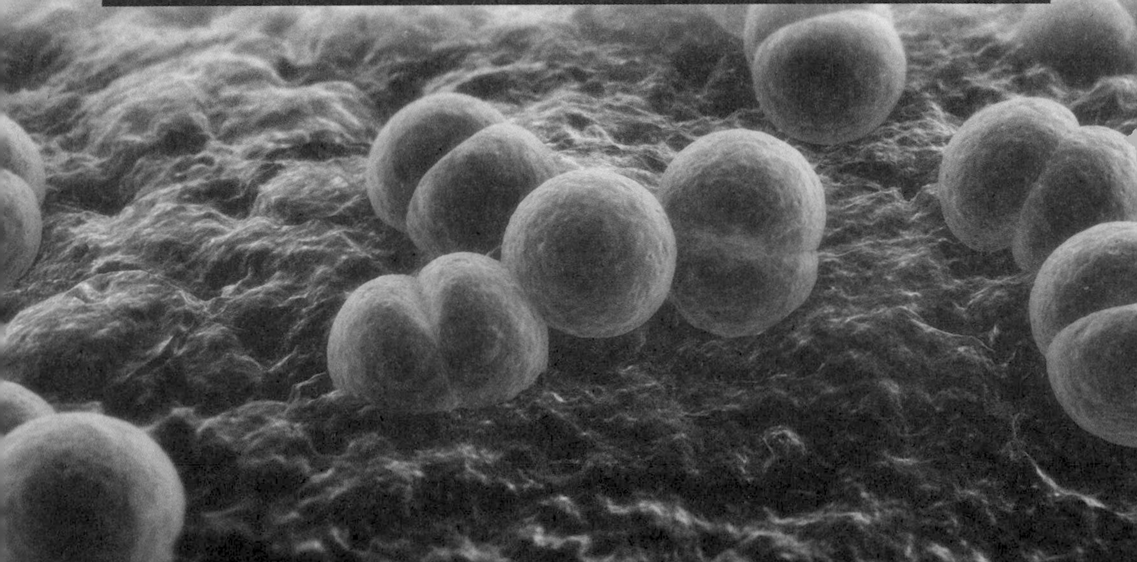

Meteorite strike 62

(and other objects falling from the sky)

The dinosaurs were apparently wiped out 65 million years ago by two giant meteorites that struck the Gulf of Mexico and the Ukraine. Evidence for human deaths in the more recent past is difficult to verify, however.

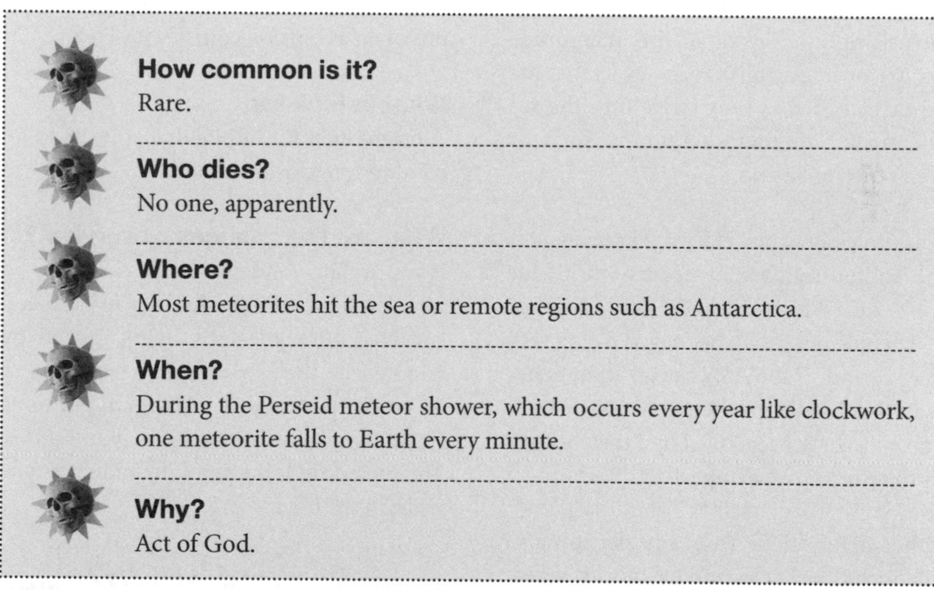

How common is it?
Rare.

Who dies?
No one, apparently.

Where?
Most meteorites hit the sea or remote regions such as Antarctica.

When?
During the Perseid meteor shower, which occurs every year like clockwork, one meteorite falls to Earth every minute.

Why?
Act of God.

'The large majority of lethal events ... [would be] caused by bodies that are so small, so faint, and so numerous that the cost of the effort required to find, track, predict, and intercept them exceeds the cost of the damage incurred by ignoring them.' John S. Lewis, 1999

In Siberia, on February 12, 1947, 150 tons of iron meteorite fragments peppered an area of 2 square kilometres, creating over 200 craters, of which half were wider than a metre (3 ft) across. If this had been a populated area, thousands would have died. We are told the human death toll was zero. Surprisingly, an event of this magnitude occurs once every 10 years, but most are never recorded as they sizzle into the sea or impact on remote regions such as Antarctica or Siberia.

One professor of planetary sciences suggests the annual number of deaths worldwide from 'near-Earth asteroids' could average 250 people per year, when taken over a very long period. But NASA categorically states that: 'No human in the past 1000 years is known to have been killed by a meteorite or by the effects of one impacting.'

Other items falling from the sky can also kill, including icicles and ice blocks, which in 2010 killed five people and injured 147 in St Petersburg alone, during Russia's coldest winter for 30 years.

Why does it kill?

Being hit by a lump of rock at speeds of over 1600 km/hr (1000 mph) leaves little room for manoeuvre.

Will it happen to me?

There is a 1 in 10,000 chance that a large asteroid or comet (greater than 2 km/1.2 miles across) will collide with the Earth during the next century, causing enough disruption to kill you. You will be relieved to hear that NASA currently knows of no such object on a collision course with Earth.

What to look for

A bright light in the sky that appears to be coming very close, very fast.

What are the chances of survival?

If you are hit, you'd expect the chance to be zero. However, a 14-year-old boy in Germany survived after allegedly being grazed by a meteorite the size of a pea, travelling at an estimated speed of 48,000 km per hour (30,000 mph), while on his way to school. The meteorite left a smoking crater, a foot wide, in the road.

DID YOU KNOW?

According to the Civil Aviation Authority, five people have been hit by ice falling from planes over Britain in the past 40 years.

Neurodegenerative diseases

Many diseases, including Alzheimer's (see page 72), are associated with degeneration of nerve cells within parts of the brain or spinal cord.

How common is it?
Around 2.5 million people have multiple sclerosis worldwide; 6.3 million have Parkinson's disease; 150,000 people have motor neurone disease; Huntington's disease affects an estimated 687,000 people.

Who dies?
Women are three times more likely to develop multiple sclerosis than men; men are 1.5 times more likely to develop Parkinson's disease and motor neurone disease, while there is no gender bias for Huntington's disease.

Where?
Regions north of 40 degrees latitude have a higher incidence of multiple sclerosis; motor neurone disease is distributed evenly around the globe.

When?
An unfortunate combination of genetic, environmental and possibly lifestyle factors coincide.

Why?
Progressive loss of regulation of body functions.

In many cases, the exact cause of neurodegenerative disease is unknown, but may involve genetic mutations, or interactions between genes, a viral infection and the immune system. Progression varies from person to person and, in some cases, is associated with an earlier than normal demise. Multiple sclerosis (MS) is a demyelination disease, meaning the myelin coat that surrounds nerves, and insulates their electrical activity, breaks down. Parkinson's disease (PD) involves a progressive loss of brain cells in the substantia nigra, which coordinates movement, and reduced levels of neurotransmitters involved in movement and mood. Motor neurone disease (MND) varies, affecting different parts of the central nervous system. Huntington's disease (HD) is a rare, usually familial, condition that mainly affects a part of the brain called the basal ganglia, causing jerky, uncontrolled limb movements.

Why does it kill?

The disease is given as a cause of death in over 60% of cases; other contributory causes of death include suicide, accidents, aspiration pneumonia (due to difficulty swallowing food and saliva), poor nutrition, cardiovascular disease, sepsis (often linked with pressure sores) and stroke.

Will it happen to me?

- Multiple sclerosis: if you have Scottish or Scandinavian ancestry you may have a greater genetic risk than if you have Gypsy, Native Indian, Maori, Japanese or Inuit blood. If a first-degree relative has multiple sclerosis, your risk is around 1 in 50; otherwise, 1 in 800.
- Parkinson's disease is most common in Nebraska, USA, around ferromanganese plants in Brescia, Italy, and among people of Amish or Parsi descent. If a first-degree relative is affected, your risk is 1 in 50, compared with 1 in 100 if no relatives are affected.
- Motor neurone disease: your risk is around 1 in 85 if you are aged 20 years and have a first-degree relative who is affected, decreasing to 1 in 1683 – compared with 1 in 50,000 for the general population – if you reach the age of 80 years without showing symptoms.
- If one of your parents develops Huntington's disease, you have a 1 in 2 chance of inheriting the associated gene. Otherwise, the risk is around 1 in 14,000 – unless you live in Venezuela, where the risk is as high as 1 in 142.

HOW TO AVOID IT

A diet rich in omega-3 fish oils, folic acid and/or antioxidants may reduce the risk of developing a neurodegenerative disease.

What to look for

Symptoms vary but can include: loss of sensation, muscle spasm, weakness or tremor, slowness or difficulty controlling limbs, jerky movements, constipation, loss of bladder or bowel control, sexual difficulties.

What are the chances of survival?

Treatment may help to control symptoms in some cases, but there is no cure. People with motor neurone disease usually (with notable exceptions) die within 3 years of diagnosis; those with Huntington's disease have a life expectancy of around 20 years from the initial appearance of symptoms. People with multiple sclerosis are 2.7 times more likely to die at any age than for similar people without multiple sclerosis, and overall life expectancy is around 7 years shorter. With Parkinson's disease, life expectancy is reduced by 7–10 years.

Obesity

Also known as 'Death by Chocolate', obesity is the leading cause of supersized coffins in the Western world.

How common is it?
The International Obesity Taskforce estimates that 1 billion people are overweight and a further 500 million are obese.

Who dies?
Traditionally middle-aged adults, but obesity now affects people in their 20s and early 30s, so death due to middle-age spread is affecting younger adults and occasionally children.

Where?
Worldwide, obesity rates are highest in the USA, Albania, Australia, New Zealand and England.

When?
Your waist size expands to 102 cm (40 in) for men or 88 cm (35 in) for women; in those with Asian genes, risks increase when waist circumference exceeds 90 cm (36 in) for men, 80 cm (32 in) for women.

Why?
Overindulgence and poor dietary and lifestyle choices.

'Obesity proves that God does not help those who help themselves and help themselves and help themselves.'

Anonymous

Many factors are implicated in obesity, but it is generally accepted as a long-term imbalance between the amount (and types) of energy you eat, and the amount you burn to fuel your metabolism and activities. Genes play a major role. Human beings evolved on a frugal diet with frequent periods of famine and lots of running around while hunting and gathering food. Our metabolism is poorly adapted for today's modern, energy-rich diet and sedentary lifestyle. The very genes evolution selected to help cavemen survive are now counting against us by laying down stores for a winter of famine that never arrives.

Evolution has also designed the appetite-stimulating effects of hormones such as ghrelin (the gremlin of excess weight) and cortisol (a stress hormone) to outweigh their appetite-suppressing counterparts, such as leptin, obestatin and oxyntomodulin. When obese people say 'it's my hormones' they are probably right.

The size of the problem

If you weigh over 20% or more than your maximum desirable body weight, you are obese. This is preceded by a phase of being overweight, when you are more than 10% heavier than your ideal. Obesity rates vary throughout the world and are generally increasing.

Why does it kill?

Obesity is a 'waisting' disease. Visceral fat deposited around the internal organs secretes hormones, free fatty acids and other substances that pass directly to the liver, where they influence its normal metabolism. As well as converting your liver to pâté de foie gras (meaning it becomes increasingly fatty), these substances activate liver genes to increase production of cholesterol, clotting factors and inflammatory mediators (chemicals that cause inflammation). Rather than making you hot, red and swollen (though you frequently are) – the usual signs of inflammation in the body – these inflammatory mediators make blood cells more sticky and elevate your blood pressure. They also affect insulin sensitivity so that your glucose tolerance goes down.

Scavenging immune cells (macrophages) come to the rescue and engulf oxidized cholesterol. Overwhelmed, they form bloated 'foam' cells that try to leave the circulation by squeezing through artery walls. Like a large person trying to squeeze through a turnstile, they become trapped and form fatty plaques in artery walls (atherosclerosis).

In these ways, obesity kills via Type 2 diabetes (see page 76), heart attack (see page 114) and stroke (see page 222). It is also linked with cancer of the breast, uterus and colon.

Prevalence of excess fat in adults

Country	% overweight	% obese
Albania	49%	29%
Iceland	41%	18%
Germany	38%	21%
Australia	37%	25%
England	37%	25%
USA	35%	34%
New Zealand	35%	25%
France	33%	17%
Bahrain	32%	27%
India	9%	2%

Figures rounded upwards in more ways than one ...

Will it happen to me?

If both your parents are obese you have a 70% chance of obesity too, compared with less than 20% if both your parents are lean. This is because genes, family eating habits and activity patterns are such good predictors of weight gain. Even if your parents are lean, consuming more calories than you need will soon lead to a bigger girth.

What to look for

Wobbly bits and an expanding waistline.

What are the chances of survival?

If you are obese, even slight fat losses can prolong your life. Losing 10 kg (22 lb) reduces your risk of premature death by 20% and your risk of a diabetes-related death by as much as 30%. These benefits accrue because a 10-kg fat loss reduces:

- blood pressure by 10/20 mmHg
- fasting blood glucose levels by 50%
- triglycerides by 30%
- total cholesterol by 10%
- harmful LDL-cholesterol by 15%

Quality of life also improves, owing to less back and joint pain, breathlessness, piles, indigestion, anxiety, depression, constipation and ingrowing toenails. And your sex life will see benefits too.

HOW TO AVOID IT

- **Insulin is the main fat-storing hormone in the body. Your pancreas secretes insulin when blood glucose levels rise, so select foods with a low glycaemic load, which impacts on blood sugar levels as little as possible.**
- **Eat fruit, vegetables, salads and whole grains rather than processed white carbohydrates.**
- **Lean meats and beans provide protein that quickly triggers satiety.**
- **Eat less and exercise more. But you already know that, and it is easier said than done. If you simply can't get on top of your weight issues a gastric band may be a last option.**

65 Occupational hazards

If work is somewhere you go to escape the dangers of home (see page 84), think again.

How common is it?

Overall, occupational accidents and illness represent around 4% of global deaths.

Who dies?

Workers over the age of 65 are more likely to suffer fatal injuries, suggesting that a retirement age of 65 is a good idea; their new replacements have a 50% higher rate of injury than older colleagues, but their injuries are more likely to be non-fatal.

Where?

One in six fatal accidents occur on construction sites; small manufacturing industries are also dangerous, especially those with fewer than 10 workers.

When?

Accidents tend to kill during work hours; diseases can kill many years or even decades after the original exposure.

Why?

Lack of health and safety culture; poor management; poor government legislation and enforcement; tiredness among shift-workers.

'May my husband rest in peace until I get there.'

Dame Edna Everage

Region	*Number of work-related deaths*
China	477,000
India	302,000
Industrialized countries	297,000
Sub-Saharan Africa	265,000
Other Asia/islands	256,000
Central and Eastern Europe and Central Asia	166,000
Latin America and Caribbean	148,000
Arab-speaking world	139,000
Total	**2.2 million**

Every year, an estimated 270 million work-related accidents occur, of which 40% involve transportation; in addition, there are 160 million cases of work-related illness. Of these, 2.2 million are fatal.

Why does it kill?

Accidents represent 20% of work-related fatalities. Events such as falling off scaffolding, plunging into vats of wine, entangling with machinery, altercations with tractors and electrocution are self-explanatory. Work-related diseases, which account for the other 80% of deaths, are less easy to quantify. Exposure to hazardous substances causes 440,000 deaths a year, of which cancers and lung diseases (pneumoconioses) top the list. Among agricultural workers, who form 50% of the global workforce, pesticides cause an estimated 70,000 acute and long-term lethal poisonings each year.

Will it happen to me?

If you work, you have a 1 in 7 chance of joining these statistics every year.

What to look for

Good insurance. Worldwide, out of a workforce of over 740 million, only 40 million workers are covered by an occupational injury insurance scheme.

What are the chances of survival?

If 270 million work-related accidents and 160 million work-related illnesses result in 2.2 million deaths per year, then the overall chance of surviving is around 1 in 200.

HOW TO AVOID IT

Follow all health and safety advice and legislation; wear protective clothing and shoes; remain vigilant; do not drive or operate machinery if you are tired or under the influence of alcohol or drugs (including some prescription drugs – check leaflet inserts). Reconsider your career options if you work in one of the ten most dangerous occupations, as a: logging/timber industry worker; airline pilot; fishing industry worker; structural iron and steel worker; refuse and recyclable material collector; farmer/rancher; roofer; electrical power line installer/repairer; truck driver or travelling salesperson; taxi driver or chauffeur.

Old age 66

Average lifespans are increasing and babies born in 2040 will have an average life expectancy of 150 years. Dr Aubrey de Grey, Chief Science Officer for the Methuselah Foundation, even claims that the first person to reach the unimaginable age of 1000 years is probably already alive today – and born before 1945.

How common is it?
One in 7000 people currently reaches the age of 100, but only 1 in 5 million reaches the elite age of 110 to become a supercentenarian.

Who dies?
Women are more likely to reach the age of 100 than men.

Where?
Often peacefully in their sleep or taking a nap in a chair.

When?
Babies born in 2040 will have an average life expectancy of 150 years.

Why?
The heart just reaches the last of its allotted beats.

'All diseases roll into one – old age.' Ralph Waldo Emerson

Centenarians have an unusually lucky combination of genes that allows them to live longer than their biblically allotted three score years and ten. This, mixed with a healthy lifestyle, also means their extended years are likely to be spent living independently, with an agile body and mind. Most centenarians are physically equivalent to people 10 years their junior, while supercentenarians, who live to 110 or more, are physically equivalent to those who are 20 years younger. Their most common ailments are osteoarthritis and, poignantly, loneliness.

Why does it kill?

In those who die of 'old age' with no other obvious cause of death, the heart presumably just stops beating. Old age is given as a sole cause of death only if a doctor:

- has cared for the deceased over a long period
- has attended the deceased within the 2 weeks prior to death
- has observed a gradual decline in the patient's general health and functioning
- is unaware of any identifiable disease or injury contributing to death
- is certain there is no reason to report the death to a coroner

However, a coroner, a crematorium referee, a registrar or the patient's family may not accept 'old age' as an adequate explanation and may request further investigation.

Will it happen to me?

The United Nations estimates there could be as many as 3.2 million people aged over 100 by the year 2050. If you are not significantly overweight and do not smoke or drink alcohol to excess, you have a fighting chance of being one of them. Prudence is not the only route to longevity, however. Researchers in the USA looked at the medical histories of 424 centenarians (aged up to 119 years) to assess their resistance to 10 major illnesses: high blood pressure, heart disease, diabetes, stroke, non-skin cancer, skin cancer, osteoporosis, thyroid conditions, Parkinson's disease, chronic obstructive pulmonary disease and cataracts. They found that centenarians formed three profiles:

- Survivors (24% of males, 43% of females) had been diagnosed with one or more of these age-related illnesses before the age of 80, but soldiered on with it.
- Delayers (44% of males, 42% of females) did not develop any of these age-related illnesses until after the age of 80.
- Escapers (32% of males, 15% of females) reached the age of 100 without developing any of these common age-related illnesses.

This is good news for those with a racy lifestyle. You don't necessarily have to have lived the life of a saint, or have a clean medical record, to reach the magical age of 100.

What to look for

Longevity in your family history, especially your parents and grandparents. It also helps if family members look young for their age.

What are the chances of survival?

The principal drawback of old age is that there's no future in it. Once you reach the age of 100, your chances of living on become increasingly slim.

HOW TO AVOID IT

- Ensure you die by one of the other means detailed in this book. All the usual advice (no smoking, sensible drinking) apply, but the most important advice is: choose your parents carefully. The offspring of centenarians are more likely to live longer than those with parents of average life expectancy. They also have a lower risk of developing any age-related disease, and if these conditions do develop, they are delayed to a later age. This is thought to result from a beneficial clustering of immune and metabolic genes.
- Among older people, the food most closely associated with longevity is beans. Every 20g increase in average daily intake is linked with an 8% lower risk of death from a medical cause at any age.
- Get a good night's sleep: not too much, not too little, but just the right amount. Researchers following 21,000 twins for over 22 years found that those who slept for between 7 and 8 hours per night lived longer than those who habitually slept for shorter or longer periods.
- Floss your teeth: scientists estimate that daily flossing can add over 6 years to your life, as people with inflamed gums (gingivitis, periodontitis) have a mortality rate that is up to 46% greater than for those with healthy mouths.
- Eat an apple a day: they're full of antioxidant polyphenols, so this can reduce your risk of death from any medical cause at any age by one-third compared with those eating fewer apples.
- Eat less: restricting your calorie intake to maintain a healthy weight can significantly extend your lifespan, although you may argue that life quality is reduced.
- Take regular exercise: a study involving more than 10,000 men found that exercise reduced the number of age-related deaths from all medical causes by almost a quarter – even if exercise was not started until middle age.
- Think positive and maintain strong social networks: research suggests that people with a sunny outlook on life and who view the ageing process optimistically tend to live, on average, 7½ years longer than those with more negative thoughts.

Pancreatitis 67

The pancreas has the distinction of being both an endocrine gland (it secretes hormones directly into the bloodstream) and an exocrine gland (it secretes powerful digestive juices directly into the intestines via the pancreatic duct).

How common is it?

Pancreatitis is one of the most common diseases seen by gastroenterologists, accounting for 2% of hospital admissions in Western countries: an estimated 3,882,644 episodes of acute pancreatitis and 1,580,000 cases of chronic pancreatitis occur every year. Of these, around 820,000 people die.

Who dies?

Mostly overweight bons viveurs over the age of 50; males are seven times more likely to be affected than females.

Where?

Usually in the spring, whether or not you have gallstones or a heavy alcohol intake, suggesting a possible viral problem as the last straw.

When?

One to two weeks after eating a final fatty meal, washed down with numerous glasses of claret.

Why?

Inability of the pancreas to cope with excessive alcohol, triglycerides, gallstone-induced blockages or infection.

The digestive juices produced by the pancreas contain enzymes that rapidly process steak, chips and peas etc. into a suitable form for absorption. When they leak into body tissues, they digest them just as efficiently. This is exactly what happens when the gland becomes inflamed, either suddenly (acute pancreatitis) or in a persistent, grumbling manner (chronic pancreatitis).

Why does it kill?

Enzymes eating through tissues cause internal bleeding (sometimes seen as bruising in the flanks – Grey Turner's sign). Release of powerful enzymes and inflammatory substances can also trigger circulatory shock, adult respiratory distress syndrome, clotting in blood vessels (disseminated vascular coagulation), fluid/salt imbalances and kidney failure. Pancreatitis affects secretion of insulin and may lead to dangerously high glucose levels (diabetes).

Other causes of death include sepsis, encephalopathy (brain malfunction), heart attack and heart failure. Sometimes an underlying pancreatic cancer is rapidly lethal. When surgery is performed for undiagnosed, acute abdominal pain, few patients with pancreatitis do well – the surgeon just ends up swilling digestive enzymes around your insides. This is known as 'kiss of death' surgery (see page 231).

Will it happen to me?

The main risk factors are excessive consumption of alcohol (70% of cases), gallstones and raised blood levels of a type of fat called triglycerides. It can also result from injury, certain drugs and some infections such as mumps, malaria and dengue fever. Many cases are idiopathic (of unknown origin). Your overall risk of developing pancreatitis is 1 in 5882. Your risk of dying from pancreatitis is roughly 1 in 8380. Those with pre-existing diabetes are at greater risk.

What to look for

Severe pain in the upper abdomen, which radiates through to your back. Nausea, vomiting and memories of a recent excessively rich meal with perhaps a little too much wine.

What are the chances of survival?

There is no particular treatment apart from intensive care and pain relief. A variety of factors affect the prognosis, including age, white blood cell count, blood pressure and circulating levels of glucose, enzymes, calcium and oxygen. Mortality rates range from 2% to 100%, depending on the number of factors present and their severity. There is some good news. Two decades ago, the average mortality rate was as high as 30%. Recent studies suggest improved medical support has reduced this to 15%.

HOW TO AVOID IT

The only risk factors over which you have any control are your alcohol intake and consumption of excessively fatty, rich meals, both of which significantly elevate your blood triglyceride levels. Don't overindulge.

Peritonitis 68

The peritoneum is a flimsy membrane that resembles a giant, closed plastic bag.

How common is it?

One in ten people experience localized peritonitis as a result of appendicitis; of these, 22,000 worldwide die from perforation and secondary peritonitis; abdominal injury kills over a million people a year through lack of basic surgical interventions following road traffic accidents or interpersonal violence; peptic ulcer disease kills 270,000 people per year; 30% of patients with ascites (fluid in the abdominal cavity) due to end-stage liver cirrhosis develop spontaneous bacterial peritonitis.

Who dies?

Infants under the age of a year, as well as elderly and immunocompromised people, who show few signs of the disease. Appendicitis is most common between the ages of 10 and 30. Before the age of 25, males are twice as likely to develop appendicitis as females.

Where?

Low- and middle-income countries.

When?

Lack of access to surgery.

Why?

Although most people die through lack of access to antibiotics and surgery, some die despite surgery (failure to resolve the cause) and a few die because of surgery (accidental bowel perforation).

The outer layer of the peritoneum is attached to your abdominal wall, while the inner layer is wrapped around your intestines. This leaves a potential cavity in the middle called the intraperitoneal space, which contains a small amount of slippery fluid so the two layers slide easily over one another. Most people remain unaware of their peritoneum until it becomes inflamed. Then, thanks to the millions of nerve endings it contains, you develop severe abdominal pain. This can result from chemical irritation or infection. As the gut is a major route through which disease enters the body, it is perhaps surprising this doesn't happen more often. Peritonitis triggers the formation of a fibrinous fluid that forms bands of scar tissue in an attempt to contain the chemicals causing the infection. This often backfires by protecting bacteria from antibiotics and your immune system, leading to an abscess.

Causes of peritonitis include:

- appendicitis
- perforated peptic ulcer
- complications of surgery or endoscopy
- strangulated gangrenous bowel
- pancreatitis
- injury
- inflammation of the gallbladder (cholecystitis)
- intra-abdominal abscess
- spread of infections such as tuberculosis
- inflammatory bowel disease (ulcerative colitis, Crohn's disease)
- pelvic inflammatory disease (especially due to gonorrhoea)
- spontaneous bacterial peritonitis from chronic liver disease
- ectopic pregnancy
- spread of infection up the Fallopian tubes after delivery of a baby
- ruptured ovarian cyst
- perforated sigmoid colon due to diverticulitis, volvulus, inflammatory bowel disease or colorectal cancer
- peritoneal dialysis in patients with kidney failure

DID YOU KNOW?

The appendix is a blind-ending pouch that branches off from the start of the large bowel. It averages 10 cm (4 in) in length, but can vary between 2 cm and 22 cm (1–9 in). Although often viewed as a vestigial 'useless' organ, it contains lymphoid tissue and may play a role in gut immunity. Appendicitis develops when the narrow opening along its length becomes blocked. This may result from swelling of lymphoid tissue in the wall of the appendix, or from a buildup of 'dried' faeces. Blockage encourages bacterial overgrowth within the appendix, leading to appendicitis. Although it is becoming less common, appendicitis remains the most frequent cause of an acute abdominal emergency.

Why does it kill?

Peritonitis leads to overwhelming sepsis and shock.

Will it happen to me?

Your lifetime risk of appendicitis is 8.6% for males, and 6.7% for females. Your lifetime risk of developing peritonitis is around 10%.

What to look for

Increasing abdominal pain (made worse by moving and coughing), fever, rapid pulse, abdominal distension, abdominal tenderness with guarding (tensing leading to washboard rigidity), diminished or absent bowel sounds when examined.

What are the chances of survival?

If left untreated, peritonitis is fatal in at least 90% of cases. A lucky few survive when their fibrinous fluid, and the fatty apron hanging from their intestines (omentum), wall off an area of infection, allowing their immune system to get on top of it. With antibiotics and surgery, there is a 90% chance of survival for otherwise healthy patients, falling to 60% in elderly people. The mortality rate of acute appendicitis is less than 1% with surgical removal. If you need laparoscopy (which uses a small incision) to diagnose abdominal pain, the mortality rate is around 1 in 70. If you progress to open laparotomy (which requires a large incision), the risk of death increases to 1 in 5, as most patients are usually very sick with widespread peritonitis and a serious underlying cause such as volvulus (see page 62).

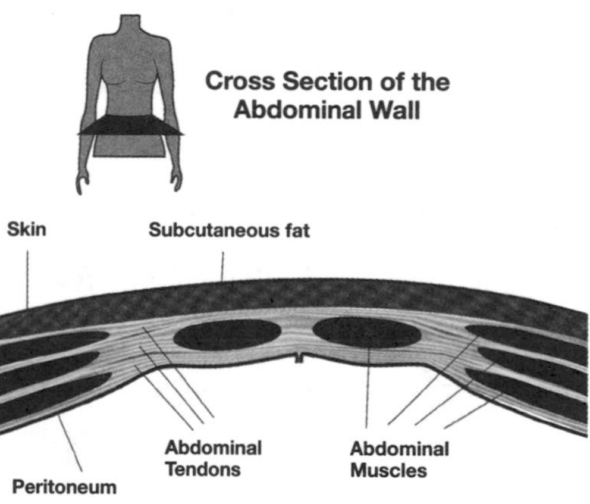

HOW TO AVOID IT

- Moderating your intake of alcohol reduces the risk of spontaneous bacterial peritonitis associated with cirrhosis of the liver.
- Surgeons sometimes remove a healthy appendix when accessing your insides for other reasons. This spares you from future appendicitis but does take away a 'spare part' that may prove useful for future reconstructive operations. The benefits of this procedure – known as incidental appendectomy – decrease significantly in people over the age of 30 (in whom appendicitis is relatively rare).

Plague

Plague is caused by the bacterium *Yersinia pestis*, which is transmitted by contact with infected rat fleas. Plague was a major killer in the Middle Ages. Between 1347 and 1353, for example, the so-called Black Death felled an astonishing one-third of the world's population. Three centuries later, the Great Plague of London (1665–66) saw off another 100,000 people.

How common is it?
Around 200 deaths are reported each year, mostly in Africa.

Who dies?
Those who are not rapidly diagnosed and treated.

Where?
It remains endemic in parts of Africa, the former Soviet Union, the Americas and Asia.

When?
Pneumonic plague can kill within 24 hours after inhalation of infected droplets.

Why?
Because rat fleas find human beings tastier than their original host.

Thanks to antibiotics (and rat control), plague is less of a problem nowadays, though it is making a comeback in parts of India, Indonesia and Algeria after 'silent' periods of 30–50 years.

Why does it kill?

The bacteria produce factors that suppress normal immune mechanisms and avoid destruction by immune cells. This allows it to multiply in the body unchecked. Death usually results from sepsis and shock.

Will it happen to me?

Unless you have contact with rat fleas, or handle infected carcasses or laboratory specimens in endemic areas, you are not at great risk. Pneumonic plague can spread from person to person in respiratory droplets, but the chance of it happening isn't something that should keep you awake at night.

What to look for

Flu-like symptoms develop 1–7 days after infection. Fever, chills and vomiting are followed by one of three clinical syndromes: swollen lymph nodes (bubonic plague), septicaemic plague or pneumonic plague, which is the most deadly version.

What are the chances of survival?

The mortality rate remains high, at up to 60%, if left untreated. This decreases to 15% with appropriate antibiotics (streptomycin, tetracyclines), so rapid diagnosis is essential.

DID YOU KNOW?

- **Bubonic plague is named after the 'buboes', or swollen lymph glands, that develop in the groin.**
- **In 1940, fleas infected with *Yersinia pestis* were allegedly dropped from a Japanese plane flying over China, causing an outbreak of plague that killed 121 people.**

HOW TO AVOID IT

- **Give rats and their fleas a wide berth.**
- **Plague vaccines are available but are generally recommended only for high-risk groups, such as laboratory personnel who are likely to be exposed to *Yersinia pestis*.**

70

Plane crash

An apocryphal tale – supposedly disseminated by the London *Times* – suggests that more people are kicked to death by donkeys every year than die in plane crashes.

How common is it?

Globally, around 46 aviation accidents every year result in at least one fatality; the majority involve small private aircraft. In addition, around 20 people per year die on a plane in a flying-related incident not due to crashing, such as a pulmonary embolus (a clot lodging within a lung artery – usually having travelled from a deep vein in the leg).

Who dies?

Usually passengers and crew when a plane hits the ground.

Where?

In or near a plane after it hits the ground in an uncontrolled fashion.

When?

The most dangerous parts of the flight are takeoff, when the plane is fully fuelled (12% of accidents), and landing (25%). Crashes are less common during the initial climb (8%), during 'flaps-up' climb (10%), while cruising (8%) and during descent (4%). Risks rise again during initial approach (10%) and final approach (11%). Accidents during taxiing, loading and unloading, towing and while parked add a further 12%.

Why?

Inability of a plane to take off, stay in the sky or land properly, owing to factors such as: pilot error, weather, mechanical failure, air traffic controller errors, improper loading, fuel contamination, bird strike and sabotage.

If the donkey statistic opposite is true, then, annually, over 1200 people must be sent to their maker by an ass.

Why does it kill?

The sudden change in velocity when a plane hits the ground leads to blunt force trauma and internal injuries, such as a ruptured aorta. Smoke inhalation, fire, drowning and hypothermia are other possible causes of death. Depending on where you land, cannibalism cannot be ruled out.

Will it happen to me?

On a fatality-per-mile basis, air transport is six times safer than travelling by car and twice as safe as rail, according to a BBC report. The annual risk of being killed in a plane crash is about 1 in 11 million for the average person. (The average person makes only one round trip per year, of just over 1000 air miles.)

Risks increase dramatically if you own a frequent-flyer loyalty card – and yet are still extraordinarily low: if you flew on a plane every day, your chance of dying in a plane crash would be once every 19,000 years.

What to look for

A look of panic on the face of your previously calm flight attendant.

What are the chances of survival?

When technology magazine *Popular Mechanics* examined data from 20 commercial jet crashes in the USA, they discovered that passengers sitting at the back of a plane were more likely to survive a crash than those in the front. Those slumming it in the rear cabin (behind the trailing edge of the wing) had an average survival rate of 69% compared with 56% when sitting over the wing, and 49% when lounging in first or business class at the front. However, experts say there is no such thing as a safe seat, as all crashes are different. So all you can do is buckle up, sip that complimentary orange juice, and hope for the best ...

HOW TO AVOID IT

Don't fly. If you must, at least listen to the flight attendant's safety speech.

Consider carrying a parachute in hand luggage (why is there a lifejacket but no 'chute under each seat?). However, you don't actually have to be in a plane to die in an aviation accident. Every year, several spectators are injured, sometimes fatally, when air show stunt displays go horribly wrong. Working in an airport also carries dangers.

Plant attack 71

Plants (including, for the purposes of this chapter, fungi) can be just as deadly as animals, but they tend to lure you into eating them rather than chasing after you.

How common is it?

Of the 1.8 million AIDS deaths that occur each year, between 624,700 and 1,125,000 are due to opportunistic fungal infections; thousands of cases of plant poisoning are reported each year, and several hundred deaths are recorded, mostly due to eating unripe ackee fruit, bird-lime thistle, yellow oleander and sea mango.

Who dies?

Children under six are most at risk of plant poisoning; those with immunosuppression from cancer or HIV/AIDS are most at risk of disseminated fungal infections.

Where?

Everywhere, but mostly in Asia where plant poisoning is a popular method of both suicide and homicide, and where people with cancer or HIV have less access to appropriate treatment.

When?

Poisonous plants are ingested, or opportunistic fungi invade immunocompromised patients.

Why?

Lack of antitoxin; those that are available are too expensive for use in developing countries, where they would make the most difference.

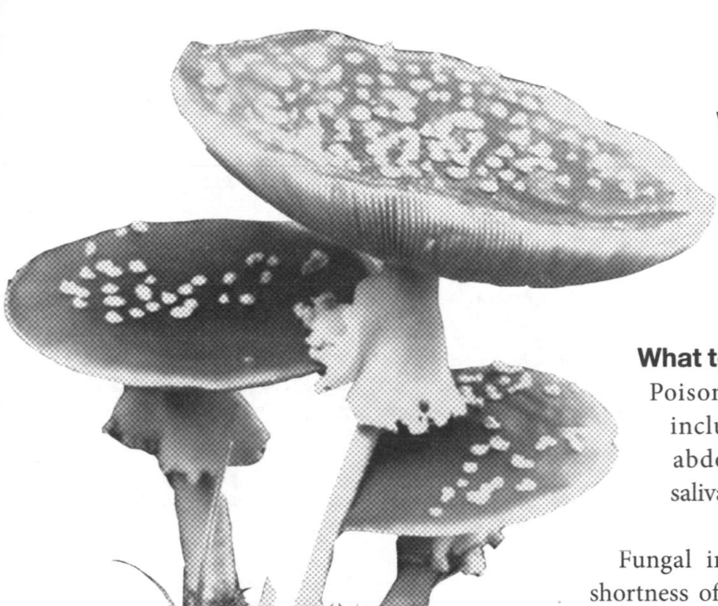

Some plants attack only if you are already immunosuppressed. Those people with cancer or HIV, for example, may develop life-threatening invasive infections of opportunistic fungi, such as *Aspergillus fumigatus, Pneumocystis juroveci, Cryptococcus neoformans, Coccidioides immitis, Histoplasma capsulatum, Candida albicans* and even *Penicillium marneffei*, which can spread throughout the body to affect just about every organ.

Why does it kill?

Opportunistic fungi cause death from pneumonia, kidney failure, liver failure, meningitis or encephalitis. Ingested plant poisons interfere with biological cell functions, especially in the heart and brain (see table on pages 188–9).

Will it happen to me?

If you eat unidentified mushrooms, fruit or leaves, or if your immunity is reduced through serious illness, it is a possibility.

What to look for

Poisoning: common symptoms include vomiting, diarrhoea, abdominal pain, changes in salivation (see table overleaf).

Fungal infections: report any fever, shortness of breath or feelings of illness if you have cancer, HIV or other serious illness.

What are the chances of survival?

Poisoning: mortality rates with supportive medical treatment are typically 5% to 10% in the Western world, rising to greater than 66% with bird-lime thistle poisoning in Asia.

DID YOU KNOW?

Paralytic shellfish syndrome is a life-threatening condition caused by eating shellfish that are contaminated with a plant – a toxic red alga (*Alexandrum* species). There is no antidote but many people survive with intensive medical care.

'Fear is the deadly nightshade of the mind.' Edward Walker

Plant	*Poisonous parts*	*Symptoms*
Ackee apple tree ***Blighia sapida***	Unripe fruits and the seeds contain hypoglycins A and B.	Hypoglycaemia, seizures, coma and death.
Angel's trumpets ***Brugmansia sp./ Datura sp.***	All parts, especially the seeds and flowers, contain the alkaloids scopolamine, hyoscyamine and atropine.	Delirium, hallucinations, blurred vision, hyperthermia, rapid pulse, seizures, coma and occasionally death.
Autumn crocus ***Colchicum autumnale***	All contain the alkaloid colchicin, especially the bulb. Do not mistake the pistils for saffron.	Fever, vomiting, bloody diarrhoea, abdominal pain, weak pulse, shortness of breath, kidney failure, death.
Bird-lime thistle ***Atractylis gummifera***	Contains glucosides such as atractyloside and carboxyatractyl-oside. Do not mistake for globe artichoke.	Vomiting, abdominal pain, diarrhoea, headache, convulsions, coma and death.
Castor oil plant ***Ricinus communis***	All parts, especially the seeds, contain the alkaloid ricinine, and the toxalbumin ricin (see page 193).	Headache, vomiting, abdominal pain, bloody diarrhoea, shortness of breath, seizures, kidney failure, shock and death.
Daffodil ***Narcissus sp.***	All parts, but especially the bulbs, contain toxic alkaloids such as lycorine, galanthamine and narcissine. Do not mistake bulbs for onions.	Vomiting, diarrhoea, seizures and death.
Deadly nightshade ***Atropa belladonna***	All parts contains alkaloids such as atropine, scopolamine, hyoscyamine and belladonnine. Do not mistake the black, cherry-like fruits for edible berries.	Dizziness, dry mouth, flushing, vomiting, dilated pupils, blurred vision, weakness, rapid heartbeat, respiratory failure and death.
Deathcap and related mushrooms ***Amanita phalloides; A. bisporigera, A. verna***	All parts contain amatoxins such as amantin and amanin. Choose your mushrooms carefully.	Vomiting, abdominal cramps, diarrhoea, delirium, convulsions, liver failure, kidney failure.
Foxglove ***Digitalis purpurea***	All parts, especially the stems, contain the cardiac glycosides digitoxin, gitoxin and digoxin. Do not mistake leaves for sage.	Vomiting, diarrhoea, abdominal pain, hallucinations, delirium, slow pulse, arrhythmia, seizures, heart block and death.
Hemlock ***Conium maculatum***	All parts contain the alkaloids coniine, methylconiine, conhydrine, pseudoconhydrine and coniceine. Do not mistake leaves for parsley.	Vomiting, dilated pupils, muscle paralysis, respiratory failure and death.

Plant	*Poisonous parts*	*Symptoms*
Lily of the valley ***Convallaria majalis***	All parts contain poisonous glycosides including convallatoxin, convallarin, convallamarin and majaloside.	Headache, vomiting, slow pulse, excessive urination, and death.
Monkshood/ wolfsbane ***Aconitum napellus***	All parts contain the alkaloid aconitine, especially young tubers. Sometimes known as 'plant arsenic'.	Pins and needles, salivation, vomiting, diarrhoea, paralysis, rapid pulse, respiratory and cardiac failure and death.
Oleander ***Nerium oleander***	All parts, especially the sap, contain cardiac glycosides such as oleandrin and neriine.	Vomiting, salivation, abdominal pain, diarrhoea, irregular pulse, seizures, coma and death.
Opium poppy ***Papaver somniferum***	All parts, except the seed, contain a white milky resin that contains opiate alkaloids such as morphine, papaverine and codeine.	Vomiting, depression, sleepiness, respiratory suppression, coma and death.
Pheasant's eye ***Adonis vernalis***	All parts contain cardiac glycosides such as adronidine, cymarin, adonitoxin, strophanthin and convallatoxin.	Vomiting, diarrhoea, slowed heartbeat, arrhythmia, cardiac arrest and death.
Sea mango or Suicide tree ***Cerbera manghas***	All parts, especially the milky sap, leaves, fruit and kernels contain the cardiac glycoside cerberin. Do not mistake for mango. Do not burn the wood – even the smoke is poisonous.	Vomiting, diarrhoea, slowed heartbeat, arrhythmia, cardiac arrest and death.
Strychnine tree ***Strychnos nux-vomica***	All parts, especially the bark, flowers and seeds, contain the alkaloids strychnine and brucine.	Vomiting, diarrhoea, muscular spasm, paralysis, high blood pressure, respiratory failure, heart failure and death.
Yellow oleander ***Thevetia peruviana***	All parts, especially the milky sap and seeds, contain the cardiac glycoside thevetin.	Vomiting, diarrhoea, slowed heartbeat, arrhythmia, cardiac arrest and death.
Yew ***Taxus baccata***	The leaves contain diterpene taxanes. Do not mistake its leaves for rosemary or its fruits for juniper berries, or make utensils from its wood.	Vomiting, salivation, abdominal pain, diarrhoea, shortness of breath, muscular spasm, cardiac arrest and death.

HOW TO AVOID IT

- **Don't eat unfamiliar plants.**
- **Ask your doctor about antifungal prophylaxis if your natural immunity is suppressed.**
- **Wash hands regularly and maintain good hygiene practices.**

Pneumonia 72

Pneumonia is an infection of the lungs.

How common is it?

Worldwide, pneumonia is the number one cause of death in children under the age of five. Among adults in Western countries, it is the fourth to sixth most common cause of death. Not counting TB (see page 250), 4 million people die from pneumonia every year, including 1.6 million children under the age of five – one every 20 seconds. This represents almost 1 in 5 childhood deaths – more than die from AIDS, malaria and TB combined. These figures do not include the 26% of neonatal deaths due to pneumonia that are classified separately.

Who dies?

Mostly children, smokers, adults over the age of 60 and those who are bedridden or immunocompromised; 1 in 20 patients admitted to hospital with other problems will develop hospital-acquired (nosocomial) pneumonia. Women are more likely to succumb than men, possibly because they tend to have smaller lungs.

Where?

Everywhere, but 85% of childhood deaths occur in South Asia and sub-Saharan Africa.

When?

Virulent organisms enter the lungs – usually through inhalation, but sometimes via the bloodstream from infection elsewhere in the body; admissions to hospital peak during cold weather.

Why?

Compromised oxygen and carbon dioxide gaseous exchange in the lungs.

When mainly confined to the airways, the infection is known as bronchopneumonia. When it spreads to affect the air sacs within a lung, which fill with pus and secretions, it is known as lobar pneumonia.

Like meningitis, pneumonia can be caused by viruses, bacteria or fungi, and many of the same culprits are involved. Bacterial lobar pneumonia is commonly due to *Streptococcus pneumoniae* (the pneumococcus), *Haemophilus influenzae* type B (HiB) and *Moraxella catarrhalis*. Bronchopneumonia may be due to *Staphylococcus aureus, Klebsiella pneumoniae, E.coli* or *Pseudomonas aeruginosa*, which are often 'hospital-acquired' by debilitated or elderly patients. Other atypical forms of pneumonia due to such organisms as *Legionella pneumophila* (Legionnaires' disease), *Bordetella pertussis* (whooping cough) and *Mycoplasma pneumoniae* are also significant killers.

Viral pneumonia (20% of cases) is often caused by the respiratory syncytial virus, but can complicate influenza and measles virus infections. In those with HIV, fungi such as *Pneumocystis jiroveci* are involved.

Why does it kill?

Respiratory failure (see page 206) or sepsis (see page 208).

Will it happen to me?

Pneumonia is spread via infected droplets (coughs, sneezes) and infected items (fomites) such as bedding and clothing. Everyone is potentially at risk but vaccination, good nutrition and sanitation mean most cases occur in developing countries.

What to look for

Shortness of breath, cough, fever, chills, loss of appetite and, sometimes, wheezing.

In children, the lower chest wall may seem to draw in rather than expanding when breathing in. Sputum may be purulent (pus-filled) or blood-stained.

What are the chances of survival?

Prognosis depends on the organism involved, your age, whether or not you smoke, and your underlying health. Bacterial forms of pneumonia, which are the most lethal, can be treated with appropriate antibiotics. For patients hospitalized with pneumonia, survival rates are 10% to 25%. For patients who develop pneumonia while in hospital for another condition, the death rate is significantly higher, at 50% to 70%.

Worldwide, more than 20% of children do not receive the lifesaving treatment they need for pneumonia.

HOW TO AVOID IT

Pneumonia in children can largely be prevented by vaccination (against *Haemophilus influenzae* type B (HiB), *Streptococcus pneumoniae*, measles and pertussis), combined with good nutrition, sanitation and hygiene. Overcrowding and exposure to cigarette smoke and other forms of air pollution increase the risk. Breastfeeding is protective.

Poisoning 73

A poison disrupts biological reactions in the body, causing damage that could be lethal.

How common is it?

More than 350,000 people die worldwide from unintentional poisoning. Pesticide ingestion accounts for 370,000 successful suicides per year – more than one-third of all suicides. In rural Asia, 60% of successful suicides involve pesticide poisoning – 160,000 people in this region alone. Poisoning is involved in 1% of homicides, accounting for at least another 50,000 deaths per year.

Who dies?

Poisoning is the fourth-leading cause of death in Russia; worldwide, it is the ninth most common cause of death in adults aged 15–29 years; accidental poisoning is particularly common among children under the age of five.

Where?

Most low- to middle-income countries.

When?

A poison enters the body in sufficient quantity and is given time to work.

Why?

Accident or design.

'Poison is in everything, and no thing is without poison. The dosage makes it either a poison or a remedy.' Paracelsus

Poisons may be naturally occurring chemicals (elements, salts, gases), manmade substances (drugs, agricultural, industrial or household chemicals), or substances produced by bacteria (see pages 41, 55, 203 and 225), plants (see plant attack, page 186) or animals (see page 22). Most poisons enter the body through swallowing, but they can also be inhaled or injected, or passed through the skin.

Hundreds of substances are poisonous. Among the most well known are:

- acetone
- alcohol
- ammonia
- arsenic
- atropine
- curare
- ergotamine
- formaldehyde
- hydrogen cyanide
- iron
- lead
- mercury
- nicotine
- organophosphates
- opiates
- paracetamol/ acetaminophen
- ricin
- selenium
- strychnine
- vitamin A
- warfarin

Why does it kill?

Disruption of metabolic reactions involved in various cell functions, which can induce failure in the brain, liver, kidney or heart, or cardiac arrest.

DID YOU KNOW?

The word 'poison' comes from the Latin *potare*, meaning 'to drink', as adding poison to wine or beer was a popular means of assassination in ancient Rome.

Will it happen to me?

Anything is harmful in excess, and everyone is potentially at risk.

What to look for

Symptoms that can occur include: nausea, vomiting, diarrhoea, abdominal pain, changes in pupil size, dry mouth or excessive drooling, difficulty breathing, dizziness, confusion, weakness, sweating, clammy skin, rash, blurred vision, abnormal skin colour, drowsiness or hyperactivity, seizures or coma. However, many poisons cause no immediate symptoms until it is too late.

What are the chances of survival?

Some poisons have antidotes, but many do not. Medical treatment to remove the poison (stomach pump) and/or to administer an antidote can save lives. If you think you or someone else has been poisoned, call an ambulance or go to the nearest hospital emergency department without delay. Do not try to induce vomiting yourself. If easily available, take a sample of any substance that may have been the source of poison.

HOW TO AVOID IT

- **Keep medicines, cosmetics, cleaning products, DIY and garden chemicals safely out of the reach of children.**
- **Keep all chemicals in their original containers, preferably with childproof lids.**
- **Fit carbon monoxide detectors in your home (see page 55).**

Poliomyelitis 74

Poliomyelitis is caused by an intestinal enterovirus that is spread via the faeco-oral route (one person defecates it, others ingest it from contaminated food and water).

How common is it?

In 2010, 946 cases were reported; 200 people died during a polio outbreak affecting 500 people in the Congo alone.

Who dies?

Mainly children under the age of five, which is why it has the pseudonym of 'infantile paralysis'; however, in the latest outbreaks most victims were aged 15–29 years.

Where?

Polio remains endemic in just four countries; Afghanistan, India, Nigeria and Pakistan. Imported infection may have become re-established in Angola, Chad, the Democratic Republic of the Congo and Sudan.

When?

During the acute infection.

Why?

Damage to spinal and brain cells regulating vital automatic functions such as heart rate and breathing.

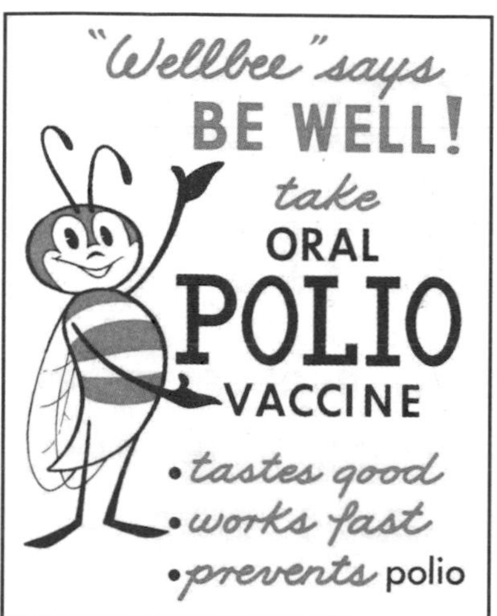

Although polio is highly infectious, many cases do not cause symptoms and go undiagnosed. In the late 1980s, polio affected as many as 350,000 people a year. Now, thanks to improved access to vaccination, the annual number of cases has dropped dramatically to less than 1000. One in 1000 children and 1 in 75 adults who get polio develop irreversible paralysis, usually affecting one or both legs. Up to 1 in 10 is unable to breathe unaided, owing to paralysis of their respiratory muscles. The mortality rate is as high as 47% in some outbreaks.

Why does it kill?

If the virus enters the central nervous system, it replicates in spinal motor neurones, causing damage that leads to paralysis. If it invades nerve cells in the brain stem (bulbar polio), the resulting encephalitis (brain inflammation and swelling) can kill. When cranial nerves are affected, the regulation of swallowing and breathing can lead to suffocation from mucus and spit accumulating in the lungs, or from paralysis of respiratory muscles and the diaphragm. This usually lasts for one or more weeks and, without access to artificial ventilation, death rapidly ensues. Paralysis can also kill by affecting blood pressure control or the heartbeat.

Will it happen to me?

If you are vaccinated, then no.

What to look for

After entering through the mouth, poliovirus multiplies in the intestines and may invade the nervous system to cause fever, headache, sore throat, fatigue, vomiting, stiff neck and painful limbs. Spasm and paralysis of one or more limbs may occur. Breathing may become increasingly difficult owing to paralysis of respiratory muscles.

What are the chances of survival?

Of those who are unvaccinated and infected, there is a 1 in 2 chance of surviving. Of those who survive, 1 in 2 develops post-polio syndrome with progressive muscle weakness, severe fatigue and muscle pain 15–40 years later.

HOW TO AVOID IT

Vaccination is essential. Oral and injected versions are used. The primary course of three doses is usually given in infancy, with boosters at 5 and 10 years later. Additional boosters may be needed if travelling to at-risk areas.

Pregnancy and birth 75

Pregnancy is not a disease, but sadly it can still kill. At least one woman dies every minute from a complication relating to pregnancy or childbirth.

How common is it?

Between 360,000 and 530,000 women die every year as a result of a maternity-related condition.

Who dies?

Of pregnancies that end in death, 99% involve women living in developing countries, especially those in rural areas. Complications relating to pregnancy and birth are the leading cause of death among adolescent girls in developing countries.

Where?

The risk of maternal death is highest in Africa (1 in 26), Oceania (1 in 62) and Asia (1 in 120). More than half of all deaths occur in sub-Saharan Africa and one-third in South Asia.

When?

Pregnancy and delivery are not supported by trained healthcare professionals.

Why?

Poverty, insufficient education and lack of access to health services, as well as cultural practices.

'Even people who aren't sick may not have optimal wellness.'

Brian Carter

DID YOU KNOW?

- Maternal deaths are classed as those occurring during pregnancy, or within 42 days afterwards, irrespective of the duration of pregnancy.
- They include deaths from any condition caused or aggravated by pregnancy, but not those that are accidental or incidental.

In addition to the statistics opposite, more than 3 million babies are stillborn every year, and an additional 3 million newborns die soon after birth.

Why does it kill?

Haemorrhage (25%), infections (15%), high blood pressure (12%), obstructed labour (8%), abortion (13%). Other causes include stroke, pulmonary embolism and heart attack.

Will it happen to me?

A woman's lifetime risk of a maternity-related death in a developed nation is 1 in 4300, compared with 1 in 120 in a developing country.

What to look for

Good healthcare screening and support during pregnancy, delivery and the postnatal period.

What are the chances of survival?

Most pregnancies follow a smooth path, and even when complications develop, there is a greater than 99.9% chance of survival if expert medical treatment is immediately available.

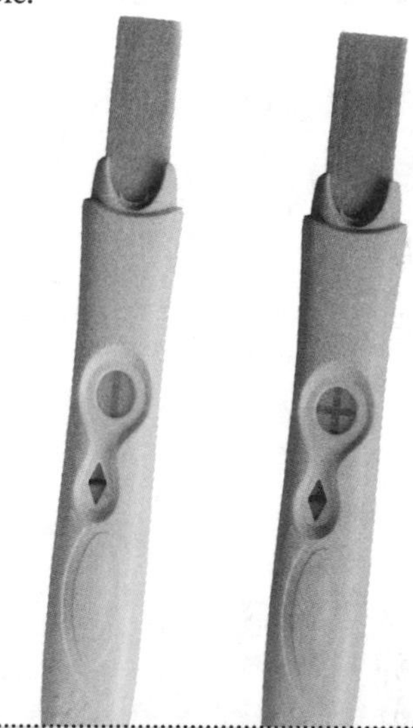

HOW TO AVOID IT

- Move to Ireland, where a woman's lifetime risk of a maternity-associated death is the lowest in the world at 1 in 48,000.
- Don't plan to have a baby in Niger where the risk is highest (1 in 7).
- Attend all maternity screening visits to which you are invited.
- Carefully weigh up the pros and cons of a hospital versus home birth, as 15% of deliveries need previously unpredicted emergency obstetric care.

Pulmonary embolism 76

Pulmonary embolism (PE) is due to a wandering clot that lodges in an artery within a lung.

How common is it?

Deep-vein thrombosis affects 1 in 2000 people in the general population (ranging from fewer than 1 in 3000 in people under the age of 40 up to 1 in 500 in those over 80). An estimated 6,873,180 people develop pulmonary thromboembolism each year, of whom 10% (687,300) will die within the first hour; another 30% will die later from recurrent embolism.

Who dies?

Twice as many women as men are affected as pregnancy and the contraceptive pill add to other risks such as immobility and recent surgery.

Where?

In continual cramped conditions; when bedridden.

When?

After being immobilized for at least 4 hours.

Why?

Increased stickiness of blood, or sluggish or restricted blood flow in the legs can cause a blood clot to develop in the deep veins – e.g. during long-haul air travel or pregnancy, or with hormone therapies, blood-clotting disorders, prolonged bed rest, injury, infection, surgery or diseases such as cancer. Increasing age and being overweight also make deep-vein thrombosis and pulmonary embolism more likely.

Clots often break off from a thrombus in the deep veins of the leg. Obstruction of blood flow through the lungs increases pressure within the right ventricle of the heart, leading to difficulty breathing, chest pain and palpitations. In severe cases, low blood pressure and collapse are followed by sudden death.

Economy class syndrome

Deep-vein thrombosis (DVT) that develops during a long flight has been dubbed 'economy class syndrome', as cheaper seats tend to have less leg room, encouraging minimal movement. DVT can also occur when travelling in business (club) or first class, and when travelling by car, train or bus. The risk doubles after sitting still, for any reason, for more than 4 hours. If you have a pre-existing risk factor such as recent surgery, the risk triples after sitting still for more than 3 hours. Those who are more vulnerable include pregnant women, obese people, those whose feet don't reach the floor when sitting (so seats place pressure on the backs of the legs), elderly people, smokers, women taking the contraceptive pill, and those with coronary artery diseases and certain blood conditions. As the risk of a pulmonary embolism remains elevated for a month afterwards, taking multiple flights over a short period of time is particularly dangerous. Young, fit, athletic people are at risk, too. Although most of the deaths occur within hours of stepping off a plane, some happen weeks later when the link may not be so obvious.

ARE YOU AT RISK OF DEEP-VEIN THROMBOSIS?

In general, the risk of pulmonary embolism is greater in people who:

- are over 40 years of age
- are overweight
- smoke
- have had previous blood clots
- have a family history of blood clots
- have cancer, heart or lung disease, or circulation problems
- have certain blood diseases, especially abnormal blood-clotting factors
- have been immobilized because of recent illness, injury or surgery, especially orthopaedic surgery such as a hip- or knee-replacement

In women, deep-vein thrombosis is more common in those who:

- are pregnant
- have recently had a baby
- are taking the oral contraceptive pill
- are on hormone replacement therapy (HRT)

The more risk factors you have, the greater the risk of a pulmonary embolism. For example, being overweight has been shown to double the risk of thrombosis, but in women who are both overweight and take the oral contraceptive pill, the risk increases 10-fold.

Why does it kill?

Acute respiratory failure and circulatory collapse.

Will it happen to me?

The risk of a deep-vein thrombosis after sitting still for more than 4 hours is 1 in 6000. If you develop a DVT, the risk of dying from a pulmonary embolism is 1 in 100. If you develop a pulmonary embolism, the risk of dying as a result is 1 in 10.

What to look for

Deep-vein thrombosis causes pain, tenderness, redness and swelling of the affected area – most often in the lower leg. This is different from the mild ankle swelling that many people get during long-haul flights, and usually (though not always) affects just one leg. The pain may be worse when bending the foot upwards towards the knee.

Pulmonary embolism can cause a sudden shortness of breath, chest pain, rapid pulse, cough, haemoptysis (coughing up blood), blue discoloration of the lips (cyanosis).

What are the chances of survival?

At least 1 in 10 people with pulmonary embolism will die. The risk of death rises to 50% if the pulmonary embolism is massive enough to cause circulatory shock (low blood pressure with systolic BP < 90 mmHg). Rapid treatment with clot-busting drugs can be life-saving.

HOW TO AVOID IT

Nobody gives much thought about fitness to fly – anyone can get on a plane. Before travelling, ask yourself: am I fit to fly? If not, seek medical advice. When travelling:

- Get comfortable in your seat.
- Bend and straighten your legs, wriggle your toes and flex your ankles every half-hour or so while seated during the flight; press the balls of your feet down hard against the floor or foot-rest to increase blood flow.
- Do not cross your legs; upper-body and breathing exercises can further improve circulation.
- Get up regularly to walk around on a plane, train or bus.
- Take regular stops when travelling by car.
- Drink plenty of water.
- Avoid drinking too much alcohol on a train or plane.
- Consider wearing graduated compression stockings.
- Avoid taking sleeping pills, which also cause immobility.
- Blood-thinning drugs (low-molecular-weight heparin, fondaparinux) and leg-compression devices reduce the risk of deep-vein thrombosis and pulmonary embolism following surgery.
- Postpone a long-haul flight until 3 months after surgery.

Rabies 77

Rabies is a viral disease caused by a lyssavirus that is transmitted through contact with the saliva of infected wild and domestic animals. Culprits include dogs, bats, foxes, raccoons, skunks, jackals, mongooses and other wild carnivores. The rabies virus homes in on the brain, causing rabid behaviour and frothing at the mouth.

How common is it?
More than 55,000 people die every year.

Who dies?
Rabies is most common in children under 15, and the majority are male.

Where?
Rabies is present in more than 150 countries or territories; 95% of deaths occur in Asia and Africa.

When?
After contact with infected saliva through a pre-existing wound or a rabid bite – in 99% of cases from a dog; once symptoms develop (2–84 days, occasionally up to 2 years late) death follows within 2–10 days. The majority of victims are male.

Why?
Dogs are the source of 99% of human rabies deaths, and children (especially boys) are instinctively drawn to play with man's best friend.

As the virus is transmitted through contact with saliva, especially via a bite, it greatly increases the chance that it will be passed on. An estimated 3.3 billion people live with a significant risk of contracting rabies from dogs.

Why does it kill?

After entering the body through a wound, the rabies virus enters nerve endings and travels up nerve axons to reach the central nervous system. Inflammation of the brain (encephalitis) and spinal cord lead to either:

- furious rabies (70%) with hyperactivity, excitability, hydrophobia (so-called fear of water) and death by cardiac and respiratory arrest; or
- paralytic rabies (30%) with gradual paralysis, coma and death

The latter form is often misdiagnosed, so incidence is higher than is reported.

Will it happen to me?

The incubation period is anywhere from 9 days to many months, so if you've been bitten during the past year, there's still time to worry.

What to look for

Initially fever, headache, weakness and pain or sensations of tingling and burning at the wound site. This may be followed by insomnia, agitation, mania and delirium with hallucinations and paranoia. Copious amounts of infective saliva (and tears) are accompanied by painful muscle spasms, especially around the mouth when trying to drink. This is the basis of the classic frothing and so-called fear of water (hydrophobia). Alternatively, paralysis leads to coma within 2–10 days.

What are the chances of survival?

If immunization is not given before the onset of symptoms (usually within 6 days), it is almost always fatal. The controversial Milwaukee protocol, in which patients showing symptoms are placed in a chemical coma and given antiviral drugs, has a survival rate of 8%. This has allowed five patients to survive rabies without vaccination. In a revised version, two out of 10 patients treated survived, possibly improving the chance of survival to 20%, though numbers are small.

HOW TO AVOID IT

- **Stay away from unfamiliar animals, especially dogs and bats.**
- **Rapid wound cleansing (soap and water, iodine) and immunization within a few hours of being bitten can prevent rabies.**
- **Immunization delivers six doses of inactivated virus to stimulate an immune response. Rabies immunoglobulin may also be given.**
- **A course of three injections is given to those at risk of exposure, such as laboratory staff, quarantine centre staff and animal handlers. Boosters are needed every 2–3 years.**
- **Immunizing dogs against rabies can significantly reduce risk.**

Radiation poisoning 78

Radiation poisoning is a natural gift from our environment. We are continuously exposed to ionizing radiation from sunlight, cosmic rays and radioactive chemicals in the Earth's crust, and in our food and drink.

How common is it?

Radon causes 1 in 10 lung cancer deaths – 140,000 per year, on average. Ultraviolet radiation is linked with 3 million non-melanoma skin cancers and 132,000 melanoma skin cancers worldwide each year. One in every three cancers diagnosed is a skin cancer.

Who dies?

We are all at risk from natural radiation exposure; those working with radioactive isotopes or receiving cancer radiotherapy are at risk of accidental exposure. Those most at risk of skin cancer from ultraviolet rays are people with fair skin, who have a tendency to burn rather than tan, with multiple moles and freckles.

Where?

Anywhere in or on the planet.

When?

When radiation sufficiently damages your DNA.

Why?

Because that's how the universe works.

We tend to take these risks in our stride. Instead, we worry about irradiation from nuclear accidents, although the risk is relatively low.

Irradiation

The effective amount of radiation to which you are exposed can be measured in a traditional unit called the roentgen (rem) or a modern SI (Système international) unit called the sievert (Sv). The low level of natural background radiation is described in fractions of these units: thousandths of a rem, or millirems (mrem); thousandths of a sievert, or millisieverts (mSv); and millionths of a sievert, or microsieverts (μSv).

- 1 Sv = 100 rem
- 10 μSv = 1 mrem
- 1 mSv = 100 mrem

The average person is exposed to 360 mrem (3.6 mSv) radiation per year from natural sources. If you work in a nuclear power station, you receive an additional whole body equivalent dose of 300 mrem (3 mSv) per year on top of your background exposure. Flight crew spending 1000 hours on board planes acquire an additional radiation dose of 200–500 mrem (2–5 mSv).

One of our biggest sources of background irradiation is radon – a colourless, odourless, tasteless, radioactive gas formed naturally as uranium decays in rocks, soil, bricks and concrete. Radon seeps into our homes and workplaces from the ground (especially if you live over granite) and is exhaled from building materials.

Depletion of the ozone layer is letting through more ultraviolet rays. It is estimated that a 10% decrease in ozone levels will cause an additional 300,000 non-melanoma and 4500 melanoma skin cancers worldwide.

Why does it kill?

Radiation ionizes molecules in your body,

CHERNOBYL

In 1986, the Chernobyl nuclear power plant exploded in the Ukraine, with radioactive contamination spreading over Belarus, the Russian Federation and Ukraine. An estimated 5 million people lived in these contaminated areas. As a result, an additional 8250 solid cancers (especially thyroid cancer due to radioactive iodine) and 680 leukaemias are expected during the lifetimes of those exposed.

Dose	*Time of onset of symptoms*	*Risk of death without treatment*	*Risk of death with treatment*
100–200 rem (1–2 Sv)	2–6 hours	5%	0%
200–600 rem (2–6 Sv)	1–2 hours	75%	25%
600–800 rem (6–8 Sv)	10–60 minutes	100%	75%
> 800 rem (8 Sv)	<10 minutes	100%	100%

including your DNA (see page 107). This increases the chance of genetic mutations. A large dose causes acute radiation sickness, in which cells cannot divide or function properly. Damage to intestinal lining cells prevents the absorption of water or nutrients. Harm to bone marrow causes anaemia and reduced immune function, leading to sepsis. Cell damage increases the long-term risk of a cancer death by 0.08% per rem for doses received rapidly (acute), and 0.04% per rem for doses received over a long period (chronic).

Will it happen to me?

Your risk of dying from radiation poisoning is 1 in a million (unless you smuggle radioactive isotopes for a living).

What to look for

Varying degrees of nausea, headache, blood-stained vomit, bloody diarrhoea, weakness, poor wound healing, dizziness, disorientation and collapse. If you survive long enough, you can also expect some hair loss and an increased risk of cancer.

What are the chances of survival?

This depends on the dose of radiation to which you are exposed.

- <50 rem (0.5 Sv) produces changes that may go unnoticed (e.g. temporary low blood cell count).
- 100 rem (1 Sv) may cause mild nausea within 24–48 hours but rarely kills.
- Doses above this start to get serious (see box above).

HOW TO AVOID IT

- **Don't eat bananas, whose potassium-40 content is allegedly high enough to activate some radiation sensors.**
- **Have the radon levels in your home measured and take steps to reduce high levels, such as fitting special ventilators and sumps.**
- **Avoid the sun between 11 a.m. and 3 p.m. during summer (and when near the equator).**
- **Wear sunblock (but take vitamin D supplements to replace what you won't make in your skin).**
- **Avoid sun lamps and sunbeds.**

Respiratory failure

Respiratory failure is, as its name suggests, a life-threatening condition in which the lungs don't work as well as they should. The most common cause is chronic obstructive pulmonary disease (COPD), which includes chronic bronchitis and emphysema.

How common is it?

Over 3 million people die of COPD every year – 5% of global deaths; of these, 700,000 are due to indoor air pollution.

Who dies?

More women now die from lung disease than men; in the UK, for example, COPD has overtaken breast cancer as the fourth biggest female killer.

Where?

About 90% of deaths are in low- and middle-income countries.

When?

Twenty or more years after starting smoking or regular exposure to air-borne pollutants – diagnoses escalate from age 40 onwards.

Why?

Slow asphyxiation from lack of oxygen.

COPD is mostly related to cigarette smoke and exposure to indoor air pollution (burning solid fuels without a chimney), outdoor air pollution (industrialization, diesel fumes) and occupational exposure to dust, chemical vapours, irritants or fumes. Lung tissue can also be damaged by frequent episodes of pneumonia, especially during childhood.

Worldwide, an estimated 210 million people have COPD, and this figure will increase by more than a third over the next 10 years.

Why does it kill?

Damaged airways become stiff, inelastic and narrow. Inflammation triggers excess production of sputum, which further obstructs air flow and is easily infected (chronic bronchitis). Destruction of delicate walls between the lung air sacs (alveoli) reduces the surface area available for gaseous exchange (oxygen in, carbon dioxide out) – a condition known as emphysema. As lung function deteriorates, oxygen levels fall and carbon dioxide builds up in the circulation (hypercapnia), producing a narcotic effect – patients slowly lose consciousness and stop breathing. Death can also result from bronchopneumonia or heart failure (cor pulmonale) as the heart struggles to pump blood through stiff, damaged lungs.

Will it happen to me?

If you are regularly exposed to cigarette smoke, air pollution or inhaled chemicals, then most likely, yes.

What to look for

Shortness of breath, desperate gasping for air, persistent coughing and excessive production of sputum and catarrh. Two clinical types are seen: 'Pink Puffers' primarily have emphysema and manage to get enough oxygen to stay pink by huffing and puffing. 'Blue Bloaters' primarily have chronic bronchitis, and tend to become blue (cyanosed) through lack of oxygen while swelling with fluid (heart failure). It's preferable to be a 'Pink Puffer'.

What are the chances of survival?

If you remove yourself from the pollution damaging your lungs (stop smoking), the progress of COPD will slow. Airway constriction may partially recover, but structural damage to the alveoli is irreversible. COPD usually kills within 10 years of diagnosis. In some countries, however, diagnostic facilities are not readily available, even though it only involves blowing into a tube to measure the volume of air you can exhale (spirometry).

HOW TO AVOID IT

- **Never smoke, actively or passively.**
- **Avoid air pollutants.**
- **If walking, cycling or exercising in polluted areas, including near heavy traffic, consider wearing a face mask that filters out fine particles.**

Sepsis 80

Sepsis – often referred to as septicaemia or blood poisoning – is a life-threatening condition in which bacteria multiply within the bloodstream.

How common is it?

Sepsis is the second – if not the first – leading cause of death in non-heart patients in the world. Experts have claimed it is the cause of 1 in 4 hospital deaths and 70% of all child deaths, and at least the tenth most common cause of death overall – yet it is poorly recognized and poorly understood. An estimated 20 million cases occur worldwide each year (although only 1.8 million are documented), of whom at least 7 million die – almost 20,000 per day.

Who dies?

Anyone; the young and elderly are most at risk, especially if already ill and undergoing invasive medical or surgical procedures; people without a spleen, which filters bacteria from the blood and produces IgM (immunoglobulin M) antibodies, are also at increased risk.

Where?

Usually in an intensive care unit.

When?

When antibiotics, intravenous fluids, artificial ventilation, dialysis and drugs to increase blood pressure fail to resolve the situation.

Why?

The wrong bacterium, secreting the wrong toxin, in the wrong host, with the wrong immune response, at the wrong time; in other words, a combination of lots of bad luck.

DID YOU KNOW?

Bacteria are introduced into the blood circulation just by brushing your teeth. In most cases, the immune system eradicates them and they do not survive long enough to multiply.

Sepsis-causing bacteria trigger immune reactions and release toxins that can lead to septic shock with low blood pressure and an inability of the internal organs to work properly. Most of the damage occurs from the body's overwhelming immune response.

Although sepsis can result from even the slightest infected scratch, most cases occur as a result of medical procedures (such as insertion of a central intravenous line), surgery or perforation or rupture of the intestines. Sepsis can also complicate other sources of infection, such as an abscess, meningitis or urinary tract infection. At a recent Global Sepsis Alliance meeting, 150 experts from 18 countries declared that sepsis is responsible for the majority of deaths associated with HIV/AIDS, malaria, TB, pneumonia and other serious infections.

Why does it kill?

Circulating bacterial toxins can lead to widespread blood clotting (disseminated intravascular coagulation), and to multiple organ dysfunction syndrome, which results in respiratory failure, liver failure, kidney failure and/or heart failure.

Will it happen to me?

Your annual risk of developing sepsis is much greater than your risk of developing lung cancer, bowel cancer or breast cancer.

What to look for

You will feel very ill with fever, chills, rigors (shakes), rapid pulse, rapid breathing, vomiting, collapse.

What are the chances of survival?

Even with intensive care, the mortality rate is 35%, rising to 60% if shock (low blood pressure) is present.

HOW TO AVOID IT

- **Breastfeeding helps to protect infants**
- **Have recommended vaccinations**
- **Maintain good hygiene practices**
- **Clean wounds thoroughly**
- **Avoid having your spleen removed unless absolutely essential**
- **If your spleen is removed, take prophylactic antibiotics long term**
- **Consider probiotics to help boost immunity**

Shock 81

The popular idea of shock is one of emotional stress in the face of a terrifying or traumatic event – like seeing a ghost. Although this can lead to death by heart attack, medical shock is a different thing entirely and describes a catastrophic circulatory collapse.

How common is it?

Technically, everyone dies of shock when their heart stops beating as their circulation and blood pressure then collapse. Mortality rates for shock are not available, as deaths are attributed to the underlying injury or disease rather than the person's physical state just before death. Cardiogenic shock is diagnosed in 10% of patients admitted to hospital with a heart attack (however, many will already have succumbed before reaching hospital). Septic shock is diagnosed in 3% of hospital admissions.

Who dies?

Anyone.

Where?

Usually just before, during or after arrival in hospital.

When?

Following a heart attack, infection, surgery or other problem.

Why?

Inability to maintain blood pressure.

'Death is a once-in-a-lifetime experience.' Anonymous

The resulting low blood pressure (usually less than 80/60 mmHg) and reduced blood circulation means organs such as the brain and heart do not receive the oxygen, glucose and other nutrients they need. Unless blood pressure is restored, and quick, death soon follows.

Why does it kill?

Lack of blood to the vital organs, especially the heart and brain.

Will it happen to me?

If it does, hope that someone else calls for an urgent ambulance with lights and bells; you are unlikely to be aware of what is happening.

What to look for

Rapid weak pulse (more than 100 beats per minute), rapid shallow breathing, clammy and mottled peripheries, low blood pressure, low urine output, dizziness and faintness, confusion and loss of consciousness. Fever may be present in septic shock. If you experience chest pain that could be a heart attack (see page 114), seek immediate medical attention. Don't wait for shock to set in.

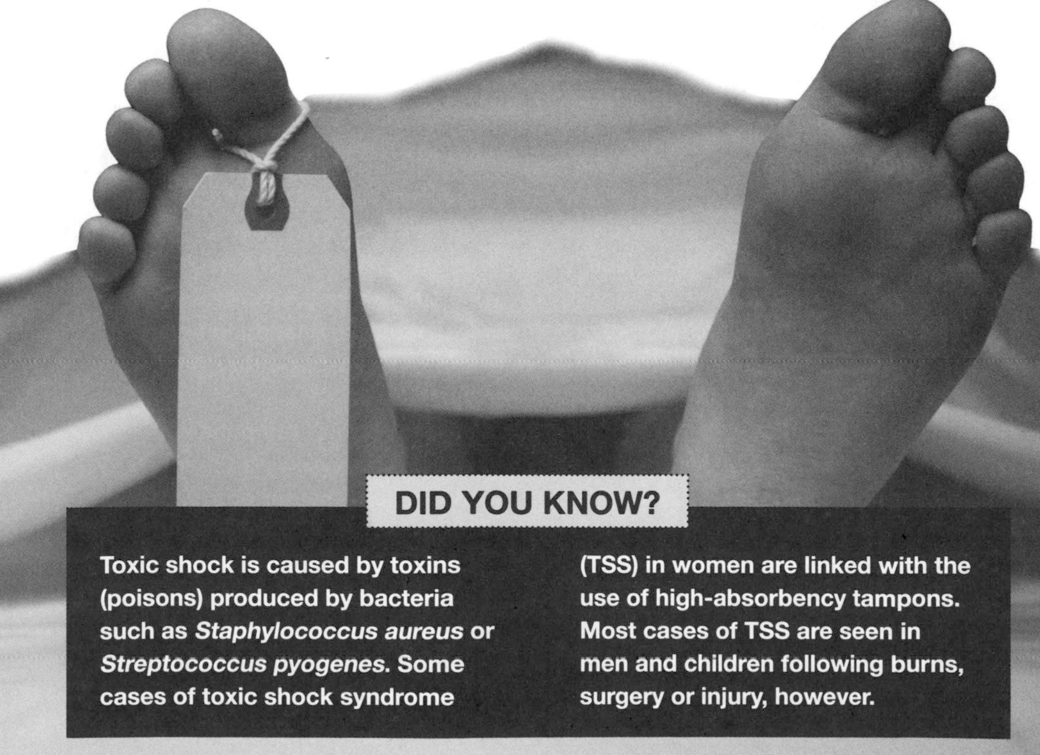

DID YOU KNOW?

Toxic shock is caused by toxins (poisons) produced by bacteria such as *Staphylococcus aureus* or *Streptococcus pyogenes*. Some cases of toxic shock syndrome (TSS) in women are linked with the use of high-absorbency tampons. Most cases of TSS are seen in men and children following burns, surgery or injury, however.

What are the chances of survival?

With excellent medical care, the mortality rate for septic shock is 50%, while for cardiogenic shock (see page 210) it has decreased from 85% to around 60% thanks to treatments such as 'clot-buster' drugs.

Cause	*Type of shock*
Loss of blood (haemorrhage) or body fluids (widespread burns, dehydration)	Hypovolaemic shock
Heart pump failure	Cardiogenic shock
Infection	Septic or toxic shock
Allergic reaction	Anaphylactic shock
Spinal damage	Neurogenic shock
Obstruction of blood flow (aortic stenosis, tension pneumothorax)	Obstructive shock
Surgery (when other causes are ruled out, shock during an operation may be related to fasting, anaesthesia, oxidative stress or reperfusion injury, in which inflammatory chemicals are washed back into the circulation from ischaemic tissues such as the liver when blood flow is re-established)	Surgical shock

HOW TO AVOID IT

As the most common type is cardiogenic shock, your best bet is to follow all the usual advice on how to prevent a heart attack (see page 116). To reduce the risk of tampon-associated toxic shock syndrome:

- **Always read the manufacturer's instruction leaflet.**
- **Wash hands before and after inserting the tampon as a part of normal hygiene practice. Use the lowest absorbency necessary for your flow. If, on changing the tampon, it is dry and difficult to remove, the absorbency is too high.**
- **Change the tampon at least as often as the manufacturer's instructions (4–8 hours).**
- **If instructions on the pack permit overnight usage, insert a fresh tampon last thing at night and remove it first thing in the morning.**
- **Vary the use of tampons with towels every now and then throughout the period.**
- **Never insert two tampons at the same time.**
- **Make sure the last tampon used during a period is removed.**

Sleeping sickness 82

Most of us would love nothing more than to lie down and sleep for a few days to recharge our physical and mental batteries. Unfortunately, many of those who do achieve this have sleeping sickness – one of the deadliest diseases in the world. Without treatment, it kills within days.

How common is it?

As recently as 1995, 60 million people were at risk, with an estimated annual death toll of 270,000. By 2004, increased fly control reduced deaths to an estimated 52,000 per year. The number of deaths is now estimated at between 10,000 and 50,000 per year and elimination is considered feasible.

Who dies?

Poor people living in remote rural areas of Africa, especially along the Congo river.

Where?

In bed, asleep, in one of 36 countries in sub-Saharan Africa, especially Angola, the Democratic Republic of the Congo and Sudan.

When?

Several months, sometimes years, after being bitten by an infected tsetse fly.

Why?

Lack of medical treatment.

Sleeping sickness, or human African trypanosomiasis, is caused by a single-celled parasitic protozoan. Ninety per cent of cases are due to *Trypanosoma brucei rhodesiense* (East Africa) and 10% to *T. b. gambiense* (West and Central Africa), which infects cattle, pigs and human beings. Another strain, *Trypanosoma evansi*, which usually infects horses and camels, has caused a handful of human cases in India. These parasites are injected into the circulation by the bite of the blood-sucking tsetse fly (*Glossina sp.*), which resembles the common housefly except that it has a sharp needle-like proboscis, and when at rest it folds one wing on top of the other along its back.

Once in the body, the parasites multiply in the lymph and blood for a variable amount of time (stage 1). *T. b. rhodesiense* tends to cause acute disease within weeks to months, while *T. b. gambiense* tends to lie hidden for several years. It then invades the brain (stage 2) and is soon fatal unless diagnosed and treated.

Why does it kill?

The parasite crosses the blood–brain barrier into the central nervous system, invading the brain to cause psychosis, seizures, sleepiness, coma and then death.

Will it happen to me?

If you visit an endemic area and are bitten by an infected tsetse fly, then yes. Sexual transmission is theoretically possible but probably rare.

What to look for

Initially headaches, fever, sweating, itching, weakness and stiff painful joints. Swelling of lymph nodes along the back of the neck is a classic giveaway, known as Winterbottom's sign. As the parasite crosses the blood–brain barrier into the central nervous system, it results in major sleep-cycle disturbances and personality changes before death.

What are the chances of survival?

Without treatment, sleeping sickness is always fatal. Medical treatment with drugs such as eflornithine plus nifurtimox, are usually effective at producing a cure. Reinfection is common when returning home, however.

HOW TO AVOID IT

- **No vaccines are available. Avoid endemic areas. If you must visit, take insect repellents and a fly swat and sleep under an insecticide-impregnated net.**
- **Avoid the need for an urgent blood transfusion.**
- **Eradication is being attempted by releasing sterile male flies into endemic regions. The females usually mate only once, so if her partner is sterile, fly numbers rapidly plummet.**

Smoking 83

Smoking is a leading cause of statistics. Out of more than 1 billion smokers worldwide, an estimated 5 million die every year as a direct result of their chosen habit. And if current trends continue, another 1000 million will die a smoking-related death during the 21st century.

How common is it?

Smoking-related diseases kill 1 in 10 adults across the world.

Who dies?

One in two smokers dies of a smoking-related cancer, often taking an unsuspecting passive smoker with them.

Where?

Asia houses one-third of the world's population but over half the world's smokers. The highest rates of smoking-related deaths are reported in Bangladesh, Pakistan, China, Japan and Vietnam.

When?

Prematurely, often in middle age.

Why?

Smoking is often started in an attempt to look sophisticated, which backfires.

It's hardly surprising that the World Health Organization condemns smoking as the single greatest cause of preventable death across the globe.

Why does it kill?

Cigarettes expose smokers to 4000 different chemicals, of which at least 60 are carcinogenic and 400 are toxic. These include benzene (petrol additive), ammonia (toilet cleaner), acetone (nail varnish remover), arsenic, cyanide and formaldehyde, which, perhaps appropriately, doubles up as embalming fluid.

These chemicals infiltrate the body to trigger a smörgåsbord of diseases ranging from gangrene to the increased accumulation of belly-button fluff. Although some resulting conditions, such as impotence and halitosis, only kill your ardour, others are eventually lethal. Half of all smokers will die from cancer while the other half will succumb to diseases such as heart attack (see page 114), asthma (see page 34), chronic bronchitis and emphysema (see page 206), gangrene, pneumonia (see page 190) or stroke (see page 222).

TWELVE TOP TIPS TO QUIT

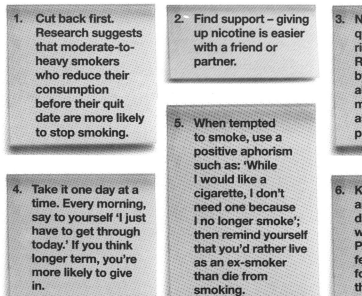

1. Cut back first. Research suggests that moderate-to-heavy smokers who reduce their consumption before their quit date are more likely to stop smoking.
2. Find support – giving up nicotine is easier with a friend or partner.
3. Name the day to quit and get into the right frame of mind. Reduce temptation by throwing away all smoking papers, matches, lighters, ashtrays and spare packets beforehand.
4. Take it one day at a time. Every morning, say to yourself 'I just have to get through today.' If you think longer term, you're more likely to give in.
5. When tempted to smoke, use a positive aphorism such as: 'While I would like a cigarette, I don't need one because I no longer smoke'; then remind yourself that you'd rather live as an ex-smoker than die from smoking.
6. Keep a quit chart and tick off every day you achieve without a cigarette. Promise yourself a feel-good reward for every week that you complete successfully.

'People are so rude to smokers. You'd think they'd be nicer to people who are dying.' Anonymous

And these terminal diseases rarely strike singly or quickly. They frequently go round slowly, in pairs. Most puffers develop two or more smoking-related illnesses and suffer a lingering death attached to an oxygen cylinder or confined to bed. Sadly, half of these deaths occur during middle age.

Will it happen to me?

Undoubtedly if you smoke. You are also at risk if your mother or father smoked before, during or after your conception. Those exposed passively in the home, workplace or when trapped in a car with a smoker should complain as quickly as possible. Legislation in many countries now bans smoking in public buildings, including pubs and nightclubs.

What to look for

If you smoke, it is safe to assume that any symptom you experience is smoking-related, whether it's an unexpected lump, pain, blood-stained secretion or ingrowing toenail. Report any persistent symptoms to your doctor and mention your smoking habit.

7. **Keep your hands busy – model-making, DIY, worry balls, painting, embroidery, knitting or origami help overcome the hand-to-mouth habit that is difficult to break.**
8. **Identify situations where you used to smoke and either avoid them or practise saying 'No thanks, I've given up.'**
9. **Ask friends and relatives not to smoke around you.**
10. **Using hypnotherapy or nicotine replacement therapy can make quitting easier.**
11. **When you have an overwhelming urge to smoke, go for a brisk walk – exercise releases opium-like endorphins in your brain to curb withdrawal symptoms. As a bonus, it's good for your heart and lungs.**
12. **Try chewing sugar-free gum or suck on an artificial cigarette made from celery or carrot sticks to help cope with urges.**

What are the chances of survival?

All is not lost. Each year thousands of people successfully stop smoking and dramatically improve their chances of a longer and healthier lifespan. Most people who smoke realize the health dangers. Surveys suggest 79% of smokers want to give up, but nicotine is highly addictive, making it difficult to quit. Withdrawal symptoms of tension, aggression, depression, insomnia and both physical and psychological cravings will do their utmost to derail you. These symptoms are not insuperable, however, and once you do quit, your risk of death starts to decrease almost immediately.

- Within 20 minutes: blood pressure and pulse rate will fall significantly as arterial spasm decreases.
- Within 8 hours: levels of carbon monoxide in your blood drop to normal, so your blood oxygen levels can rise.
- Within 48 hours: the stickiness of your blood and the quantity of blood-clotting factors present will fall enough to halve your risk of a heart attack or stroke.
- Within 1–3 months: the blood supply to your peripheries (hands, toes, penis, brain) increases, and your lung function will improve by up to a third.
- Within 5 years: your risk of lung cancer will have halved. Within 10 years: your risk of a smoking-related cancer will have reduced to almost normal levels. Within 15 years: your risk of a heart attack is back to the same level as if you had never smoked at all.

HOW TO AVOID IT

- **It is never too late to quit smoking. If you can give up in middle age (assuming you make it that far) you have a good chance of avoiding a smoking-related death.**
- **The quit rate with nicotine replacement therapy is two or three times higher than when trying to give up unaided.**
- **Antidepressant drugs such as bupropion or nortriptyline are sometimes prescribed to help people quit smoking. Their effectiveness appears to be similar to that of nicotine replacement therapy.**

Snoring 84

Snoring kills, and not just because of the homicidal tendencies it may evoke in your room mate or bed partner.

How common is it?

Snoring affects 45% of the population from time to time, and an estimated 25% of middle-aged adults are habitual snorers. Over 40% of those who snore have obstructive sleep apnoea (OSA) but most are unaware they are affected. It is estimated that, overall, 6% of men and 2% of women have clinically significant OSA. Incidence rises with age.

Who dies?

Men are three times more vulnerable than women; it is four times more common in men with Type 2 diabetes than those without, even after taking weight into account.

Where?

In whatever passes for your bed.

When?

During sleep.

Why?

Often (but not always) because fat around the neck obstructs the airway; most sufferers have a collar size greater than 17 inches (43 cm) for men, or 16 inches (41 cm) for women.

Snoring is associated with obstructive sleep apnoea (OSA), in which you literally stop breathing during sleep. Occasionally, you fail to restart.

OSA results when your throat muscles relax and your upper airway sags, or your tongue falls back. This stops you breathing while you are asleep. Carbon dioxide (the body's exhaust gas) builds up in the circulation to activate a survival mechanism in your brain so that breathing restarts. As your airway jerks open again, a gasp occurs and you may briefly wake up. These apnoeic episodes last for at least 10 seconds. The severity of OSA is classified according to the number of times per night you stop breathing or experience significantly reduced airflow. Those with moderate to severe OSA (15 or more episodes per hour) are six times more likely to die over a 14-year follow-up period than those without OSA.

Why does it kill?

Accidents from daytime sleepiness. OSA also increases the risk of high blood pressure, heart failure, coronary heart disease and stroke. Sometimes breathing just fails to restart.

Will it happen to me?

If you are overweight, with fat stored around your neck, and/or have enlarged glands (tonsils, adenoids or thyroid) or a nasal obstruction (polyps, deviated septum), or drink alcohol, smoke cigarettes or take sleeping tablets, then you are potentially at risk.

DID YOU KNOW?

- Playing the didgeridoo can improve snoring and sleep apnoea by strengthening throat muscles in the upper airway.
- At least one person per year is murdered because of their snoring.
- In very obese people, OSA is referred to as Pickwickian Syndrome – named after Joe, the fat, red-faced boy in Charles Dickens' novel *The Pickwick Papers*.

What to look for

An angry glint in your bed partner's eye most mornings, and complaints about your snoring. Other giveaways include:

- waking up feeling hungover – even though you've had no alcohol
- waking up with a frightening sensation of choking and fighting for air
- morning headaches
- excessive daytime sleepiness
- lack of concentration
- poor memory – thoughts peter out mid-sentence
- constant yawning from lack of oxygen
- poor driving skills, which can lead to accidents
- low sex drive

What are the chances of survival?

If you lose weight, stop smoking, take up exercise and use antisnoring devices, your chances are good. A stimulant drug, modafinil, is licensed in some countries to treat excessive sleepiness in people with OSA. Dental appliances worn at night may stop the tongue falling back or may lift the soft palate or uvula (the dangly part on a stalk at the back of your throat) to keep the airway open. If the weight continues to pile on, however, you may want to explore surgical options (a gastric band to lose weight, or surgery to trim a floppy soft palate).

HOW TO AVOID IT

- **Lose any excess weight (though 50% of sufferers aren't clinically obese) and increase your level of physical activity to improve muscle tone.**
- **Raise the head of your bed about 10 cm (4 in) to help stop your tongue flopping back.**
- **Try using special antisnoring pillows, devices and/or sprays.**

Stroke 85

When you imagine a stroke victim do you think of a frail old lady, or an overweight middle-aged businessman? Think younger.

How common is it?

Stroke accounts for an estimated 8.6% of all deaths in males and 11% of deaths in females. Worldwide, 3 million women and 2.5 million men die from stroke every year. Some experts have suggested that stroke may eventually become the most common cause of death worldwide, as cancer and heart disease treatments improve.

Who dies?

Adults of all ages; women in their late 40s and early 50s are twice as likely to have a stroke as men in this age group.

Where?

The highest number of deaths from stroke occur in India, China and the Russian Federation.

When?

More people die of ischaemic stroke in the spring than in any other season – this effect has been noted worldwide. Significantly more strokes occur during the day than at night, with two peaks: between 8 a.m. and 10 a.m. and between 4 p.m. and 6 p.m.

Why?

Sudden loss of blood supply to part of the brain.

Although stroke is the third-leading cause of death (after heart attack and cancer) in people aged over 60, it is also the fifth-leading cause of death in people aged 15–59 years.

Stroke – also known as a cerebrovascular accident, apoplexy or (less elegantly) a brain attack – is caused by a sudden interruption of blood flow to part of the brain. There are two main types:

- ischaemic stroke owing to interruption of blood supply – from a blood clot forming within a brain artery (thrombosis, 45% of cases) or from a clot formed elsewhere lodging within the brain (embolism, 35%)
- haemorrhagic stroke, in which a ruptured blood vessel bleeds into or over the brain (20%)

Why does it kill?

When deprived of blood supply, brain cells (neurons) stop functioning within 90 seconds, from lack of oxygen and glucose. Anaerobic respiration leads to abnormal brain cell function and a buildup of acids and other toxins. If good blood supply is not reinstated within 3 hours, these cells will die (although rapid chilling can prolong their survival). Death of brain tissue is known as cerebral infarction. If the affected area regulates vital functions (e.g. respiration, heart rate), then death of the patient may result. Other causes of death include increased pressure within the skull.

Will it happen to me?

If you live to the age of 85 years, you have a 1 in 5 chance of experiencing a stroke. Your risk of dying from a stroke is increased by:

- 420% if you have had a previous stroke or TIA (mini-stroke)
- 140% if you have atrial fibrillation (fast, irregular heartbeat)
- 84% if you have high blood pressure
- 83% if you have impaired glucose tolerance
- 38% if you have coronary artery disease

SURVIVAL GUIDE

If two or more of these apply to you (or you don't know the answer), see your doctor for assessment:

- **you are a man aged over 45, or a woman over 55**
- **your father or brother had a heart attack before age 55, or your brother or sister had one before they were 65**
- **you have had heart disease, a heart attack, a stroke or abnormal heartbeat**
- **you smoke (either actively or passively)**
- **your total cholesterol or LDL-cholesterol is raised or your 'good' HDL-cholesterol is low**
- **your blood pressure is 140/90 mmHg or higher**
- **you don't exercise for at least 30 minutes most days**
- **you are overweight by 9 kg (20 lb) or more**

However, a third of strokes are unpredicted, and may result from a congenital weakness or abnormality in the brain circulation, such as a small 'berry' aneurysm.

What to look for

Symptoms and signs vary, depending on the part of the brain affected, but they usually come on quickly. A stroke may produce the following:

- sudden loss of consciousness
- confusion or loss of memory
- loss of movement of part of the body (e.g. a limb) or several parts, usually on just one side (e.g. left arm, left leg and left side of the face)
- numbness in part of the body
- difficulty speaking or understanding speech
- problems with swallowing
- trouble seeing with one or both eyes
- difficulty walking
- dizziness and/or loss of balance or coordination
- severe headache with no known cause
- fainting or unconsciousness

If you suspect a stroke – call an ambulance.

What are the chances of survival?

Even though stroke is the leading cause of disability in many countries (suggesting a good survival rate), the risk of death approaches 60%. A clot-dissolving drug (tPA, or tissue plasminogen activator) can reduce death and long-term disability when given within 3 hours of an ischaemic stroke.

The chance of surviving a TIA (transient ischaemic attack) is highest as, by definition, symptoms resolve with 24 hours. There is somewhat less chance of surviving a stroke caused by carotid stenosis (narrowing of an artery in the neck). There is even less chance of surviving a stroke due to a blockage of an artery, while a ruptured cerebral blood vessel is the most dangerous type of all.

HOW TO AVOID IT

- **Smoking increases the risk of stroke by two- to three-fold. Lack of exercise and unhealthy diet are the other two main risk factors.**
- **Know your blood pressure – for every 10 people who die of stroke, four could have been saved if their blood pressure had been controlled.**
- **Ensure your cholesterol and glucose levels are well controlled, exercise regularly and maintain a healthy weight.**
- **On the diet front, cut back on salt and alcohol intake while increasing your intake of fruit and vegetables – five or six portions daily can reduce the risk of stroke by up to 30%. Eating fish on a weekly basis may reduce the risk of stroke by 12%, with possible additional reductions of 2% per serving per week (or take fish oil supplements).**

Substance abuse 86

Persistent substance abuse is perpetuated by an addiction that produces cravings and unpleasant symptoms ('cold turkey') on withdrawal for any length of time.

How common is it?

Every year, alcohol abuse kills 2.5 million people (3.8 % of total, see page 13); illicit drug use kills 200,000 (0.4% of deaths); tobacco kills 4.9 million people (8.8% of all deaths, see page 215) and is predicted to kill 10 million per year by the mid 2020s. Eight times as many young people die from solvent abuse as from illegal drugs.

Who dies?

Usually the most vulnerable and marginalized members of society; 70% of deaths occur in developing countries; three times as many adolescents die from solvent abuse as from illicit drug use.

Where?

Everywhere, in all sectors of society.

When?

The amount inhaled or consumed exceeds the body's ability to cope.

Why?

Boredom, experimentation and a need to escape from reality.

'I'm on so many pills now, I'll need a childproof lid on my coffin.' Paul O'Grady

Worldwide, at least:

- 2 billion people abuse alcohol
- 1.3 billion abuse tobacco
- 185 million abuse illicit drugs; of these:
- 147 million abuse cannabis
- 14 million abuse opiates, including 9.2 million who use heroin
- 13 million abuse cocaine

Globally, 29 million children have abused a volatile solvent (sniffing or huffing glue, lighter fuel, cleaning fluids, petrol) at least once, by the age of 12, to get high.

Why does it kill?

Volatile solvents have an anaesthetic effect that can cause sudden heart arrhythmia, or coma and death during acute intoxication. Pressurized liquids such as butane cool rapidly to −20 °C (−4 °F) as they expand, and when inhaled can cause frostbite and prolonged laryngospasm (throat constriction) and hypoxia (lack of oxygen). Half of deaths occur through accidents, choking on vomit or suffocation.

Will it happen to me?

Some people are more prone to chemical dependency than others. Several major risk factors have been identified:

- genetic inheritance – if a parent is dependent on alcohol each offspring has a 40% chance of the same problem
- childhood experiences – dysfunctional or abusive families
- current peer group – the stronger the pressure to 'fit in' by experimenting, the more likely you are to succumb
- current life situation – the more desperate you are to escape, the more likely you are to indulge
- the addictive potential of the substance(s) to which you are exposed

What to look for

Paint stains on fingers, mouth or clothes, vomiting, red or watery eyes or nose, chemical odour on the breath, dazed or dizzy appearance, irritability or excitability.

What are the chances of survival?

Continuing addiction usually leads to premature loss of life, whether through chemical damage to the body, accidents or brushes with violence. If you successfully kick a habit for life, then you have a good chance of surviving. Unfortunately, most addictions are like a revolving door – no sooner are you out then you're right back in again. Compulsions are powerful things.

HOW TO AVOID IT

If anyone really knew the answer to this there would already be significantly fewer addictions and deaths from substance abuse. If you think you are at risk of an addiction, don't try to manage it on your own. Seek help.

Sudden arrhythmic death syndrome 87

Sudden arrhythmic death syndrome is as scary as it sounds. A seemingly healthy, usually young, person simply drops dead for no apparent reason. One minute they're fit and well. The next they are not.

How common is it?

Worldwide, an estimated 1 in 7000 people have something called long QT syndrome; 1 in 330 people in the West and 1 in 70 in Asia have Brugada syndrome; 1 in 10,000 people have CPVT (see page 228 for more on all of these). The number of cases of sudden adult death syndrome is unknown but, based on typical figures, 55,500 cases worldwide is a reasonable estimate.

Who dies?

Usually fit young adults; sudden death due to Brugada syndrome is unusually common in Asia, especially Thailand and Laos.

Where?

On the sports field, walking round town, at home, in bed – anywhere.

When?

Often during exercise or emotional upset; some are made worse by exercise, some by sleep.

Why?

Abnormal heart rhythm or abnormality of the heart conduction system.

If a cause of death is not apparent at autopsy, it is assumed to result from an abnormal heart rhythm. Those that occur during sleep are known as sudden unexpected nocturnal death syndrome. These awful events are thought to result from an underlying abnormality of electrical conduction in heart muscle, involving the membrane channels through which salts flow in and out of heart muscle cells (ion channels) or the electrical pathways in the heart. Similar abnormalities, sometimes hereditary, may account for many cases of sudden infant death syndrome.

Potential causes of sudden arrhythmic death syndrome, which can be diagnosed only with a heart tracing (electrocardiogram or ECG) during life, include: conditions called long QT syndrome and short QT syndrome; Wolff-Parkinson-White syndrome; Brugada syndrome; catecholaminergic polyventricular tachycardia (CPVT); progressive ventricular fibrillation; and sodium channel disease.

When an underlying cause of sudden death is found during autopsy, this will be cited on the death certificate instead – e.g. heart attack, cardiomyopathy, congenital heart disease, valvular heart disease, viral inflammation of the heart (myocarditis), pulmonary embolism or stroke.

Why does it kill?

Sudden cessation of heartbeat due to abnormal flow of electrolytes or electrical signals in the heart. This causes a short-circuit and stops the propagation of the signal that usually triggers the heartbeat.

Will it happen to me?

Your risk of experiencing a sudden unexplained death is approximately 1 in 124,000 per year – not something to worry about unless you have a family history of it.

What to look for

Sometimes there are no warning signs, or victims complain of dizziness or feeling faint, or experience palpitations, unusual chest discomfort or shortness of breath. Seek medical advice even if you feel fit and well.

What are the chances of survival?

Brugada syndrome was first recognized from the abnormal heart tracings (ECG) of men who were resuscitated from sudden arrhythmic death syndrome, so it can be survived with rapid medical intervention. If diagnosed during life, certain conditions can be treated with drugs that reduce heart arrhythmias (e.g. betablockers) or with surgery.

HOW TO AVOID IT

- **If sudden adult death has occurred in your family, ask to have cardiac tests (including an electrocardiogram, or ECG) to see if you could have one of the known underlying heart conduction abnormalities associated with this condition.**
- **Avoid competitive sports and severe exertion.**
- **Invest in a home defibrillator and make sure the people you live with know how to use it.**

Suicide 88

The global suicide rate is 16 per 100,000 people, representing almost 2% of deaths overall. Unsuccessful attempts – known as parasuicide – are 15–20 times more prevalent. Europe has the world's highest suicide rate and, tragically, the incidence is increasing among younger people. In those aged 15–24, suicide is the second most frequent cause of death after road accidents.

How common is it?
Globally, around 1 million people kill themselves each year, equivalent to one person every 40 seconds.

Who dies?
Women are more likely to attempt suicide; men are three times more likely to succeed.

Where?
Often away from home, to save loved ones the trauma of discovery.

When?
More often in spring and summer, usually after drinking alcohol.

Why?
Feelings of desperation and hopelessness; in many cases, suicide is associated with an untreated mental illness such as depression.

'My work is done. Why wait?' George Eastman's suicide note

DID YOU KNOW?

- The term 'suicide' comes from the Latin *sui caedere*, meaning to kill oneself, which suggests it may have been a problem in ancient Rome.
- Someone who has attempted suicide once is 100 times more likely to do so again.
- 40% of people who die by suicide have attempted suicide before.

Why does it kill?

Suicide is the result of self-poisoning or self-harm. The exact cause of death depends on the method chosen, which will impair the function of vital organs such as the brain, heart or lungs in some way.

Methods vary depending on the situation and equipment available. At one time, putting your head in a gas oven was popular in the UK, but the switch from coal gas to natural gas (which lacks carbon monoxide and smells unpleasant) has virtually eradicated this method. Other chosen modes of death include: drug overdose; eating/drinking poison; inhaling car exhaust fumes; shooting; hanging; jumping from a height; throwing oneself in front of a train or other vehicle; slashing wrists; drowning; suffocation; falling on a sword (or knife); driving into a wall at speed; and 'suicide by cop', in which a deliberately threatening manner attracts a lethal response from law-enforcement officers.

Women are more likely to commit suicide by taking an overdose, slashing their wrists or drowning. Men are more likely to shoot or hang themselves.

Will it happen to me?

Suicide is the 13th-leading cause of death worldwide. The overall risk that anyone will die from suicide is approximately 1 in 6900. In practice, however, only those experiencing extreme physical or emotional pain (beyond a level they can continue to endure) will contemplate this mode of death.

What to look for

If life no longer feels worth living, please seek immediate help.

HOW TO AVOID IT

If you feel depressed, that life is no longer worth living, or that you have no future, it is vital to seek help from your doctor. Don't try to cope on your own. You will also find it helpful to talk to someone in confidence. Befrienders Worldwide at www.befrienders.org provides contact details (24-hour helplines, websites, email) for organizations that provide emotional support and help to reduce suicide in your country.

Surgery and its complications

Every year, an estimated 235 million surgical operations are carried out throughout the globe. Even when an operation is deemed a success, the patient can still die, as most countries define a surgery-related death as one that occurs within 30 days of the procedure.

How common is it?
The overall risk of dying during surgery averages 1 in 200,000, but this includes people with serious underlying health problems.

Who dies?
Potentially anyone under the knife, but risks increase if you are obese, elderly, smoke or have a pre-existing condition such as angina, diabetes or chronic bronchitis.

Where?
On the operating table or during recovery in hospital; occasionally at home.

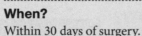

When?
Within 30 days of surgery.

Why?
From a number of shorter- and longer-term complications, including human error (see list under 'Why does it kill?').

'Before undergoing surgery, arrange your affairs – you may live.' Remy de Gourmont

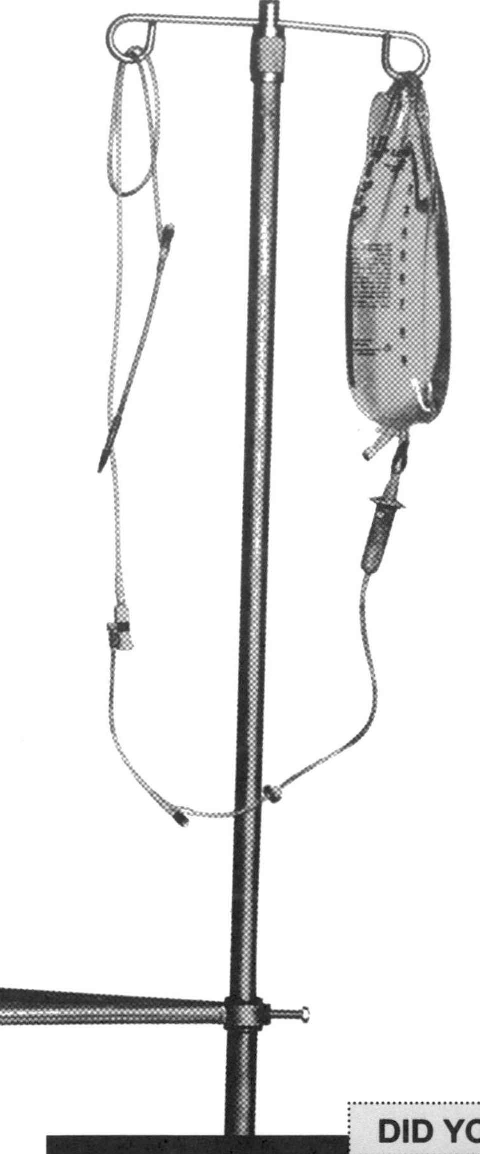

To improve safety, the WHO recently implemented a Surgical Safety Checklist. Dramatic results from a year-long pilot, in eight countries, suggest this could reduce the rate of complications and deaths by as much as one-third. This list reminds theatre staff to double-check incredibly basic things like the patient's name, operative site, allergies, airway access, risk of inhaling crowns, false teeth, anticipated blood loss, the number of instruments, sponges and needles used, and whether or not any malfunctioning equipment has been sorted out. Sometimes it's the little things that make the difference between life and death.

Why does it kill?

Before the days of anaesthesia or infection control, surgical mortality was high, with shock, sepsis and gangrene topping the list. Today, surgical mortality is more likely to result from one of the following complications, some more rare than others:

- receiving wrong gas mixture or other human error
- equipment failure
- compromised airway
- fluid and electrolyte imbalances
- haemorrhage

DID YOU KNOW?

Skilled at amputating a limb in 2 minutes, Scottish surgeon Robert Liston (1794–1847) performed the only known operation with a mortality rate of 300%. He managed to kill his patient (gangrene), his assistant (sepsis after losing his fingers) and a distinguished spectator who dropped dead from 'fright' (heart attack) when his coat tails were slashed. In another case, Liston's enthusiasm removed a patient's testicles along with his leg.

'Any fool can cut off a leg, but it takes a surgeon to save one'.

Anonymous

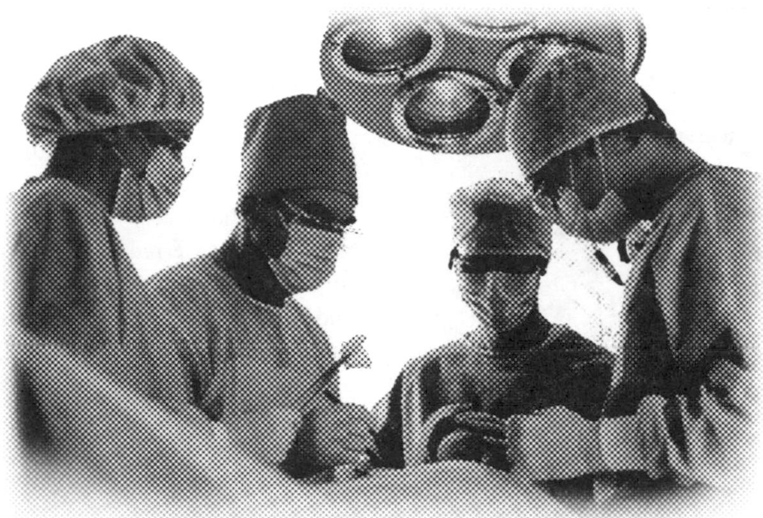

- low blood pressure (surgical shock)
- heart rhythm abnormalities
- heart attack
- pulmonary embolus
- stroke
- seizure
- pneumonia
- peritonitis
- sepsis
- allergic drug reaction
- asthmatic attack
- aspiration pneumonia
- collapsed lung (pneumothorax)
- pulmonary embolism
- perforation of internal organs
- elevated temperature (hyperthermia)
- blood transfusion mismatch
- acute kidney failure
- congestive heart failure
- respiratory failure
- multi-organ failure
- leakage of surgically joined intestines (anastomosis)
- hospital-acquired superbug
- picking up a blood-borne infection
- unexplained coma

Will it happen to me?

All surgical operations entail some risk. In the 1950s, the death rate just from general anaesthesia (without the surgery) was estimated at 1 in 10,000 in otherwise healthy people. Now, the mortality rate from anaesthesia alone is considerably lower at 1 in 200,000. When surgery is added, the mortality rate climbs to 1 in 125 overall. Before implementation of the WHO Surgical Safety Checklist, however, it was 1 in 67. The exact risk depends on the underlying condition in the body where the surgeon is daring to tread.

Surgical procedure	*Mortality rate*
Emergency laparotomy	1 in 5*
Colorectal resection	1 in 25
Coronary-artery bypass graft	1 in 30
Hip replacement	1 in 100
Carotid endarterectomy	1 in 260
Carpal tunnel release	1 in 400
Thyroidectomy	1 in 500
Open prostatectomy	1 in 1000
Hysterectomy	1 in 1250
Caesarean section	1 in 10,000
Tonsillectomy	1 in 15,000

* *This rate is high as patients are usually very sick, often with widespread infection of the abdominal cavity (peritonitis).*

What to look for

You will remain blissfully unaware when serious complications arise during the operation itself.

What are the chances of survival?

Mortality rates depend as much on your age, weight and general health as on the procedure and the skill of your surgeon. Some operations carry such a high mortality rate they are referred to as 'kiss of death' surgery. Few surgeons, for example, will undertake abdominal surgery during acute pancreatitis. Most blanch at the thought of a ruptured aortic aneurysm (see page 29). Typical mortality rates for common procedures are shown in the opposite table.

HOW TO AVOID IT

- View your hospital's mortality statistics.
- Choose your surgeon and anaesthetist carefully.
- Some countries even publish the personal mortality rating for individual surgeons. However, this can mislead as statistics are skewed when a surgeon performs only a small number of cases, dares to take on emergency patients or attempts kiss-of-death surgery that others (with an eye on their rating) have turned down.
- Try to be as fit and healthy as your condition allows.
- Lose at least some excess weight beforehand.
- If you smoke, do your utmost to stop.
- Ensure your hospital has implemented the WHO Surgical Safety Checklist.
- In general, keyhole surgery, in which a surgeon makes a tiny hole, is safer than traditional open surgery (with a larger wound).

Syphilis 90

Syphilis, also known as the Great Pox, is a sexually transmissible disease caused by a bacterium, *Treponema pallidum*. This affliction has shaped history.

How common is it?

There are 12 million cases worldwide each year, with an estimated 155,000 deaths.

Who dies?

Currently prevalent in middle-aged divorced males with 'safe-sex fatigue'; if not treated, it kills a decade or two later in their 50s and 60s; it also crosses the placenta to cause an estimated 492,000 stillbirths and infant deaths each year.

Where?

Traditionally in developing countries, where testing is not widely available, but infection rates have increased 10-fold in developed countries over the past decade.

When?

Ten to twenty years after untreated infection.

Why?

Exposure to *Treponema pallidum* from infected body fluids.

When rife in 16th-century Europe, the English called syphilis the French disease, the French called it the Italian disease, the Italians called it the Spanish disease and Spain retaliated by declaring war on England. Or something like that. After the discovery of penicillin in the mid-20th century, syphilis waned in popularity as a cause of death. It is now making a comeback, which is surprising as it is a totally curable infection. In fact, syphilis is so easily treated with penicillin, erythromycin or doxycycline that you can almost get away with sniffing the drugs rather than taking them. Toxins released when the causative bacteria succumb cause a 'healing crisis' known as the Herxheimer reaction, with fever, chills, headache and muscle pain in 50% of those with primary (first-stage) syphilis and 90% of those with secondary (second-stage) syphilis.

Why does it kill?

Gummatous syphilis causes tumour-like lesions that erode and invade the skin, organs and bones. Cardiovascular syphilis attacks the aorta, leading to aneurysm or valve disease. Neurosyphilis (general paralysis of the insane, paralytic dementia) attacks the brain and spinal cord, leading to paralysis, blindness and dementia. In its heyday, neurosyphilis accounted for 20% of admissions to asylums. The Herxheimer reaction during treatment is occasionally fatal.

Will it happen to me?

If you have unprotected sex, then it remains a possibility. The risk of acquiring *Treponema pallidum* after a single, unprotected sexual contact with an infected person is around 30%. It can also enter the body through damaged skin or during wet kissing. There is no evidence that it can be acquired from toilet seats.

There is a complex interaction between syphilis and HIV infection – having one increases the susceptibility to, and virulence of, the other.

What to look for

In medical circles, syphilis is known as The Great Impostor. Its symptoms and signs mimic a myriad of other maladies. Like a certain lager, the bacteria disseminate throughout the blood and lymphatics to reach the parts other bacteria cannot reach. The symptoms of primary syphilis appear

DID YOU KNOW?

Syphilis was the scourge of kings, queens and dictators. Among the famous and infamous who allegedly had syphilis were: Abraham Lincoln, Al Capone, Bathsheba, Beethoven, Catherine the Great, Charlemagne, Cleopatra, Columbus, Goya, Henry VIII, Herod (whose private parts were 'putrefied and eaten by worms'), Hitler, Ivan the Terrible, Julius Caesar, Keats, Lenin, Mussolini, Napoleon, Schubert, Tolstoy and van Gogh.

9–90 days after infection to cause:

- a painless ulcer (chancre) at the site of infection (genitals, mouth, anus, finger, occasionally big toe), which heals after 4–8 weeks
- enlarged, rubbery lymph nodes

Secondary syphilis appears 6–12 weeks later and persists for a year or more with malaise, headache, fever, loss of appetite and fatigue. A dusky-pink skin rash is transient and often unnoticed. Widespread lymph node enlargement occurs and some people get snail-track ulcers on mucous membranes, diffuse hair-loss ('moth-eaten' alopecia) or moist, flat, wart-like lesions (condylomata lata) on the genitals.

Syphilis then enters a latent phase in which it is no longer infectious. If untreated, 1 in 3 people develop tertiary (third-stage) syphilis, usually within 10 years (occasionally up to 40 years). This is the stage that kills by destroying tissues and attacking the aorta, brain or spinal cord.

The 'sailor's handshake' was designed to detect enlarged glands around the elbow – a dead giveaway that the owner had syphilis.

What are the chances of survival?

In all stages of syphilis, treatment can cure the disease, but in tertiary syphilis the damage that has already occurred cannot be reversed. Follow-up blood tests are recommended at 3 months, then 6-monthly for 2 years, and annually thereafter to detect any reactivation or reinfection.

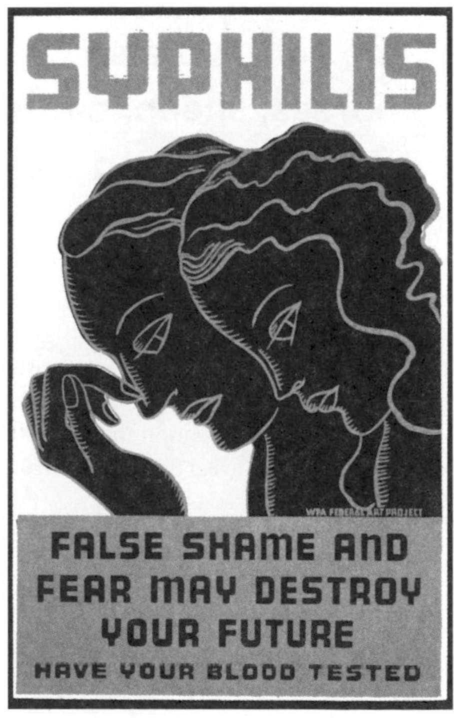
SYPHILIS
WPA FEDERAL ART PROJECT
FALSE SHAME AND
FEAR MAY DESTROY
YOUR FUTURE
HAVE YOUR BLOOD TESTED

HOW TO AVOID IT

Don't have sex. If you must, use condoms, although safer-sex practices offer only limited protection – none at all if your partner's chancre is on their finger or tongue.

Tetanus 91

Tetanus is due to a toxin made by the bacterium *Clostridium tetani*, which is universally present in the soil. It is also found in the gut (and faeces) of horses, sheep, cattle, dogs, cats, rats, guinea pigs, chickens and 1 in 4 people – especially farm workers.

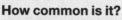

How common is it?

Worldwide, 10,000 cases are reported every year. In addition, unreported neonatal tetanus kills more than 60,000 newborn infants annually, an improvement on the 213,000 deaths in 2002 (of which 198,000 were in the under-fives) thanks to a vigorous WHO vaccination campaign.

Who dies?

The unvaccinated, especially the newborn (umbilical stump infection), the over-60s (tetanus boosters often long overdue) and heroin injectors.

Where?

Mostly rural areas in undeveloped countries with warm, damp climates.

When?

Four to fourteen days after a wound is infected.

Why?

Non-immune exposure to *Clostridium tetani* spores.

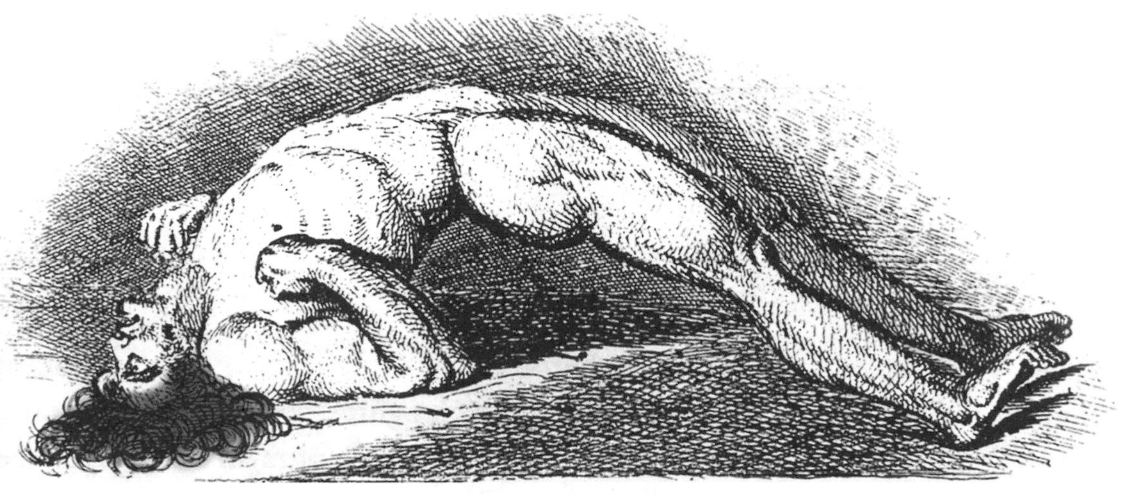

Greek illustration of a man suffering Opisthotonus (the backward spasm) and lockjaw, the terrifying symptoms of tetanus. For Greeks, spasms in general were diseases, not symptoms; the simplest was shivering.

Related to the germs that cause botulism and gas gangrene, these micro-organisms are classed as obligate anaerobes – meaning they are poisoned by oxygen. *Clostridium tetani* produce oval spores, giving them a characteristic drumstick appearance. These are not the sort of drumsticks you'd want to riff with, however. When spores enter your body through a penetrating wound, they germinate in your warm, low-oxygen environment to release a potent neurotoxin. Known as tetanospasmin, this acts on the nervous system to paralyse your skeletal muscles. Nature usually has a reason for everything, but producing a toxin that kills its host does not confer an obvious survival advantage on any bacterium.

Why does it kill?

Tetanus toxin causes paralytic seizures of skeletal muscles throughout the body, including the respiratory muscles. This kills as a result of brain hypoxia (lack of oxygen), bronchopneumonia and respiratory distress. Oversecretion of adrenal gland 'stress' hormones can trigger a heart attack. A marked rise in body temperature (greater than 42 °C / 107 °F) can also occur, leading to sudden circulatory collapse. On top of that, there's septic shock.

Will it happen to me?

If you do not maintain adequate tetanus antibody levels through vaccination, then yes. The causative spores are everywhere, and readily find their way into dirty wounds. Punctures from the thorns of roses, lovingly fertilized with farmyard manure, are particularly dangerous.

What to look for

Symptoms start in the small masticating muscles of the face, hence the popular name of 'lockjaw'. This early symptom precedes violent spasms and rigidity of skeletal muscles in the limbs and trunk. The lips are drawn back in a sardonic smile (risus sardonicus) and the whole body arches like a bow (opisthotonus). Spasms can be severe enough to fracture bones.

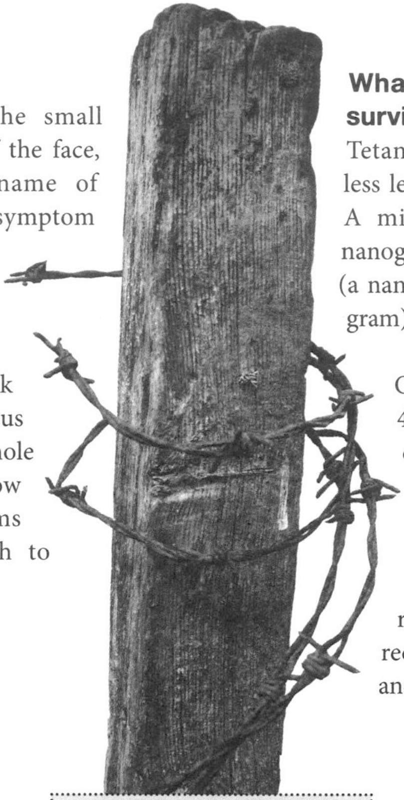

What are the chances of survival?

Tetanus toxin is only slightly less lethal than botulinum toxin. A minuscule dose of just 2.5 nanograms per kilogram can kill (a nanogram is one-billionth of a gram).

Overall, the mortality rate is 45%. With first-class medical care, the chance of survival is 94% if you have previously received one or two doses of tetanus toxoid, falling to 85% for the unvaccinated. Death rates are highest in people requiring artificial ventilation, and in the over-60s.

HOW TO AVOID IT

- **Vaccination with inactivated tetanus toxoid provides good protection. After the primary course (three doses in early infancy, plus preschool booster), regular boosters are needed every 10 years to maintain a protective level of antibodies. Even those who have survived tetanus need vaccination, as the lethal dose is too small to stimulate a natural immune response. Good wound hygiene is also vital.**
- **Check your tetanus vaccination is up to date (do it now).**
- **Don't grow roses. If you must, select thornless varieties and wear strong puncture-proof gloves for gardening.**
- **Wash wounds under running water for 10–15 minutes and ensure all dirt and debris are removed; cover with a sterile dressing.**
- **If you experience a puncture wound, and your last tetanus booster was more than 5 years ago, have another within 48 hours of the injury.**

Thunderbolts and other forces of nature

92

In ancient mythology, thunderbolts were the gods' weapon of choice for punishing mankind. Today, a staggering 1800 thunderstorms are in progress somewhere on the Earth at any given moment. Other natural disasters include earthquakes, tsunamis, volcanic eruptions, avalanches and floods.

How common is it?

An average of 397 natural disasters occur each year, with 67,000 deaths; this figure fluctuates wildly from lows of 10,000 to highs of 236,000 or more in the wake of a 'mega-disaster'. The Earth is pelted with 3 million lightning flashes per day.

Who dies?

Most lightning deaths (85%) affect the under-35s during outdoor recreations; national disasters affect all age groups.

Where?

65% of natural disasters affect developing countries; 40% hit Asia, especially the Philippines and China, and 89% of victims are Asian.

When?

Natural disasters are most common during the summer months.

Why?

Acts of God.

Each spark of lightning reaches the unimaginable temperature of 28,000 °C (50,000 °F) and delivers 100 million volts. Unless it strikes a fuel depot or downs a plane, however, lightning usually picks us off one at a time. Even so, it claims an estimated 24,000 victims per year worldwide and causes an additional 240,000 injuries. Equatorial Africa, especially the Congo, is most affected – on one occasion, all 11 members of a football team were killed by a single bolt of lightning. The opposing team remained uninjured.

Natural disasters

Other forces of nature come in a variety of shapes and sizes, but can be divided into four main types: ground-, water-, storm- and climate-related (see page 243). Individually, they have the power to claim hundreds, thousands, hundreds of thousands or even millions of lives in a short space of time.

Why does it kill?

Lightning stops the heart, short-circuits the brain, and burns flesh. Other disasters may kill through internal injuries, starvation, dehydration, heat stroke, hypothermia or

Continent	*Country/state*	*Lightning flashes per square kilometre per year*
Africa	Democratic Republic of Congo	158
South America	Colombia	110
Asia	Northern Pakistan	87
North America	USA/Florida	59
Europe	Northern Italy	28

Force of nature	*Your lifetime risk of dying as a result*
Flood	1 in 30,000
Tsunami (coast-dweller)	1 in 50,000
Tornado	1 in 60,000
Lightning strike	1 in 83,930
Earthquake	1 in 131,890
Tsunami (non-coast-dweller)	1 in 500,000

'The trouble with quotes about death is that 99.99% of them are made by people who are still alive.' Joshua Burns

Ground-related	*Water-related*	*Storm-related*	*Climate-related*
Earthquake	General flood	Tropical cyclone	Heatwave
Volcano	Flash flood	Extratropical cyclone	Cold wave
Rockfall	Coastal flood	Local storm/Lightning	Drought
Landslide	Tsunami	Blizzard	Wildfire
Avalanche	Limnic eruption (lake overturn)	Hail or ice storm	
Subsidence		Wind/tornado	

drowning. Numbers are swelled by stress, lack of post-disaster support, infectious disease, homicide, suicide and loss of social cohesion and livelihood. Although most deaths are contemporaneous with the event, some may occur months or even years later (e.g. after coma).

Will it happen to me?

Depends where you live and your lifestyle. The overall lifetime risk of dying in a natural disaster has been calculated – with spurious precision – as 1 in 3357. If you live in an earthquake zone, on a flood plain, in a hurricane belt or on the side of a volcano, your risk is higher, especially if you ski off-piste during your holidays.

What to look for

High insurance premiums.

What are the chances of survival?

Lighting-strike victims survive in 80% of cases, but 70% of these have serious long-term after-effects.

DID YOU KNOW?

Lightning *can* strike twice and more – one US park ranger has been struck seven times.

World's worst disasters

Year	*Disaster*	*Death Toll*
1931	Floods, China	2.5 million – 4 million
1970	Cyclone 'Bhola', Pakistan	500,000 to 1 million
1970	Avalanche, Peru	20,000
1972	Blizzard, Iran	4000
1976	Earthquake, China	779,000
2003	Heatwave, Europe	40,000
2004	Tsunami and earthquake, Indian Ocean	310,000
2008	Cyclone Nargis, Myanmar	138,366
2010	Earthquake, Haiti	316,000
2011	Earthquake, Japan	28,000

From www.emdat.be

HOW TO AVOID IT

- **Take shelter if you hear thunder less than 30 seconds after a lightning flash. Go indoors.**
- **Never shelter under a tree or other object that is the highest around. If in an open area, crouch down to reduce your height (but don't lie flat). Avoid water.**
- **Don't use a land phone, as lightning can strike through the phone wires.**
- **During an earthquake, go under a strong desk or table or next to an interior wall. If outdoors, move to an open area away from buildings, power lines and trees.**
- **If the sea suddenly withdraws further than usual, run the other way. A tsunami is coming.**

Tropical viral diseases 93

Some of the most lethal tropical diseases are due to viruses that invade the liver, disrupt the body's clotting system and lead to severe haemorrhaging, sometimes accompanied by jaundice.

How common is it?

- Yellow fever: 200,000 cases per year, with 30,000 deaths.
- Dengue fever: over 100 million people are infected with dengue every year, of whom 500,000 people have dengue haemorrhagic fever; mortality rate without specialist medical care is 20%, reduced to 1% with intravenous fluids to maintain blood pressure.
- Lassa fever: 500,000 cases per year with 5000 deaths; only a handful of deaths from Ebolavirus and Marburgvirus occur each year, on average, with occasional outbreaks killing several hundred people.

Who dies?

Children and pregnant women are most at risk.

Where?

Mostly Africa, Latin America, Asia and Western Pacific, with different viruses endemic in different regions.

When?

Two to twenty-one days after infection.

Why?

Fluid loss and haemorrhage.

Some tropical diseases are harboured by monkeys in tropical rainforests and transmitted to people by insect bites.

- Dengue is a mosquito-borne infection caused by a flavivirus. During an epidemic, up to 90% of people who are not immune from previous exposure develop symptoms. Dengue can be complicated by haemorrhagic 'breakbone' fever. Numbers are increasing, and 2.5 billion people – two-fifths of the world's population – are at risk.
- Ebola haemorrhagic disease is due to a thread-like member of the *Filoviridae* family of viruses known as Ebolavirus. It is transmitted by direct contact with infected blood and other body secretions (including soiled clothes and bedding). The virus infects and destroys so many cells that the internal organs turn to mush. Outbreaks are sporadic and have a mortality rate that can be as high as 80%.
- Lassa haemorrhagic fever is caused by a member of the *Arenaviridae*. The animal carrier is a rat-like rodent (*Mastomys*) that sheds the virus in its urine and faeces. Eight out of ten human cases show no obvious symptoms; the remaining 20% develop severe multi-organ failure of the liver, spleen and kidneys.
- Marburg haemorrhagic fever (also known as green monkey disease) is due to a thread-like member of the *Filoviridae* family of viruses known as Marburgvirus. Like its close relative Ebolavirus, transmission is via infected blood and body fluids. Outbreaks are sporadic and have a mortality rate approaching 90%. The virus has been detected in semen 7 weeks after the patient's recovery.
- Yellow fever, due to a flavivirus, is an acute haemorrhagic viral disease transmitted by infected mosquitoes. It is named after the jaundice it causes, and cases are increasing. A billion people are at risk of infection. After an initial apparent recovery, 1 in 6 patients suddenly develop jaundice and bleed from the mouth, nose, eyes and other orifices.

DID YOU KNOW?

Some haemorrhagic viral diseases are transmitted via human body fluids, and may be sexually transmissible.

For most haemorrhagic viral disease, there is no cure, only supportive treatment (fluids, coagulation factors) while patients fight for their life. The antiviral drug ribavirin may be effective against Lassa fever.

Why does it kill?

In a variety of ways: bleeding and loss of fluids lead to circulatory failure (hypovolaemic shock, see page 212) and kidney failure. Seizures and coma are common.

Will it happen to me?

If you travel to an endemic area, then it is a distinct possibility.

What to look for

Fever, headache, sore throat, flu-like aches and pains, lethargy, nausea and vomiting, and sometimes diarrhoea, shivers, loss of appetite and abdominal pain. Jaundice or a rash may be evident on the skin. Liver enlargement may be noticed. Bleeding starts from a variety of orifices.

What are the chances of survival?

There is less than a 1 in 2 chance of surviving some haemorrhagic fevers.

Dengue virus spends part of its life cycle in the human body and part in the mosquito

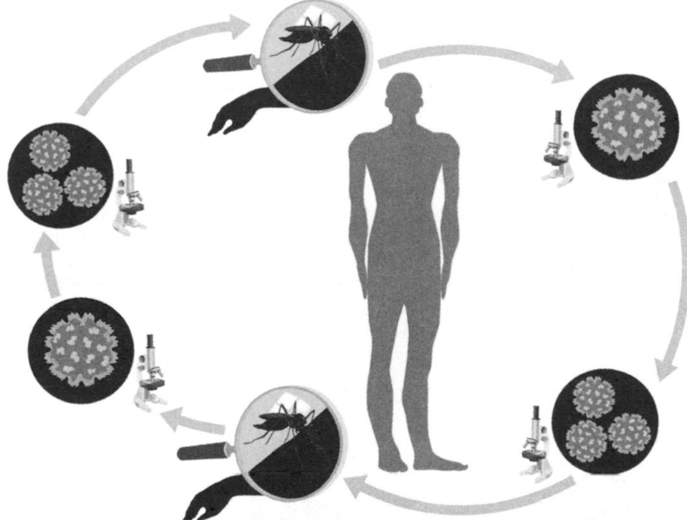

HOW TO AVOID IT

- **Avoid travel to endemic areas, especially during an outbreak.**
- **Vaccination can protect against yellow fever in 95% of cases, and is mandatory for travel to some areas. Vaccines are in development against dengue and Ebolavirus.**
- **Avoidance of mosquito bites (see page 157) is the main preventive measure against many haemorrhagic fevers.**

Tropical worms 94

In the West, parasitic worms are relatively benign, and mostly cause itchy bottoms (thread worms). Those who are particularly unlucky may experience visual loss from a childhood encounter with *Toxocara canis* in dog faeces. Elsewhere in the world, worm infestations – known collectively as helminthiases – can kill.

How common is it?

Intestinal nematode infections kill 6000 people per year; schistosomiasis kills 200,000 a year in Africa alone; cysticercosis due to tapeworms causes 50,000 deaths per year.

Who dies?

Those infested with worms who have no access to treatment.

Where?

Sub-Saharan Africa, the Americas, China, India and the Pacific.

When?

After eating worm or fluke eggs or larvae in faeces, soil or contaminated food or drink. Some are acquired after eating muscle and offal in which worms or flukes lie dormant inside a protective coat to form a cyst.

Why?

In the battle against parasite and host, the worm wins.

Lymphatic filariasis (elephantiasis with gross enlargement of a limb, genitals or breast) is transmitted by infected mosquitoes. The pork tapeworm, *Taenia solium*, causes cysticercosis with hundreds of larvae holing up in organs such as the brain. Worldwide, this is both the most common parasitic infection of the human nervous system, and the most frequent preventable cause of epilepsy. The beef tapeworm, *Taenia saginata*, can live for 25 years, and grow up to 20 m (66 ft) long in the intestines.

Scolex (head) of a beef tapeworm, Taenia saginata

Guinea-worm disease (dracunculiasis) is transmitted by tiny water-fleas living in stagnant water. Hookworm larvae in soil and *Schistosoma* fluke larvae in water can actively penetrate the skin.

Why does it kill?

Obstruction of the intestines, lymphatic system, blood vessels, invasion of the liver, heart, kidneys or brain; anaemia from chronic blood loss; compromised nutritional status (so other infections are more likely to kill). Bladder cancer is a late sequel of schistosomiasis. Neurocysticercosis causes epilepsy and deteriorating brain function.

Will it happen to me?

If you visit an endemic area and come into contact with eggs, larvae or infested mosquitoes or water-fleas, or eat infected meat, then yes.

What to look for

Skin lesions, diarrhoea, abdominal pain, unusual creatures in your poo (wriggly things, square packets of eggs), general malaise, weakness, reduced growth, swollen belly, swollen limb, genitals or breast, blood in urine.

What are the chances of survival?

If you have visited an endemic area, and notice possible symptoms of worm infestation, seek immediate medical advice. Most worm infestations are readily treated with anthelminthic drugs.

HOW TO AVOID IT

- **Good sanitation and access to safe drinking water and hygienically prepared food are vital.**
- **Don't buy food, fruit, vegetables – anything – from street markets where hygiene and hand-washing after visiting the loo are probably not a priority.**
- **Check meat is visually free from cysts in endemic areas; cook all food well.**

95 Tuberculosis

Tuberculosis is a contagious pandemic caused by *Mycobacterium tuberculosis*, or the tubercle bacillus (TB) – a close relative of the villain in leprosy, *Mycobacterium leprae* (see page 143).

How common is it?

One-third of the world's population is infected with TB – more than 2 billion people – though only 10% will develop clinical disease. Every year, 9.5 million people are newly infected, 6 million cases of TB are diagnosed, and almost 2 million people die from it – 4700 deaths per day.

Who dies?

Those who are overcrowded, poorly nourished, with poor sanitation and inadequate medical care; the risk is highest in children, elderly and homeless people and those living with HIV or cancer; once infected, women of reproductive age are more susceptible than men, making TB among the three greatest causes of death in this group, worldwide.

Where?

All areas, but especially sub-Saharan Africa, India and China.

When?

If left untreated, 1 in 2 of those who develop TB symptoms will die, with most deaths occurring within 10 years.

Why?

Wasting effects of chronic infection, sepsis or organ failure.

Region	*% of cases detected*	*Number treated for sputum-positive pulmonary TB*	*Treatment success rates*
Africa	50%	570,000	80%
Americas	79%	110,000	77%
Eastern Mediterranean	70%	170,000	88%
Europe	80%	70,000	66%
South-East Asia	65%	1,010,000	88%
Western Pacific	70%	650,000	93%

The immune system usually gets on top of TB infection, walling it off in the lungs. Undaunted, the bacillus secretes a waxy coat and hunkers down, lying dormant until its host's defences drop. In 1 in 10 cases, it eventually rears its less than pretty head. Although reactivated TB usually affects the lung, it can spread to any organ and cause a myriad of different symptoms. This makes it particularly difficult to diagnose. Only those with the active pulmonary form are infectious, however. Without treatment, reactivated TB kills 1 in 2 of its victims.

TB is making a resurgence in the West but, globally, the death rate has fallen by a third over the past 20 years.

Why does it kill?

The complications of TB include pneumonia, pleural effusions (excess fluid), bleeding from the lungs (haemoptysis), sepsis and meningitis. It can spread to multiple organs, including the liver, kidneys, brain, bones, ovaries and testicles – you name it, it can get there. Once it takes root, tissue destruction commences. Untreated victims often fade away as a result of weight loss – traditionally described as 'consumption'.

Will it happen to me?

TB spreads in the same way as cold viruses via coughs, sneezes and spittle from someone who has an active lung infection. Worldwide, the chance of being infected is 1 in 3. Once you are infected, there is a 90% chance your immune system will keep it at bay, if you are otherwise fit and well.

What to look for

Fever, night sweats, swollen glands, blood-stained sputum and/or unexplained weight loss.

What are the chances of survival?

In Western countries, the overall mortality of TB is 8%. Worldwide, 4 in 5 people (86%) with sputum-positive TB are successfully treated. Those who do not respond are usually elderly, have underlying poor nutrition, HIV, cancer or a particularly virulent multi-drug-resistant strain.

HOW TO AVOID IT

Have screening and vaccination if you are at risk. If you are unsure of your risk status, ask your doctor.

Umbrellas 96

Who'd have thought umbrellas could be so dangerous? The most famous 'Death by Umbrella' involved the Bulgarian dissident Georgi Markov. An assassin fired a hollow pellet into his thigh, using a black umbrella as a compression gun. The pellet contained the deadly natural poison ricin, extracted from the castor bean plant.

How common is it?
Rare – fewer than one a year.

Who dies?
Mostly those with enemies in high (presumably rainy) places.

Where?
On the end of an umbrella.

When?
Soon after being stabbed, hit or blown off balance by an umbrella.

Why?
A good question.

In other cases, an umbrella has been used as a murder weapon to beat someone to death, or to stab them in the head. It is also possible to be blown off a cliff if your golfing umbrella is snatched by a strong gust of wind.

HOW TO AVOID IT

Never use your own umbrella. And stay as far away from other people's umbrellas as possible.

'And I can never be perfectly certain whether Helen was got with child by Leonard Bast or by his fatal forgotten umbrella. All things considered, I think it must have been the umbrella.'

Katherine Mansfield on E.M. Forster's novel *Howards End*

97

Valvular heart disease

Damage to the heart valves is just as lethal as coronary artery disease but it keeps a lower profile since the advent of penicillin.

How common is it?

Worldwide, acute rheumatic fever, one of the main causes, leads to 90,000 deaths per year. As many as 30 million children and adults who survive acute rheumatic fever go on to develop chronic rheumatic heart disease, of whom 298,000 die each year as a result.

Who dies?

Those aged 5–15 are most at risk of acute rheumatic fever (only 20% of cases are in adults); death from the effects of chronic valve damage occurs later in life at an average age of 67 years; the prognosis is worse for females, and for those of Maori or Hawaiian descent.

Where?

Often where there is overcrowding and poor hygiene (which spreads haemolytic streptococcal infections) and a lack of medical diagnosis and treatment.

When?

Rheumatic fever typically develops between 1 and 5 weeks after a strep sore throat or scarlet fever.

Why?

An unlucky combination of the right bacterium in the right host with the right genetic profile.

'Be careful about reading health books. You may die of a misprint.' Mark Twain

One of the main underlying causes of valvular heart disease is rheumatic fever. However, this has been reduced to just a handful of cases per year, since antibiotics became available to treat haemolytic streptococcal infections such as sore throats and scarlet fever. If left untreated, however, the body makes antibodies against these bacteria, which consider it within their job description to attack your body tissues if you have the right genetic profile. This auto-immune reaction can lead to acute heart muscle inflammation (myositis) and damage to heart valves, which thicken and acquire ugly, wart-like growths.

Damaged heart valves either fail to open properly (stenosis), fail to close properly (incompetence) or both. This interferes with the correct flow of blood through the heart, which ends up pooling in the body and/or lungs.

The heart

The heart acts as a double pump, each half of which is divided into two chambers: an upper atrium and a lower ventricle. The right side of the heart receives deoxygenated blood from the body and delivers it to the lungs for oxygenation. The left side of the heart then receives the refreshed blood and pumps it back out to the body via the aorta. For this to work properly, each heart chamber is fitted with a non-return valve that ensures blood flows only in one direction. This prevents unwanted back-flow as the heart contracts. The sound of these valves opening and closing produces the familiar lub-dub of the heartbeat.

Heart valves can also become narrowed or incompetent as a result of congenital malformations, connective tissue diseases, bacterial colonization (endocarditis), cancer, other auto-immune conditions, injury, taking certain drugs or just plain old age; in

Valve	*Location*	*Likelihood of being damaged during acute rheumatic fever*
Mitral valve	Separates the left atrium from the left ventricle (high-pressure valve)	70%
Aortic valve	Left side of the heart, protecting the entrance to the aorta, which takes oxygenated blood from the heart to the rest of the body (high-pressure valve)	25%
Tricuspid valve	Separates the right ventricle from the right atrium (low-pressure valve)	10%
Pulmonary valve	Right side of the heart, protecting the entrance to the pulmonary artery, which takes blood from the heart to the lungs (low-pressure valve)	<1%

DID YOU KNOW?

The heart beats over 2760 million times and pumps over 225 million litres (475 million pints) of blood during the average lifespan.

the latter they frequently become stiffened and calcified.

Why does it kill?

Acute inflammation of the heart muscle (myocarditis), abnormal heart rhythms, heart muscle weakness (cardiomyopathy), congestive heart failure (see page 117) or heart attack (see page 114); or blood clots forming on damaged valves may flick off to cause pulmonary embolism (see page 198) or stroke (see page 222).

Will it happen to me?

In most developed countries, the risk is low at around 1 in 100,000. If you have native Hawaiian or Maori genes your risk may be higher.

What to look for

A persistent sore throat. Acute rheumatic fever can cause joint, skin and other soft tissue inflammation that mimics rheumatoid arthritis. Rheumatic heart disease often causes symptoms around 20 years later, with changing heart murmurs, purplish-red cheeks (from mitral stenosis), fainting (from aortic stenosis), shortness of breath, swelling of ankles and rapid heart rate.

What are the chances of survival?

Those with acute rheumatic fever have a 99.9% chance of surviving with modern medical care and a 3% to 39% chance of developing chronic rheumatic heart disease. If valve stenosis or incompetence occurs, surgical repair or artificial replacement is available. In developing countries, however, there is a 10% chance of dying from acute rheumatic fever and a 70% chance of progression to chronic rheumatic heart disease. This figure jumps to 90% with subsequent attacks.

Internal anatomy of the heart

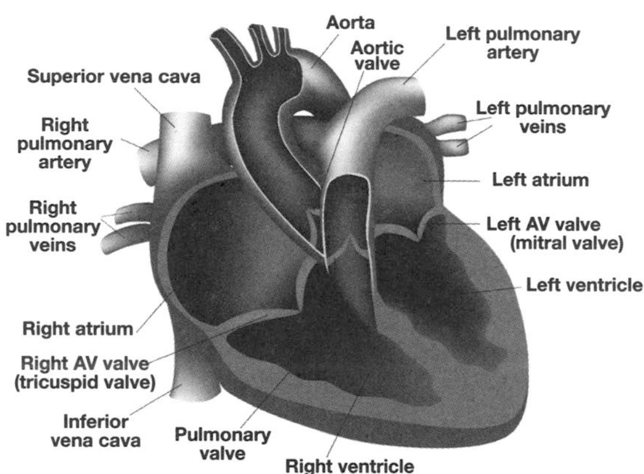

HOW TO AVOID IT

Although most sore throats are viral, if symptoms are prolonged beyond 5 days, see your doctor for a throat swab to rule out a streptococcal infection. Taking penicillin long term (for at least 10 years) may prevent recurrent infection and worsening valve damage.

War 98

War and genocide should be the stuff of legends from medieval times. Sadly, at least eight major military conflicts are currently waging around the globe, each of which inflicts over 1000 battlefield deaths per year. Then there are the lesser skirmishes whose fatalities soon add up.

How common is it?

Over a recent 50-year period, up to 8.7 million violent deaths occurred as a result of war in 13 countries (especially Vietnam) – an average of 174,000 per year. This is three times higher than suggested from passive surveillance data as many deaths occur where eyewitnesses fear to tread.

Who dies?

Mostly young, fit males aged 15–44.

Where?

Mostly in the eight current areas of major conflict (see table).

When?

Aggressiveness peaks during summer months.

Why?

Usually territorial, political, religious or ethnic disputes.

'War does not determine who is right – only who is left.'

Bertrand Russell

DID YOU KNOW?

During a typical war, around two-thirds of casualties are 'military' and one-third 'civilian'.

World War I killed an estimated 15 million people, of whom around two-thirds were military and one-third civilians. World War II killed a minimum of 50 million people, making it the most deadly war so far. We don't know how many will die during World War III, but the results will be so catastrophic for the human race that World War IV is likely to be fought with sticks and stones.

Why does it kill?

Homicide on a scale that has been dubbed 'multicide' results from mortar fire, artillery shells, bombs, land mines, bullets, bayonets, machetes and so on. Significant numbers also die of suicide, famine and disease among those who are displaced or subjected to forced labour.

Current conflicts or wars with more than 1000 deaths per year	*Cumulative death toll*
Afghanistan	2 million
Iraq	1,120,000
Somalia	400,000
Sudan	50,000
North-West Pakistan	31,000
Mexico	32,000
Yemen	17,000
India	11,000

Will it happen to me?

If visiting an area of conflict, then quite probably. Even shopping in the high street of any Western city carries a small risk of death from terrorism – in fact, a 1 in 9.3 million chance.

What to look for

Bomb craters, destroyed buildings, bullet pock-marks and so on.

What are the chances of survival?

A lack of medical facilities and good hygiene in war-torn countries mean any injury can be lethal unless you are evacuated (medevacced) out of the area.

HOW TO AVOID IT

Peace talks and negotiation.

Whooping cough 99

Whooping cough is a highly contagious respiratory disease caused by the bacterium *Bordetella pertussis*. Paroxysms of violent, uncontrollable coughing make breathing almost impossible. Each bout is followed by a desperate whoop as the victim tries to draw in enough air to breathe before the next episode starts.

How common is it?
An estimated 16 million cases of pertussis occur worldwide, with 195,000 deaths.

Who dies?
Mostly infants and young children; pertussis is more common in girls than boys.

Where?
Globally, 95% of cases and deaths occur in developing countries.

When?
About 6–20 days after infection; peak season is in the summer months.

Why?
Unvaccinated exposure to the causative bacterium.

'Love, Cough and Smoke can't well be hid.' Benjamin Franklin

DID YOU KNOW?

In 2008, 82% of all infants in the world received three doses of pertussis vaccine, preventing an estimated 687,000 deaths.

What are the chances of survival?

Early treatment with antibiotics (erythromycin) and oxygen may minimize the duration of disease and infectivity. Mortality rates can be as high as 50%, but decrease to less than 0.2% (1 in 500) with excellent medical care.

During bouts of whooping cough, loss of consciousness can occur through lack of oxygen. Coughing can last from 4–8 weeks. It can affect anyone of any age, but tends to be less severe in older people.

Bordetella pertussis *bacteria in trachea*

Why does it kill?

Pneumonia is a relatively common complication. Death can also occur from inability to breathe (apnoea), lack of oxygen (hypoxia), dehydration, seizures, encephalitis (infection of the brain) or stroke.

Will it happen to me?

If you have been vaccinated against pertussis, then serious disease is unlikely. You may, however, still develop mild symptoms.

What to look for

Mild fever, runny nose, vomiting and, sometimes, diarrhoea are accompanied by sudden bursts of coughing and the declarative whoop. In the very young, pneumonia may occur instead.

HOW TO AVOID IT

Pertussis can be prevented by vaccination. The primary course, given in infancy, consists of three doses, with boosters around 3 years later and every 10 years thereafter.

100

Zzzzzzzzzzzzzz

We all have to leave this Earth somehow and, arguably, dying in our sleep is one of the kindest ways to go.

How common is it?

Around 11% of deaths occur between midnight and 8 a.m.

Who dies?

Victims include those experiencing sudden death due to 'old age' (see page 174), obstructive sleep apnoea (see page 219), sudden unexpected nocturnal death syndrome (see page 227), carbon monoxide poisoning (see page 55), sleeping sickness (see page 213), hypothermia if you are single (see page 127), heart attack (during dream sleep, around 6 a.m., see page 114), unexplained 'dead-in-bed' syndrome associated with Type 1 diabetes, and sudden unexpected death in epilepsy (see page 92).

Where?

In bed.

When?

The most common time to die in your sleep is between midnight and 1 a.m., and again between 6 a.m. and 7 a.m.; the risk of a heart attack is increased during the 2 hours after sex.

Why?

General powering down of body systems, followed by a sudden stressful surge as systems 'reboot' just before waking.

'Sleep … Oh! How I loathe those little slices of death.'

Longfellow (possibly, though often attributed to Edgar Allan Poe)

If you sleep for 8 hours per day, and do not take part in dangerous activities during your waking hours, then, all things being equal, the chance of dying while asleep is 1 in 3. However, all things are not equal.

In sleep, the body experiences distinct diurnal rhythms that influence blood pressure, heart rate and brain activity. As a result, you are three times less likely to die between midnight and 6 a.m. than you are between 6 a.m. and 12 noon. You are also 18% more likely to die on a Monday than on a Sunday, suggesting that the stress of returning to work and the Monday Blues is a real phenomenon. You are also 25% more likely to die during the depths of winter than in the peak of summer.

ZZzzzzzzzzzzzz

DID YOU KNOW?

Sleep is a form of unconsciousness that is our natural state of rest. As well as allowing muscles and joints to recover from constant use during the day, most of the body's repair work is done at night when growth hormone is secreted.

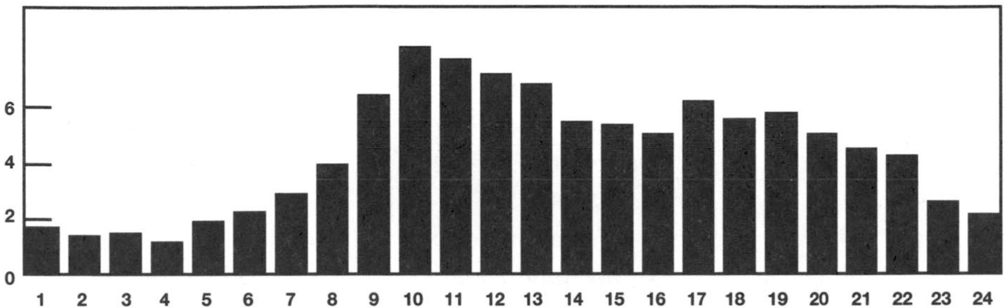

Why does it kill?

Changes in blood pressure, heart rate, heart rhythm, ability of the heart to respond to hormone triggers, vascular tone, raised blood stickiness, increased tendency of blood to clot when lying inactive. The exertions of recent sex may play a role in some cases.

Will it happen to me?

Although we get less and less sleep as we get older, our risk of dying in our sleep increases.

HOW MUCH SLEEP DO YOU NEEED?

- A baby needs 14–16 hours a day.
- A five year old needs around 12 hours.
- The average adult sleeps for 7 hours 12 minutes per night.
- Those over 75 need least sleep of all – often as little as 5 hours.

What to look for

Dreaming of a long tunnel with a bright light at the end.

What are the chances of survival?

Extremely low unless you are shocked out of it by an emergency response team with a portable defibrillator.

HOW TO AVOID IT

- Avoiding sleep isn't an option as sleep deprivation itself can result in premature death.
- Sleeping with a bed partner increases the chance that, should you wake in extremis, someone can call for help or give resuscitation (but sex just before sleep may not be a good idea).
- Ensure your bedroom is a comfortable temperature – neither too hot nor too cold.

Index

E

F

G

H

N

O

P

Q

R

S

T

PICTURE CREDITS

1 and 3 © Eric Isselée/Shutterstock.com, 8–9 © InterNetwork Media/Digital Vision/Getty Images, 11 © BioMedical/Shutterstock.com, 17 © C Squared Studios/Photodisc/Getty Images, 18 © martan/Shutterstock.com, 20 © irin-k/Shutterstock.com, 21 © Fatseyeva/Shutterstock.com, 23 (scorpion) © Photodisc/Getty Images, 23 (crocodile) © John Kasawa/Shutterstock.com, 24 © Shutterstock.com, 27 © sagasan/Shutterstock.com, 28 © Carolina K. Smith, M.D./Shutterstock.com, 30 © rob3000/Shutterstock.com, 36 (dust mite) © Sebastian Kaulitzki/Shutterstock.com, 36 (pollen) © Knorre/Shutterstock.com, 36 (egg) © Photodisc/Getty Images, 36 (nuts) © C Squared Studios/Photodisc/Getty Images, 40 © iStockphoto.com, 42 © Jiri Hera/Shutterstock.com, 43 © CandyBoxPhoto/Shutterstock.com, 48 © irin-k/Shutterstock.com, 58 © vetpathologist/Shutterstock.com, 59 © iStockphoto/lpkoe, 61 © Ragne Kabanova/Shutterstock.com, 64 © Sebastian Kaulitzki/Shutterstock.com, 67 © easaab/Shutterstock.com, 73 © alxhar/Shutterstock.com, 80 © Artifan/Shutterstock.com, 83 © Dr Kari Lounatmaa/Science Photo Library, 85 © Photodisc/Getty Images, 87 © Philip Lange/Shutterstock.com, 100 © iStockphoto.com/Peter Austin, 103 © Four Oaks/Shutterstock.com, 111 © Phiseksit/Shutterstock.com, 113 © Photodisc/Getty Images, 121 © Photodisc/Getty Images, 128 © Smileus/Shutterstock.com, 130 © Rob Byron/Shutterstock.com, 132 © CLIPAREA l Custom media/Shutterstock.com, 135 © GeoM/Shutterstock.com, 137 © Sebastian Kaulitzki/Shutterstock.com, 148 © Photodisc/Getty Images, 151 © Sebastian Kaulitzki/Shutterstock.com, 154 Sebastian Kaulitzki/Shutterstock.com, 156 © Kurt De Bruyn/Shutterstock.com, 158 © Kletr/Shutterstock.com, 164 © Sebastian Kaulitzki/Shutterstock.com, 166 © Triff/Shutterstock.com, 170 © Chris Shorten/Cole Group/Photodisc/Getty Images, 181 © Alila Sao Mai/Shutterstock.com, 183 © Photodisc/Getty Images, 185 © Photodisc/Getty Images, 187 © addimage/Shutterstock.com, 195 courtesy CDC/Mary Hilpertshauser, 197 © Bomshtein/Shutterstock.com, 204 © Becky Stares/Shutterstock.com, 211 © @erics/Shutterstock.com, 216 © Karlosk/Shutterstock.com, 218 © ManuelSchäfer/Shutterstock.com, 220 © Svetlana Mihailova/Shutterstock.com, 221 © Michael Pettigrew/Shutterstock.com, 226 © iStockphoto.com, 232 © Comstock, 233 © Dmitriy Shironosov/Shutterstock.com, 239 © NYPL/Science Source/Science Photo Library, 240 © iStockphoto.com, 242–3 © Don Farrall/Photodisc/Getty Images, 244 © C. Lee/PhotoLink/Photodisc/Getty Images, 246 © Oleg Kozlov/Shutterstock.com, 247 © Mark Giles/Science Photo Library, 249 © Pasieka/Science Photo Library, 253 © Jupiterimages, 256 © Alila Sao Mai/Shutterstock.com, 258 © Trinacria Photo/Shutterstock.com, 260 © NIBSC/Science Photo Library, 262 © Dwight Smith/Shutterstock.com.

Quercus Publishing Plc
55 Baker Street
7th floor, south block
London
W1U 8EW

First published in 2011

A catalogue record of this book is available from the British Library

UK and associated territories: ISBN 978 0 85738 610 6

Printed and bound in China

10 9 8 7 6 5 4 3 2 1